HERESY IN THE MIDDLE AGES

HERESY IN THE MIDDLE AGES

A HISTORY OF AUTHORITY AND EXCLUSION

ANDREA JANELLE DICKENS

FORTRESS PRESS
Minneapolis

HERESY IN THE MIDDLE AGES
A History of Authority and Exclusion

Copyright © 2024 by Fortress Press, an imprint of 1517 Media. Published by Fortress Press, an imprint of 1517 Media. All rights reserved. Except for brief quotations in critical articles or reviews, no part of this book may be reproduced in any manner without prior written permission from the publisher. Email copyright@1517.media or write to Permissions, Fortress Press, PO Box 1209, Minneapolis, MN 55440-1209.

Library of Congress Cataloging-in-Publication Data

Names: Dickens, Andrea Janelle, author.
Title: Heresy in the Middle Ages : a history of authority and exclusion / Andrea Janelle Dickens.
Description: Minneapolis : Fortress Press, [2024] | Includes bibliographical references and index.
Identifiers: LCCN 2024000186 (print) | LCCN 2024000187 (ebook) | ISBN 9781506498218 (paperback) | ISBN 9781506498225 (ebook)
Subjects: LCSH: Christian heresies--Europe--History--To 1500. | Religious thought--Europe--Middle Ages, 600-1500.
Classification: LCC BT1319 .D53 2024 (print) | LCC BT1319 (ebook) | DDC 273/.6--dc23/eng/20240213
LC record available at https://lccn.loc.gov/2024000186
LC ebook record available at https://lccn.loc.gov/2024000187

Cover image: Sir John Oldcastle being burnt for Lollard heresy and insurrection in 1414. Woodcut print, first published in Holinshed's Chronicles (1577); and details from The Picture of the Hanging and Burning of Diverse Persons Counted for Lollards, in the First Year of the Reign of King Henry V, woodcut print from 'Acts and Monuments' by John Foxe, 1563.
Cover design: Kristin Miller

Print ISBN: 978-1-5064-9821-8
eBook ISBN: 978-1-5064-9822-5

For Diana, Maxwell, and Andrew

For Dana, Maya Eli, and Andrew

CONTENTS

	Acknowledgments	ix
	Preface	xi
	Introduction *Laying a Foundation for Heresy*	1
1.	The Petrobrusians and Henricians *The Monastic Influence on Heresy*	11
2.	The Cathars *The Turn to Force against Group Heresies*	31
3.	The Waldensians *Heresy and Reunion*	53
4.	The Beguines and Beghards *The Rhetoric of Defining a Heresy*	75
5.	The Templars *Power, Publicity, and Authority in Heresy*	99
6.	The Spiritual Franciscans *Apocalyptic Literature and Claims to Authority in Heresy*	121
7.	Wycliffe and the Lollards *The Academic and Public Face of Heresy*	143
8.	The Hussites *The Sociopolitical Nexus of Heresy*	167
9.	Late Medieval Witchcraft *The Movement Back Toward Individual Heresy*	189
10.	Conclusions	213
	Notes	221
	Bibliography	245
	Index	257

ACKNOWLEDGMENTS

Good colleagues help make research and writing worthwhile, and I am very grateful for all the assistance I have received, some financial, some archival, and much collegial. Without the great assistance of my network of friends and coworkers, near and far-flung, this book would not have been possible. First and foremost, I'd like to thank the Wabash Center for Teaching and Learning in Theology and Religion for a grant that helped make much of the early research possible. I'd like to thank the librarians at both the Bodleian Library and Arizona State University for their help with tracking down and acquiring resources. Many colleagues have helped me articulate ideas or have read pieces of this book, including Dan Joslyn-Siemiatkoski, Monica Coleman, Horace Six-Means, and Marianne Kabir. Thanks to Carey Newman, a friend and colleague for many years, for encouraging me to finish this book and let it see the light of day. And finally, thanks to my intrepid colleague Sarah Duerden, who had the fortitude to read through late drafts of the entire project.

PREFACE

The Middle Ages saw an extraordinary blossoming of faith. Starting in the twelfth century, the church saw the creation of many new ways to live out a Christian charism, and it saw reforms meant to encourage deeper religious fervor. It saw the creation of new orders: the Cistercians, with their monastic austerities, who lived on the edges of society; double monasteries, with men's and women's houses in the same compound; the mendicants, wandering preachers such as the Franciscans and Dominicans; and the beguines, who lived single lives in lay communities and served as nurses and artisans within urban centers. It saw the founding of universities dedicated to the study of theology and the hashing out of particular thinking behind theological positions. In short, religion was flourishing in a way it had not done for centuries. Yet while all these new expressions of faith were occurring, many were to be suppressed as well; the High Middle Ages saw new ways of repressing some of these new charisms—although some were approved, other charisms continued to arouse suspicion. Here is where this story begins.

The idea of the medieval heretic conjures up a very different set of images than those listed in the previous paragraph. In the heretic, one sees the unrepentant sinner being tossed onto an auto-da-fé pyre. Heresy conjures images of inquisitors arresting, questioning, and torturing those who misbelieve. Heresy makes people think of force, violence, and a church that bends the world to fit its will. Heresy is based on there being clear limits as to what counts as right belief.

This book probes this clash of cultures to uncover a more truthful image of the times, to discern the consistency within both images, and to hear the stories from this conflict. To do so, it looks at a series of snapshots of the Middle Ages. In each page of this photo album, there are stories to tell: each snapshot evokes the stories of each heresy to shed light on what people thought needed reforming, on the ways the church reacted to internal threats, and who it decided would be brought back in, banished, or held in awkward, in-between states. Like a family photograph album, these snapshots tell the stories of various relatives, some known, some barely remembered.

This book begins by crossing the hills and mountains in southern France. It will eventually find its way to Alpine valleys, deep clefts in tall mountains, visiting old villages where everyone has known each other for generations. Eventually, it makes its way to the bustling trade of the cities of the Low Countries and from there to England's Midlands and the countryside of Bohemia. Beautiful, charming places to visit, each of them. Wherever this book stops, we will encounter a different movement and the people behind it. Each of these stories illuminates a different aspect of how the church wanted to define itself, how it wanted to limit the definitions of who would be seen as a right believer, and how it wanted to label some of its own as outsiders. The medieval heretics existed at a time when the church was both shoring up its power and confronting new groups outside of its faith, especially through the Crusades. In some of these stories, the centralization of power encouraged the tendency to fight so-called foreigners within Christianity itself.

This book both tells a narrative and fights against a narrative. The narrative it tells is the fragmentary, personal stories of each movement. The narrative it acknowledges but wants to resist is that the fight against heresy had a collective impetus and that the inquisitorial framework creaked into place to defend it. Each group of heretics that were examined had its own history, which may or may not have had much other connection with the development of heresy as a category other than being investigated by the same inquisitors. But the heretics have stories that illuminate much about the life of the church, just like any stories told from the seats of power do.

The challenge with medieval heretics is that history is often recorded by the machinations of power, and the record of heretical voices varies: some left behind extensive writings, and some left behind little. Some inquisitorial documents appear more objective, while others have a clear polemical sheen to them. Some heretics were trained as priests or academics or lived within religious communities; some were laypeople desperately trying to learn more about their faith through whatever means they could. Listening to their voices, as much as is possible, helps us to understand the heretics as they saw themselves: inheritors of the church traditions who wanted to find ways to reform and improve them. Understanding the heretics, their time, and their culture and the church's development enrich our ability to appreciate the development of faith and its pitfalls.

But the church isn't the only voice in this story; much of the challenge in telling it is making sure we hear many voices. Some of the information we have about the heretics comes from those who would designate them as such; work has been done to recover, where possible, the writings and records of the heretics themselves, to give them a voice. And even scholars have had to adjust the ways they listen to these distant echoes as new information and new texts have come to light. Each person we visit has a new way of telling their story. But the whole point is to let them talk, to describe their world, and to listen. They will share what they can about their place, their people, and their view on the world. They will describe their communities and narrate their experiences of God and other Christians. They will share the hospitality of faith and stories.

This book begins a couple of decades after the First Crusade. It was a time when Christianity was engaging with other faiths and having to develop the tools for how to interact with people—warriors, leaders, and intellectuals—of other traditions. From the first heresy discussed, we will see how the heretic within becomes "othered" almost like a foreigner. By the time of the late medieval witches, the rhetoric will be of outsiders within for sure. The lives and teachings of the medieval heretics can also tell us a lot about the rhetoric of defining who we are as a church community. Two of the questions lurking just below the surface of all these stories are why the church needed to proclaim each of these groups as outsiders and what were the implications of removing them for the rest of the church.

One of the fundamental challenges these groups and their detractors raise is the issue of how we think of heterodoxy and orthodoxy and the legacy of previous answers to a question churches still face today: Are heterodoxy and orthodoxy truly incompatible categories? Could there be overlap, or could they in some cases exist on a sliding scale? If one is at some point deemed heterodox, must one always be so? In modern discourse around hot-button issues, there have been attempts to figure out how to move beyond the vituperative and recriminatory rhetoric of two groups at odds with each other.[1] Here, in thinking of medieval heresy, the discussion should perhaps be easier to launch because both the heterodox and orthodox see themselves as inheritors of the same tradition, even if they express it differently.

Introduction

Laying a Foundation for Heresy

THE IDEA OF the heretic in the Middle Ages conjures up a variety of images of danger. The auto-da-fé and the public burning of books and people. Marguerite Porete going to the bonfire proclaiming that she had received the word of God and written it down. The Templars—knights who had fought so valiantly for the restoration of the Holy Land to Christian hands—later executed for idolatry and sexual indiscretions. Itinerant preachers with their sermons about dualistic worlds—good and evil pitted against one another in an eternal cosmic struggle—and the storming of their Occitan town. The Peasants' Revolt in England and uprisings against landlords. Heretical movements such as the Arians and Pelagians threatened Christianity in its early history, but large-scale movements were relatively rare between the late antique and high medieval periods. There had been a gap in executions between Priscillian in 383 and the heretics executed in Orléans in 1022, but in the eleventh century, the church would begin executing heretics once more.[1] In the early church, various movements and splinter groups tested the limits of Christianity, and in the process, the church solidified its doctrines. One way the church did so was through rehabilitating heretics and clarifying the boundaries of belief.[2] During the High Middle Ages, heresy evoked a number of anxieties: that it led to widespread instability and violence; that it caused people to be led down the road to damnation by being intellectually misled; and that it led to diabolical associations. At the heart of the heretical movements of the Middle Ages, we find again and again a church worried about leading the people—the laity—to salvation without exposing them to ideas that would lead them astray. But the rise of heresy wasn't a rise in misbelief; rather, it was an increase in attempts to exert control over the laity by defining what constituted right belief and praxis. As the issue of right belief became more and more pressing, interest in repressing divergent beliefs and channeling groups and their ideas into already approved orders of the church increased as well.

Defining Heresy

The definition of the term *heresy* will change depending on who is in charge, who is objecting, and in what social setting divergent or new beliefs arise. The word's roots, *haeresis*, do not provide a moral or ethical judgement: *haeresis* is merely a set of coordinated beliefs, a system of thought. To begin with a definition based on how it was typically viewed, heresy consists of repeated persistence in opposing the teachings of the church. There are a number of different ways to talk about inappropriate beliefs, thoughts, sayings, and actions such as blasphemy and apostasy. Heresy is also belief held contrary to the regularized belief of the Western church in the Middle Ages, as determined by either Rome or local church authorities and as upheld by church and municipal justice. Heresy was determined when a judge or other official deemed that a person or group failed to repent and return to doctrinal accord with the official wishes of the church, through a repeated failure to be obedient to such requests. This view is from the perspective of the central power, not the individual. This definition isn't perfect, but it shows one emphasis: heresy is a label applied by an authority for the purpose of ordering. In theory, under the Inquisition, the heretic was not condemned because of mere errors in thought but because they repeatedly defended a position after the church offered correction.

A prevailing sense of orthodoxy characterized the medieval church. Heresy requires both an orthodoxy and a body strong enough to enforce that orthodoxy.[3] Through the period we'll look at, heresies often differed from orthodoxy, not on core beliefs but in how one should reform the church of their time: "Whatever its forms, medieval heresy differed from orthodoxy and mere heterodoxy less in assumptions than emphasis and conclusions. It became heresy from pressing these too far. From the eleventh to the fifteenth centuries, its aspirations were common to all religious reform: namely, the desire to emulate the life and teachings of Christ and his Apostles; and more particularly to seek a return to the precepts of the gospel through a life of poverty—or one of complete simplicity—and preaching."[4] The heresy scholar Gordon Leff, for example, ignores the Cathars for this reason when discussing Christian heresy; he sees them as having non-Christian (Manichaean) origins and therefore as being adherents of another religion, not heretics.

The heresies of the early church would continue to overshadow medieval heresy to both their contemporaries and modern scholars. Heresies in the early church were named after the charismatic founders of their ideas, as the well-known Manichaeans, Arians, Donatists, and Pelagians all bear evidence. Heretics followed a leader who would stand by their doctrines even in the face of disputations by the church. Groups grew like family trees from their founders. In the High Middle Ages, some groups would have charismatic leaders. This idea would be subsumed in the Middle Ages into a belief that all heretics sprang from one root. It would also evolve into a belief by medieval and early modern contemporaries that heresy was the work of the devil, and all heretics were seen to be in Satan's service. The tension was there in the Middle Ages: Was it the work of individuals—the individuals who led heretical movements under the authority of their own intelligence—or were they working under the deceit of the devil?[5] This rhetoric continues throughout the Middle Ages, from the time of the Cathars to the accusations against the Templars regarding homosexual behavior and to the time of late medieval witchcraft, where once again women were accused of sexual relations with the devil and incest.

The Society of the Middle Ages

The Middle Ages were a flourishing age of faith. The Middle Ages oversaw the development of new orders and outreach to the laity through both volunteerism and the popularity of monasticism that could not keep up with the demand for spots. It was a time of newly developed and flourishing popular piety as well. Indeed, the Middle Ages saw the understanding of a religious vocation expand considerably: one could take vows and go off to the Crusades, retire to a monastery that celebrated elaborate liturgies, or live in a remote swamp in North Yorkshire. A vowed hermit who kept lighthouses, a master at a university, or a nurse in an urban hospital were all roles within the religious life. Yet for all the proliferation of religious vocations, the underside was a constant monitoring of how people expressed fervor. While the numbers and types of religious vocations increased, vocations outside of previously approved ones were increasingly limited. This situation leads us to a paradox: "Heresy is not a phenomenon of an anti-religious age, but appears only when people are sufficiently convinced that belief in true doctrine is a prerequisite to salvation."[6] An interest in heresy appears in the high medieval and late medieval church as a consequence of religious fervor, and accusations of heresy were often aimed at those with the most fervor.

At the time when we pick up the history of the development of heresy in the Middle Ages, there are a number of social changes and currents taking place. Traditional historical accounts have pitted two opposing cultures against one another: clerical versus lay, or learned versus vernacular, but this picture is very incomplete.[7] The Gregorian reform movement (ca. 1050–80) had undertaken a massive reorganization and renewal in the church, from institutional to lay levels. The number of schools greatly increased. Monasteries also increased in number, and monastic observance was seen as a model that could benefit all layers of society. A number of monks were raised to the papacy, especially from orders such as the Cistercians, who were reform-minded. The economy of Europe increased greatly, and new towns accommodated a burgeoning mercantile class. Universities arose, as did schools centered in cities and towns, around cathedrals, and in monasteries. Literacy became more widely established. But while secular power increased, even leading to lay societies of "textual reading" of the Scriptures, there was a concomitant rise in persecution. Textual commentaries and preaching manuals were developed for those clergy commissioned to preach, as a way of guiding correct reading and preaching. More church legislation was created to encompass all aspects related to spirituality, preaching authority, and interpretation of Scripture. But beyond controlling its own preachers, the church began to use these tools to limit the actions of lay Christians. At this time, both cities and nations were vying for political power, and the development of power beyond the local region was occurring. The church's struggle to consolidate power and establish a hierarchy of authority was part of the ethos of the times. In the first few chapters of this book, the development of an inquisitorial apparatus becomes clear: there's a momentum toward the rooting out and suppression of heresy, but it was a momentum that reflected the institutionalizing of the church. The Inquisition took a few years to develop, but until it did, there wasn't one sole department that dealt with heretics or heresies.

Studying Medieval Heresy

Scholars today have a wonderful advantage in the understanding of medieval heresy. There is greater access to more documents, from a wide variety of voices, that provide nuance to the stories we tell about the past. More documents are available with which to understand the development of lay spirituality, which was so often equated with heresy. The number of recovered, rediscovered, or newly available documents helps broaden and deepen knowledge of many medieval religious groups, particularly of the heretical groups. Understanding their thoughts in their own words helps to discern the accuracy of the church attacks. The development of social histories, particularly of lay religious movements or "popular religion," means that scholars have a clearer sense of how to understand the gap between official records and documents and the lived religious experience of many of the so-called heretical groups. The historian of heresy faces a challenge in the way that modern accounts have explained heresy. On the one hand, the records indicate that the rise of the persecution of heresy starting in the eleventh century gained momentum and was marked by intense fervor. On the other hand, current historiographical trends are to read the medieval descriptions of heresy, even outside of inquisitorial records, with a hermeneutics of suspicion, seeing them as inflammatory documents that are formulaic in their statements against alleged heretics and products of either Europe's "inner demons" (to use Cohn's phrase) or a "persecuting society" (to use Moore's categories).[8] The result is a suspicion as to whether the formulaic nature means the documents rely on manufactured charges, since heretical accusations seem so similar across time and location, or whether the inquisitors focused on "essential" elements identified within a particular group. One of the goals of this book is to bring additional voices—those of the accused heretics, their supporters, and other observers—into the conversation. In that, I hope to begin to reconcile these approaches while trying to probe why the institutional church needed to distance itself from these groups; the answers are often rooted in political, economic, and nonreligious readings.

When scholars turned to serious study of the main medieval heresies, beginning in the early twentieth century, it was often the case that they could work only from accounts written by those condemning the heretics, through documents related to heretics' condemnations and through theological disputes. In the intervening decades, more documents have been recovered from a number of the accused heretical groups. And we also stand at a point where we can see beyond the bifurcation of heretic and orthodox. The scholar Peter Biller talks of "deconstructive trends in the study of medieval heresy in the later thirteenth century."[9] He states that toward the end of the twentieth century, "these years show sharper critical scrutiny of evidence deriving from the repression of heresy, the commonplaces of polemic against heretics,

Catholic theologians' and inquisitors' labels for heretics, and the records of confessions extorted by inquisitors."[10] In short, the trend has been to view the historical records with a hermeneutics of suspicion toward their reporting of the specifics of what groups deemed heretics believed. The heresy scholar Robert Lerner perhaps used this approach to the best effect and deconstructed the Free Spirit heresy out of existence, showing that the definition of that heresy was made before the historical records can prove that any more than a handful of such "Free Spirits" actually lived. Mark Pegg followed a similar line of exploration regarding the Cathars.[11] Today, the pendulum of scholarly hermeneutics has moved again, and the challenge facing the student of heretical movements is to both understand that the Middle Ages saw heresy as a real threat and acknowledge that what was considered heresy was sometimes not heresy at all.

Recent historiography has begun questioning the narrative that held sway for so long: there was little heresy before 1100, then there was, and the groups that were identified in the following centuries up to the time of the Reformation included many of the ones in this book—the Cathars, the Waldensians, the beguines, and the Templars. Today, the challenge is to look at heresy, not merely from the perspective of those whom the church declared heretics but from their own self-assessments as well, and to see how they saw themselves within the church. There was a large uptick in new religious expressions, but what necessitated such a growth? Very few of the people written about in this book saw themselves as heretics. They saw themselves as revitalizing the church, restoring it to its apostolic interests, finding ways to help people experience God, or a dozen other positive, Christian efforts. I will show that the heresies presented in this book, while sometimes quite rightly heresies, were as often as not condemned for social, political, or economic reasons than for doctrinal reasons and that often issues of whether to reintegrate groups into the church depended on the pope or politics at the time rather than on clear theological principles. This paradox—that heretics were often both heretics and condemned for extradoctrinal issues—is where I shall begin the investigations of these groups in the following chapters.

Contemporary Theories of Heresy

As the study of heresy has improved, more methodologies—often alongside others—have helped shed new light on aspects of the phenomenon. One is the attempt to read within economic or social frameworks. For instance, heresy arose when workers at the lower strata of the socioeconomic order had no way to express their problems except by means of intellectual dissent.[12] This view has been especially popular in explaining the Cathar attempts to regulate the means of trade and set up rival social organizations in Languedoc. The Cathars were attempting, in this view, to strip power from the local landowners. Another view sees the heretics as having their source in the tensions between Christian precedent and practice.[13] Another way of reading heresy is that of Herbert Grundmann, who traced feelings of affection (rather than alienation) and saw the medieval heresies as expressions of a yearning for the *vita apostolica* (the apostolic life). According to him, the attitude of the clergy was the primary decisive factor in whether a popular religious movement would become radicalized. Those that met with opposition became more radicalized, whereas those that met with clergy support usually found a way to become of use to the church. The Middle Ages saw waves of popular religious movements. And whether they were misguided or heretical, their fervor came from the same source as those officially sanctioned movements that found the church's favor. In his work on medieval dissent, Jeffrey Burton Russell focused on categories of types of dissent. Classifying heresy more broadly as a type of dissent, meaning that it was a deviation from expected norms within medieval society and not merely a form of deviation in religious belief or practice, he identified classifications to understand the behaviors that were practiced by heretics and heretical groups. Setting heretical ideas within the enthusiasm of the twelfth-century Gregorian reform, Russell then sees that the heretics were those who were either eccentric, reactionary, or intellectual in their implementation of these reform ideals.[14] His approach looks at the effects of these groups and tries to determine groupings. It then sets the central church as the touchstone for all these groups. And while there's much benefit in this way of looking at heresy, it does not probe the true significance or precisely identify what each group believed; this approach merely labels such groups as deviants.

But this tendency to see heresy as the work of the devil means that contemporaries and historians have followed its lead—intentionally or not—and tried to tie heresies together socially and intellectually through the construction of genealogies of influence. Rather than see each heresy as a unique and separate movement, the assumption is that they must get at least some of their impetus to err from heretical predecessors; so many people could not come up with so many unique ways to diverge from the beliefs of the church, apparently. The story generally told is one in which the Bogomils of tenth-century Bulgaria are listed as the predecessors of the later high medieval heretical movements in Western Europe.[15] Thus, the genealogy constructed points to Mani, a leader of a third-century dualist group called the Manichaeans that began in what is now Iran, and the genealogy finds similarities in the cosmology constructed by Bogomil and his followers in Eastern Europe, as reported to us by the priest Cosmas. These genealogies have based themselves on similarities of doctrine, such as dualism, denial of the sacraments, disdain for clerical authority, and repudiation of the physical in favor of the spiritual. They have also tried to tie them to lines of the dissemination of ideas, such as across trade routes and major roads of travel, especially across the Alps. Following in the steps of Malcolm Lambert, authors try to trace the heresies through their Bogomil influence. While there's no doubt that there were similarities, genealogies of these movements extrapolate greatly from the few things we know and seemingly rely on the assumptions of the inquisitor, who was tasked with condemning heretics and believed all heresy had a common root.

This genealogical approach tries to find more similarity between the heretical communities than in fact existed. The movements declared heretical generally involve some sort of critique of the church, which is then seen as having gone astray. Critiques of the church come in several forms: a questioning of the basic beliefs of the church, such as the nature of the Trinity or Christ; a questioning of church ritual, such as the necessity of various sacraments or of reverence given to persons (Mary, saints) or objects (the cross, decorations, buildings); an attempt to preach; or a questioning of the clergy. All the reform movements of the church took upon themselves an attempt to reorient the spiritual life of some segment of the church population by critiquing some of these areas. The Cistercians objected to the trappings of Cluniac life (which involved elaborate art, such as richly decorated altar sets, stained glass, tapestries and vestments, and elaborately choreographed liturgies accompanied by polyphonic choral music) and thus sought a simpler way of living the monastic life. The Dominicans and Franciscans felt the clergy were not responding to the needs of the laity and sought to preach to convert people from heresy (Dominicans) or to rebuild a fervent church of believers (Franciscans). The twelfth century finally saw Aquinas outline the number of sacraments and discuss their nature. Church doctrine was becoming more fixed, but also more debatable, because its boundaries were being clearly marked. All these groups within the age focused on finding new ways to improve.

This Project

In this account, I am interested in domestic matters: how these heretical movements were in conversation with the communities and social trends of their times. It is in seeing them as being part of local and national discussions within Catholicism that we begin to understand the nature of what determined heresy and orthodoxy in these times, and just how tenuous the line between the two was. We see that the difference was not based on doctrine but on other matters, such as political allegiances, wealth, and factions between orders in the church, during a period when there was first a rapid growth of new orders and then a sudden decision to put a stop to any more new orders. For this understanding, it's important to know what the detractors said and, where possible, to know what the defenders of the groups believed or the rituals and liturgies they followed. I hope in this work to explain some of the appeal, and the internal logic of these movements, by using the reformers' own words, where possible, to present people as true to their visions as possible.

Finally, at the heart of the discussion of various heretical sects in the Middle Ages is the very question of what heresy actually is. On the one hand, it's easy to say that heresy is a derivation from the received and sanctioned beliefs of the church. But beyond this description, it becomes more difficult to define it. Do the dissenting views deal only with doctrine? What about the political power of the church? There are a number of recognized theological systems in the Middle Ages; for example, the Dominicans and Franciscans did not hold to the exact same theologies. Which divergences mattered? What about divergences in practice? Again, in examining a time when the number of distinct orders within the church was exponentially increasing, I try to address in each chapter what each "heresy" shows as far as variation from some expectation.

In this book, I want to both tell a narrative fight against a narrative. The fight against heresy had a collective impetus, and the inquisitorial framework creaked into place to fight it; but each group of heretics that were examined had their own history that may or may not have had much other connection with the development of heresy as a category other than being investigated by the same inquisitors. The inquisitorial records tell us more about the production of power than about the words or exact thoughts of the heretics.[16] We can see a similar individual-but-part-of-a-history scenario in other aspects of the time; thus, when Robert of Arbrissel developed the Abbey of Fontevrault, he had a number of models to consider. That he chose a recognized form of life—monasticism—but one that differed from how it was practiced at that time in France, inventing the double monastery with a woman in charge, shows that he was able to blend both positive examples and innovate at the same time, something we welcome in the history of the church. When looking at heresy, the temptation is to find how it might be making similar innovations. Here, I want to consider each separate group as unique, pointing to how its members viewed themselves as well as how outsiders viewed them. Hopefully, this way will begin to correct the tendency, still present in scholarship in heresy studies, to see heretics as part of one history. What this book seeks to provide are concise chapters that explain each heresy, its influences, the social milieu in which it arose, and the conditions for its recognition as a heresy. There are a great many books out there on the topic of heresy, many of which are quite good. But as of yet, one needs to be rather advanced in understanding the social and intellectual histories of movements as well as theologically adept to enter into conversation with these studies. It is the aim of this book to help initiate others into the study of this aspect of social history. The study of medieval heresy also helps us to think about the modern world and the modern churches, about the threats—real or imaged—they face, and how they construct ideas of what is right belief, right actions, or right power. Sometimes we gain the perspective we seek when we study something that looks distinct from our own time and place, only to later see the correspondences that were there.

CHAPTER 1

The Petrobrusians and Henricians

The Monastic Influence on Heresy

AT THE DAWN of the twelfth century, the church had not had to deal with widespread heresy for several centuries. The early church dealt with Donatists, Manichaeans, and Arians, whose influence spread across Europe, but by the time of Charlemagne, widespread heresy was a thing of the past. The heresies that arose between then and the twelfth century were small affairs, generally at the hands of a single wayward preacher, and responses were tailored to the threat posed by each individual.[1] Gone were the serious heretical attacks such as those posed by the Manichaeans and Arians. Thus, the heresies of Peter of Bruys (fl. 1112–31), his contemporary Henry of Lausanne (fl. 1116–48), and their followers (known as the Petrobrusians and Henricians, respectively) represent a sea change in heresy and its suppression: Peter and Henry began what were local heresies, preached by wandering preachers, that had little impact at first but would find widespread interest once the two men moved into the area known as Languedoc. Their teachings would lead to riots, challenge priests and church authorities, and threaten the political order. At the time these heresies posed a threat, the church was not ready to fight widespread heresies, and there was no established church-wide mechanism for the investigation and condemnation of heretics. The move toward a centralized system for the investigation, correction, and punishment of heresy would find its first impetus in the wake of the Petrobrusian controversy.

Although Peter of Bruys and Henry of Lausanne (who was also called Henry of Le Mans or Henry the Monk) are known as a pair of evangelists who started off as wandering preachers and grew to have a following in Languedoc, each began his preaching career independent of the other. Each preached revival of faith and encouraged a life turned away from sin and modeled on the apostolic life. Each identified the apostolic life as one of austerity and poverty, and they lived off the alms that their followers gave them. Such a way of life was unexceptional for the times, and many wandering preachers had an unofficial place within the church. Peter and Henry eventually found trouble when, after losing episcopal approval to preach and even after being asked to desist, they kept returning to preach. The increasing condemnation they came under shows how the shift from local to larger-scale activities could be branded dangerous and lead to suppression. It also demonstrates that what might start off as reform could cross over into anticlericalism and doctrines that denounced church teachings. The response shows a church that moved toward a uniform, centralized mechanism for dealing with dissent, a response that drew on organized clerical structure and centralized power of the monastic orders for its initial development and ultimately became an arm of the papacy.

Wandering preachers were a well-established phenomenon in the twelfth century and arose from a spiritual tradition that emphasized apostolic poverty and a return to a spiritual life. As such, they converted people to their message through the example of their own lives, said to be held in common with that of Christ on his ministries and that of the apostles. The wandering preacher movement gave rise to innovations when the leaders and followers settled into communities; one tendency was to gradually encourage the enclosure of such movements within the cloister, where they could be watched and carefully supervised. This practice highlights the tension within the blossoming of new spiritual expressions in the medieval church: while wandering preachers were part of the religious landscape of the time, itinerant preachers sometimes caused problems for the church. The wandering preacher Tanchelm of Antwerp, a contemporary of Peter and Henry's, preached enthusiastically about clerical reform in the Low Countries, focusing on correcting the abuses and moral laxity he saw in the clergy. Of particular focus for him was the practice of priests living with women. He also opposed the paying of tithes to the church. Eventually, he would preach against the sacraments and real presence in the Eucharist and be condemned. His example reminded the church that significant unrest could result from popular preaching if it was not in obedience to the church.

Wandering preachers found particular favor among the guild and trade workers of smaller cities, where the model of integrating spiritual discipline and labor fit workers' lives. Generally, the church appreciated and encouraged the work of wandering preachers; at the end of their travels, a number of famous wandering preachers eventually settled in one place and founded orders within the church. Among them was Norbert of Xanten (1082–1134), who grew up in privilege and was a canon, a priest living in a chapter house with other priests who would all have been bound by a rule and have duties in the nearby cathedral or other parishes. A near brush with death led him to embark on an ascetic life of penance; after three years, he visited Pope Gelasius II, who suggested that Norbert become a wandering preacher to atone for his former life of vanity, allowing him to practice both his asceticism and his pastoral duties. Norbert would eventually settle in one place and establish the Norbertine order, an order of canons regular dedicated to following the asceticism of Norbert while exercising pastoral duties in parishes. They followed the *Rule of Saint Augustine*, and their numbers quickly grew.

Contemporary with Norbert was Robert of Arbrissel, who looked like a contemporary John the Baptist as he preached his way across France barefoot and dressed in animal skins. Robert had been the advisor to the bishop of Rennes before Pope Urban II gave him permission to be an itinerant preacher in 1096. From his vantage point, Robert could see the challenge wandering preachers posed to local church authorities trying to guide their flocks. Eventually, he settled down and established his double monastery at Fontevrault, which gained several inmates of aristocratic lineage and enjoyed the support of nobles. Double monasteries—which had a house for male monastics and an attached house for female monastics—had not existed in the church for a number of centuries and were an innovation that helped both the spiritual life and economics of the conjoined communities. Part and parcel with wandering preachers were new ways of thinking about the ways to foster leadership, charismatic gifts, and spirituality within the church.

In the High Middle Ages, other calls for reform within the church resounded as well. The Cistercian order (founded 1098, officially formed 1112) and the Carthusian order (founded 1084) were both monastic reform movements; other reforms had been ongoing for centuries, such as the Cluniac reform begun in the tenth century. These various monastic reforms reevaluated everything from liturgy and music to architecture and decoration to consider how each order furthered the mission of the church. Soon an explosion of new mendicant orders and military orders would once again expand the variety of charisms supporting the church.

In addition, Pope Gregory VII (1073–85) launched the Gregorian reform around this time, focusing on developing the structure and organizational order of the church on the clergy.² According to church organization, the church was a hierarchy with the pope at the summit and the layers of cardinals, bishops, priests, monks and nuns, and laity all filling specific defined ranks and roles and serving in obedience to those directly in charge over them. This arrangement directly encouraged people to act in the way that their part of the hierarchy was intended to. One of the derivative results was a clarification of the distinct roles and charisms of each order within the church. But change also risked a sense of turmoil. When the church came to adopt some of the ideals of the Gregorian reform, the laity could feel the effects; often, laity who wished to impose stronger ideals on their own lives grew increasingly critical of individual clergy who did not live up to the reform ideals. Finally, Crusade preaching from 1095 onward had stirred up public passions and encouraged the population to see itself as a vital front in the establishment of church doctrine and protection of the faith. People, in short, wanted preachers who preached the virtues of poverty and hard work to also live a life that was in harmony with their sermons.

Peter and Henry, Wandering Preachers

Not surprisingly, wandering preachers often left few records of their own journeys and preaching. We know from others about the content of Peter's and Henry's theological views, but the chronology of their lives is incomplete. We know they both began as wandering preachers, met around 1119, and preached together for about twenty years, with Henry continuing their message after Peter's death. Both men began preaching at about the same time, but Peter of Bruys would die first, and this event painted Henry into the role of disciple who continued the movement. Peter of Bruys started preaching sometime around 1112 and certainly started no later than that decade in the village of Bruys in the Hautes-Alpes, in the foothills of the Alps.³ He likely began as a priest in the area. For the majority of his preaching life, he worked alone and had a small, local impact, with his preaching focused on reform of the church. The local prelates worked to contain the impact of Peter's preaching and were largely able to do so. As the abbot of Cluny, located geographically to the northwest, was passing through Peter's area, he became aware of the heretical teachings that had been preached and was concerned that they were not completely eradicated, only temporarily suppressed.⁴

Around 1135, Peter's influence spread into the area of Narbonne and then into Languedoc, specifically around Toulouse. Languedoc, where the Petrobrusian heresies really took hold, was a unique area occupying a wide swath of southern France. It was an area defined by uniqueness in language, culture, and society. Its residents spoke *langue d'òc*, a language linguistically distinct from that of northern France. The area's literary heritage, troubadour poetry, and culture were related but distinct from the trouvère traditions of the north of France and Low Countries. Politically, the dukes of Aquitaine, the counts of Toulouse, and the kings of Aragon-Catalonia wielded power, and the feudal system had not become as strongly developed in Languedoc as in northern France. As a result, the area did not have the same strong fealty to local lords that other places did, which meant that dissenters more easily found support. Residents also practiced the custom of partible inheritance, which allowed both sons and daughters to receive lands; an inheritance split among many offspring (rather than going entirely to the oldest son) meant that landholdings did not remain in fiefdoms.[5] Languedoc did not have a wealthy landholding class but rather many impoverished landowners who were amenable to reform messages. As Peter's influence spread, his ideas also came into cities for the first time; the cities were even more receptive to his preaching apostolic poverty.[6] His preaching had found a foothold that allowed his message to spread much faster and wider than it had in rural areas, while ensuring its suppression would require a stronger response than before.

Peter's ideas created fear in the minds of his detractors. Peter was said to stir his followers into a frenzy that led them to destroy places of worship, burn crosses, turn over altars, and beat priests and monks. His followers would also make priests marry women.[7] Peter the Venerable noted Peter of Bruys's tendency to use force to get his way, leading to the whipping of priests and forcing them to marry.[8] Peter the Venerable described that one Good Friday, a day of traditional fasting and abstinence from meat to commemorate Christ's death on the cross, Peter's followers made a fire from crosses, roasted meat on it, and invited the public to have a festival day.[9]

Around 1119, Peter came into contact with Henry, with whom he shared a similar viewpoint on many reform issues. The two men became a team. During the period of 1119–39, after Peter's initial anathema, the number of people listening to his message grew large enough that the preachers needed to begin dividing their followers into missions to lead them effectively. It was this move—handing pseudo-ecclesiastical power over to local laity—that really created consternation among church authorities because it gave the appearance of setting up a rival church that had a diocesan structure that was not subject directly to Rome.

Peter of Bruys came to an unexpected end but not at the hands of inquisitors: while preaching in Saint-Gilles-du-Gard, the crowd became overzealous as they gathered outside of a local church. Peter encouraged them to burn the church crosses, saying that such symbols of idolatry should be destroyed. After the bonfire had been started, Peter found himself tossed onto it by the outraged townspeople who had watched the burning of crosses with horror. He died a victim of the religious fervor he sought to encourage.

Unlike Peter, Henry was attracted to preaching in towns and cities rather than to rural populations. Henry began his career as a wandering preacher and former monk in the Diocese of Lausanne in eastern France near the current Swiss border. He would move clear across France to Le Mans, in northern France, by 1116.[10] That year, he received permission to preach in the Diocese of Le Mans during Lent, as the bishop (Hildebert of Lavardin) would be absent. Apparently, Hildebert thought he was dealing with a wandering preacher like many of the famous ones of the time, such as Robert of Tiron, Raoul of Fustage, and St. Alleaume, men who traveled across various provinces to increase the religious zeal of the laity and encourage them to turn away from sin.

Accounts describe Henry in standard ascetic terms: "Hair cropped, beard untrimmed, tall of stature, quick of pace, he glided along barefoot as winter raged; easy of address, awe-inspiring in voice, young in years, scornful of ornate dress; his unconventional way of life was on the surface unlike that of ordinary folk."[11] In this narrative, Henry made his preaching entrance into Le Mans on Ash Wednesday, and he is described using Old Testament archetypes of a prophet. He could tell people's sins just by reading their faces.[12] Yet after comparing Henry to the prophets, the author would add that he was really a wolf in sheep's clothing. This depiction situated Henry as a concerned reformer in the tradition of the prophets, a man whose role was to challenge the church and bring it back to God's will.

When Henry began preaching, the scene was one of anticipation. He wore pilgrim's clothing and carried an iron cross on a long staff. When he climbed onto the platform to preach for the first time, everyone was captivated: "He spoke a pictorial, popular, and very different language, it seems, [compared to] the refined language of Hildebert, this delicate one, which the panegyrist acknowledged in a vulgar, novel way, and did not always know how to put himself within the reach of the people."[13] Henry's mode of delivery was shocking to the clerics—though very effective with the people. Adding to his dramatic effect was his outward appearance: long hair, a thunderous voice, passionate gestures, and eyes that "roared like a sea fertile in shipwrecks."[14] The next day, more people came to listen, with Henry "attracting women, children, performing miracles, he soon gained immense popularity in the city."[15] His chronicler noted that the purpose of this preaching was to warn honest Christians against the hypocrisy of the church.[16] He had wandered into the city as a charismatic preacher of the Gregorian reform and preached penitence.[17] It would become evident rather quickly that Henry's preaching was leading to disarray in the city and that the bishop would have to turn back from a planned trip to Italy to remedy the situation.[18]

By all accounts, Henry was a charismatic figure who emphasized a life rejecting wealth and honors. His preaching encouraged the renewal of faith and evangelism in the local populace, emphasized poverty, and stressed the reformation of individuals; his sermons included elements of asceticism, although it was not as large of a focus in his preaching to the laity as it was for other reform preachers. Henry also insisted that the prostitutes of the city give up their trade and marry the young men; since the latter could not afford wives, he paid the wedding settlements, although the men then left the city for the suburbs and the women went back to their trade.

Upon the bishop's return, the city was in complete disarray. Henry continued preaching in a number of different cities after Le Mans, including Poitiers, Bordeaux, and Dauphiné, but he repeatedly ran afoul of the authorities. It was in Provence that Henry met Peter of Bruys, and from that meeting, he regarded Peter as his master and teacher. Henry's chronicler noted that Henry clarified his doctrines after meeting Peter.[19] They travelled together through Provence, Gascony, and Narbonne. In 1135, the archbishop of Arles brought Henry before the Council of Pisa, which denounced three tenets he held; as a result, he promised to enter the Cistercian monastery of Cîteaux and give up his life as a wandering preacher. While Henry appears to have escaped detection for a while, he never entered the Cîteaux or any other monastery, and by 1145, historical accounts of him are silent.

There are three versions of Henry's end. According to one, Henry was persuaded to leave Toulouse, though the heresy continued after he left. In the second version, he was arrested by the bishop of Toulouse and asked permission to go to Clairvaux to expiate his sins. Bernard of Clairvaux offered to let him come to the monastery, but in transit, Henry slipped away and died somewhere unknown. In the third version, Henry was arrested and placed in the custody of the bishop of Toulouse, who took him to the Council of Rheims in 1148. There, he was condemned as a heretic by Pope Eugene III and was imprisoned until his death.[20] Regardless of the end Henry faced, the movement did not fully die out; in 1151, followers of Henry were still found in Languedoc. Around 1151, the chronicler Matthew Paris noted that a young woman was preaching and bringing new followers to the doctrines of Henry once again; the movement would continue, even after this second leader's death. The exact nature of Peter and Henry's collaboration and how long or even how they worked together is largely conjecture.

Peter and Henry's Theological Beliefs

With Peter and Henry, as with many medieval heretics, the majority of records were written by those who argued against them, so it is difficult to know their theological beliefs accurately.[21] In the case of Peter and Henry, we have canons of councils that condemned them midcareer and treatises written against Peter and against Henry. Their opponents were likely to exaggerate the threat to the local laypeople. The fact that heretical sects garnered such attention was matched by the fact that clerics within the church began to write tractates against them and wrote letters to clergy in regions affected by heresy, thus providing a greater record of the beliefs, practices, and impact of the heretical groups. These twelfth-century heretics instigated a change in the way that heresy was practiced and promulgated: starting with Peter, heretic leaders were more willing to use force and to incite crimes against the established churches and overlords; they were spread more openly by active preaching campaigns; and they stimulated believers who accepted their message into a series of positive actions, such as giving up wealth and jewelry.

The time in which the Petrobrusians were initially condemned—1119–20—saw a series of uprisings within the church. The unrest showed popular discontent with the way priests lived and sought to have them outwardly live more like average believers.²² Peter's preaching included defiant rhetoric whipped up against the laziness and excesses of other clergy. His theological views, although founded on the idea of the spiritual unity of all the church, were violent (and more violent than Henry's). Peter began by insisting that the ephemeral aspects of the church—all material components, decorations, and signs of luxury—were unnecessary. The Petrobrusian emphasis was on spiritual unity, not on the material aspects of faith.²³ He condemned the use of church buildings and the practice of the veneration of the cross. Thus, his dematerialized theology supported the destruction of churches and their furnishings;²⁴ in particular, the cross received his hatred, and he insisted that every one should be chopped up and destroyed in revenge for the killing of Jesus on the cross.²⁵

Peter's antimaterialism extended far beyond church decorations: repudiating material components of religion eventually led Peter to deny the Old Testament, the church fathers, and traditions of the church. He rejected infant baptism, the doctrine of the Eucharist, the sacrifice of the Mass, and prayers for the dead.²⁶ He rejected the authority of ecclesiastical tradition, including the Old Testament, some of the New Testament other than the Gospels, and the church fathers.²⁷ His emphasis on the spiritual over and against the material de-emphasized or totally denied the incarnation of Christ and found the sacraments empty and meaningless. Given his early geographical proximity to the Cistercians and Cluny, it is likely that Peter the Venerable knew about Peter's preaching firsthand when he wrote *Contra Petrobrusianos* (*Against the Petrobrusians*) sometime before 1138.²⁸ When Peter the Venerable passed through the same area a couple of decades later, he was able to see the lingering physical and spiritual aftermath of the heresy, and it caused him to write a letter dedicated to the archbishops of Arles and Embrun and the bishops of Die and Gap. Peter the Venerable noted that Peter of Bruys, although not permitting baptism of infants, did allow adult baptism with water, so his antimaterialism wasn't consistent and wasn't complete antisacerdotalism.²⁹ His complaint about the Eucharist wasn't antimaterialism as much as it was a concern that at the Last Supper, Christ had not intended to establish the rite of the Eucharist to forever repeat in the future.³⁰ While some other heretical groups would also deny the importance of the Eucharist, Peter, Henry, and their followers were unique about why.

Henry would add a radical anticlericalism to Peter's antimaterial stance. For Henry, clergy were not the sole dispensers of God's grace. Rather, he believed each individual to be in charge of receiving God's grace. Henry justified his theology on Matthew 28:19, "Make disciples of all nations."[31] William the Monk, who wrote about Henry in his chronicle (1135), would point out that Christ chose the disciples and sent them out two by two, thus having a divine control of the process. Only those who received a charge that descended from these men had a right to evangelize. For laypeople, the charge to preach was by invitation only; the call to live like the apostles was, according to William the Monk, a metaphor and not a literal call. Henry also began to preach that people lapsed through their own fault, not original sin; baptism needed to be a person's free choice, and as such, the baptism of infants was wrong; the sacrifice of the Mass was useless; only the consent of the couple was needed in marriage; and confession of sins among the laity replaced the sacrament of confession. For Henry, these propositions showed the completely unnecessary role of the sacraments and hence the unnecessary role of the clergy. Whereas Peter of Bruys's wholesale denigration of the material aspects of the church destabilized its means of asserting control, Henry's repudiation of clergy and the ecclesiastical structure and sacraments of the church threatened to tear it all down.

Henry's position was also one of radical simplicity: like Peter, Henry did not see the need for building ornate churches, but unlike Peter, he did not call for them to be destroyed. Henry preached within churches, although he would sometimes hold services outside.[32] And although he emphasized simplicity of worship, he didn't share the particular disregard for the cross that Peter had. He also emphasized evangelical ideals but did not disdain the Old Testament as Peter had. He saw no need for a special priestly class; his ideal was a poor, moneyless clergy who were mendicant and who served pastoral, not sacerdotal, functions. To rectify the decadence of the clergy, their roles would be like Henry's, wandering preachers whose exhortations would be key to leading the people back to belief. Certainly, some of Henry's complaints about the multiplication of worship were similar to others' complaints, such as those the Cistercians lodged against the Cluniacs. Henry disapproved of church singing; the Cistercians certainly simplified the liturgy in their own reform, not eliminating singing but greatly reducing the pomp and liturgical spectacle.[33] But the real danger in a popular movement that took asceticism to extremes wasn't merely about church decoration or liturgy; the real challenge to the church was how it questioned the ecclesiastical structure of power and the diocesan system. Further, Henry preached questionable notions, including a rejection of doctrinal and disciplinary authority of the church and a belief that the only correct interpretation of the rule of faith is free interpretation of the gospel. These accusations, if at all correct, show an increasing separation between Henry's preaching and the doctrines of the mainstream church.

Condemnations

The condemnations of Peter and Henry show that there was not yet an organized response to heresy at their time. Official responses came in a variety of forms, from condemnations of local bishops to a "crusade" preached against them by the Cistercian monks Alberic, Bernard, and Godfrey. There were two treatises of significant note written against them: Peter the Venerable's treatise against Peter of Bruys and William the Monk's against Henry. There were also two councils that condemned Peter and Henry and ordered them to stop preaching. The wheels of institutional response were gaining strength and order, and they were beginning to communicate so as to allow them to work together, but they were not as focused and coordinated as they would become within the next few decades. The writers who attacked Henry's teachings were primarily monks and bishops, and their writings focus on Henry as a bad monk compared to Peter as the bringer of dangerous ideas and violence.

In 1119, Pope Callixtus II convened the Council of Toulouse, which promulgated one canon that directly addressed heretics; it is thought to be directed against Peter of Bruys.[34] The canon mentions that the followers of the condemned heretics expressed doubt about the sacrament of the Eucharist, baptism of children and infants, the priesthood, the criteria for a legitimate marriage, the priesthood, and the orders. It places both those who follow these heretical ideas and those who defend them under condemnation.[35] The story would not end here, obviously, as Peter and Henry continued preaching.

The next to take up the fight against the Petrobrusians was Bernard of Clairvaux, a monk of the Cistercian order, which had been founded only a couple of decades before. Bernard began to set up a clear set of principles that would form the response against heretics. He focused on the person of Henry and his bad past, whereas Peter the Venerable focused on the doctrine, not the character, of Peter of Bruys.[36] Bernard mentioned that he had seen a work of collected sermons that was circulated by Henricians, but he doubted the origin of the writings.[37] By 1135, William the Monk also wrote against

Henry. William the Monk provided a summation of the group and its beliefs in the work *Contra Henricum schismaticum et hereticum* (*Against the Henrician Schismatics and Heretics*). His treatise continued to focus on Henry's misdeeds, especially as they related to the clergy of Le Mans.[38]

The Council of Pisa asked Henry to return to a monastery. He agreed to enter the Cistercian abbey of Cîteaux, where Bernard was, but never made it there. In 1145, Bernard and his friend Geoffrey of Chartres went on a preaching campaign against Henry. Although the church had no apparatus for dealing with widespread heresy, it did have one for dealing with outsiders threatening Christianity. The Crusades would become the basis for how the church dealt with these heretics, seeing them as outsiders in need of conversion and as people against whom the church could act with force if needed. Peter the Venerable would also use the language of foreigners and outsiders in his treatise against the Petrobrusians.

In 1138, Peter the Venerable wrote the first draft of his arguments against the group, a letter that contains a tractate against the Petrobrusians. He used rhetoric chronicling Peter of Bruys that was milder than the preacher's end would suggest. Likely, part of the reason for the focus on the heretics of Provence was to help secure Cluny's efforts to reclaim some of its prior lands.[39] As Peter the Venerable wrote, "Since it is right that Christian charity should put the greater effort on converting heretics than on driving them out, let authority be cited to them, let reason also be added, so that they may be compelled to yield—to authority if they choose to remain Christians, to reason if they choose to remain men."[40] Peter the Venerable described the movement's preachers as foolish and impious, noting that at times they seem too bold and at other times struck with terror. He thought heretics had somehow laid aside reason to follow illogical beliefs; at heart, he believed that heretical errors were errors in understanding and the light and truth of proper preaching would set the heretics back on the correct path.

Peter the Venerable took the positions of Peter of Bruys and his followers seriously; he considered Peter to be a fair opponent who had thought through his positions and tried to back them up with reasoning, church authorities, and Scripture. Peter the Venerable enumerated five tenets of the Petrobrusian controversy that he deemed to be heretical. He describes these five main errors of the Petrobrusians as "poisonous plants" that Peter of Bruys had sown and nurtured. Underlying these is Peter of Bruys's idea that the church is essentially a spiritual church and that the earthly church, organization, and sacraments do not matter. The most public form of scandal was their insistence in not venerating crosses.[41] This type of insistence on the primacy of the spiritual and ignorance of the material not only went against the Christian focus on the incarnation, but it was also too reminiscent of a number of the dualist heresies from the ancient church, which focused solely on the spiritual and abhorred the physical.[42] The Godhead had deigned to become fully human in the incarnation—and, as such, the material was exalted and had a rightful place in the celebration of the sacraments. Peter the Venerable enumerated the errors as such:

1. Peter of Bruys's followers did not believe that infant baptism was necessary.
2. They claimed that God is everywhere, so buildings and temples were not necessary. One does not gain anything from worshipping in a church if God is omnipresent.
3. They viewed the cross as the locus where Christ was tortured and therefore not a location to be revered or an artifact appropriate for worship.
4. They claimed the transformation of bread and wine into body and blood happened only at the Last Supper celebrated with the apostles, and all subsequent celebrations did not contain the real presence of Christ in the elements. Christ did not intend to create a rite that would be repeated. Not even symbolic recreations of this supper were amenable to the group.[43] As such, they emphasized the uniqueness of the time Christ lived and walked in the Holy Land. In reality, this emphasis undermined their focus on the "spiritual" over the "material" by asserting the historicity of the Last Supper event.
5. They declared prayers and Masses for the dead to be useless and unable to change the afterlife of the deceased.

Peter the Venerable saw the overall impact of these ideas was not that Peter of Bruys was a reformer but that he was an outsider or foreigner who was not truly within the Christian community of believers.[44]

In his introduction to the *Contra Petrobrusianos*, Peter the Venerable also stated that he had begun thinking that Henry was a mere follower of Peter of Bruys, but on investigation, he learned that Henry had held a position as a wandering preacher before he became enthralled by Peter of Bruys's ideas. As such, in Peter the Venerable's mind, the two are closely though not perfectly aligned in their thoughts and deeds.[45] Peter the Venerable attempted something different in this treatise: instead of merely condemning them as the canons of councils did, he took their ideas and set them up as a series of propositions meant for debate, assuming that if they could be pronounced to be illogical, incompatible with church teaching, or incorrect in other ways, that the heresy would be defeated and the followers would return to the church. In so doing, Peter spent his time developing both doctrines but more importantly, an ecclesiology and a culture of the church that was imbued with the monastic spirit. It placed the newly formed monastic orders in a key role in protecting the orthodoxy of the church, as they explored new types of solitary and community life. That the person against whom Peter the Venerable was writing the treatise had also been a monastic or anchorite of some sort helped his point by allowing him to insert the monasteries into the discussion without having to distinguish them from the active mission of the church. So his rhetorical point was not just to condemn or exclude but also to show who should be included within the church. How one was—or wasn't—located within the church was open for interpretation at this point, as it was a time when many new orders were being created and approved. One could perhaps wonder if Peter the Venerable's true purpose was to exclude one group or to cement the inclusion of his own.

Bernard's preaching crusade against the heretics also asked them to debate; although not accepted, the proposal took the same tone and impetus as Peter the Venerable's writing. Despite Peter the Venerable's 1138 treatise against the heresy, the Henricians gained favor in a number of cities in southern France. By 1145, Pope Eugene III supported sending strong preachers to counteract the Henrician influence. Eugene III, the first Cistercian pope and a friend of Bernard's, asked Alberic, the cardinal-bishop of Ostia, to handle the situation. Alberic invited Bernard and Godfrey, bishop of Chartres, to conduct the preaching tour. In the summer of 1145, Bernard left for the south of France, in search of Henry. Bernard's tour included stops in Bergerac, Périgueux, Sarlat, Cahors, and Toulouse.[46] That summer saw the crusaders against heresy arrive in Toulouse, but they were not well received. The people at large, even people who were not Henry's followers, were not convinced Henry was a heretic; the laity saw him as an austere, holy man. Henry left in response to Bernard's arrival.

Count Alphonse Jourdain, whose rule extended over Toulouse, Provence, and Narbonne, extended protection to Henry.[47] The three preachers of orthodoxy—Alberic, Bernard, and Godfrey—moved on to Albi, where they were greeted more enthusiastically than at Toulouse. In the smaller hill-towns such as Verfeil, the heretics caused distractions to keep Bernard from being heard.[48] The experience of the orthodox preachers showed heresy had already become accepted in the local culture. It had the protection from the local lords, who were concerned with those from outside coming in and challenging their tenuous authority. It also had the support of the average people, who appreciated the straightforward, earnest message of Henry. None of these were strong doctrinal stances; they were for reasons of political expediency or due to general admiration. The years 1145 and 1146 naturally led to apocalyptic speculations: a pope had died, the third in three years; Halley's Comet passed the earth; and there were extensive famine and natural disasters. People were on edge, and all signs pointed to some sort of supernatural intervention in the world. The clash between heresy and orthodoxy took on an urgent feel in such an environment.

A year after the unsuccessful preaching tour against him, Henry was finally arrested and brought before the bishop of Toulouse. During that year, Bernard encouraged the diocese to crush the remaining heresy. These events show a change in the Cistercian understanding of the monks' roles in the lives of the church: the Cistercian order had always sought remote locations far away from established villages and towns. The emphasis of Cistercian spiritual practice was on the interior reformation of the person. Bernard's move to deal with matters outside of the monastery, particularly with lay movements, shows a nontypical Cistercian approach to the exterior world. Rather than being Mary, who contemplated the Lord's presence, Bernard was intent on becoming Martha, who bustled about, taking care of pastoral issues and promoting orthodoxy within the church.

The Legacy of the Monastic Response

Perhaps more remarkable than the content of the Petrobrusian heresy is the strong response it elicited from the Cistercians. Before the Petrobrusians, there were small heretical groups that are known only from the documentary evidence of the hearings that found them guilty. In the case of Peter and Henry, there exists a record establishing both a rhetoric for describing heretics and a world that starts to perceive them as a threat serious enough to warrant refutations of their views. The world of literature into which this heresy was born was a fragmentary one including a variety of forms. Bernard of Clairvaux, the tireless Cistercian abbot, frequently preached about heresy in his sermons delivered to his monastery. He also wrote of heresy in general and of the Henrician heresy in letters. We also know of the Henrician heresy from the writings of William the Monk. And Peter the Venerable, at the request of Bernard, also wrote a treatise against the Petrobrusians, as we saw in the last section. His writings are perhaps the most detailed description of the group.

The Petrobrusian heresy provides a glimpse into shifts that began to occur in the High Middle Ages. In particular, this heresy presented itself as the first one to merit a widespread response by the clergy and papacy since the time of the Arians. The church had to determine what tools it would use to fight heresy and how to do so effectively. At its disposal were the preachers of the church; the monastic traditions of reform, which could speak to the zeal for austerity; and the church authority, which had become gradually centralized and had begun to work in lockstep with the secular authorities as places in Europe became centralized under regional secular leaders. The Petrobrusian heresy flourished during the time of charismatic leaders, including a monastic leader who had a penchant for attacking various individuals and groups: Bernard of Clairvaux.

Bernard was a watchdog who enjoyed taking aim at any number of folks.[49] He attacked the theologian Peter Abelard of the University of Paris, seeking and receiving the condemnation of Abelard, and he criticized the scholastic logician Gilbert of Poitiers, who did not receive condemnation despite Bernard's best efforts. Bernard's statements about Henry show that Bernard viewed him as both an apostate monk and as a gyrovague, a type of wandering, unstable monk that the founder of Western monasticism, Benedict of Nursia, warned against in the beginning of his *Rule*. Bernard said that Henry "is an apostate who, having abandoned the monastic habit (for he was once a monk), has returned to the world and the filth of the flesh, like a dog to its vomit. Ashamed to live amongst kinsmen and those who know him, or rather not permitted to do so on account of his monstrous crimes, he has girded himself and taken the road to where he is not known, becoming a gyrovague and fugitive on the face of the earth."[50] Bernard also compared Henry to Judas, the treacherous apostle who betrayed Christ for a bag of silver. Worse yet is not just that Christ becomes a monetary transaction but also that this money then has an immoral purpose. "When he began to seek a living he sold the Gospel (he is an educated man), scattering the word of God for money and preaching so that he might live. If he is able to secure something over and above his keep from simple people or some elderly women, he squanders it in gambling or more shameful ways. Frequently after a day of popular adulation this notable preacher is to be found with prostitutes, sometimes even with married women."[51] It wasn't bad enough that Henry sold Christ out for a bag of money; preacher Henry used that money to gamble and hire prostitutes.

Bernard's condemnations of Henry were part of the abbot's larger view. Bernard was not content to condemn heresy only outside of the monastery. Within its confines, Bernard preached against heresy in his sermons from 1143 onward. In his sermons on the Song of Songs 2:15, he explained to the monks that he felt the need to preach a third sermon on the verse "seize for us the little foxes that are destroying the vineyard." Here Bernard warned his own monks about not being connected to a community and then moved from addressing them to talking about the dangers outside of the monastery in relation to heresy. Elsewhere, Bernard said that wandering heretics should settle down into the religious communities to prove their seriousness and orthodoxy, expressing the Benedictine concern that gyrovagues were ruthless, untrustworthy, and prone to error and seen as a monastic problem.[52] But such a response elicits two interesting conclusions. First, Bernard of Clairvaux thought Henry was a reformer, and his error was more with his way of life. Second, to Bernard, Henry's way of life was more a problem than his theological beliefs. These ideas are quite distinct from Peter the Venerable's thoughts on Peter of Bruys.

Bernard's attacks on Henry placed him as one of the reprobates within the history of Christianity. Henry conformed to the symbols of those who, like him, betrayed Christ or betrayed the life of one who follows Christ. He was someone already lost. Peter the Venerable wrote that heretics should be spoken to as a way of bringing them back into the church or treated as foreigners or under foreign influence. Understanding their errors and trying to lead them to truth was part of the pastoral responsibility of the church. Bernard tended to be more zealous. His attacks on the Petrobrusians were the first widespread heresy that Bernard went after. His letters addressed not just the

Petrobrusians but also their neighbors and potential sympathizers. The aim of his letters was both to educate and perhaps even threaten those who would offer support to heretics, seeing them as encouraging the waywardness. Letter 242, written after Bernard had returned home to his monastery, addressed the people of Toulouse and condemned the uncommissioned preaching by heretics.[53] The previous letter included Bernard's attack on Henry, containing his comments that priests were not given respect within the group and virtuous people were driven out of the church. Here Bernard developed a sense that stronger secular justice or military action must be taken against heretics. This idea would culminate in the Albigensian Crusade against the Cathars of the same region, which will be discussed in the next chapter. It was also at this time that Bernard found himself the preacher for the Second Crusade, whipping up popular opinion against the Saracens. While Bernard was clear that heretics have no place within the church, he did not make clear the mechanism for their return. He naively seemed to think that right thinking would bring most people back to the church if they could only see the errors of their ways.

In letters to Everwin, the prior of Steinfeld, about heretics in the Rhineland, Bernard also referred to the heretics in terms of deceit. They were wolves in sheep's clothing: "sheep in appearance, foxes in deceit, wolves in action." Bernard also attacked them for rejecting church authority, rejecting its teaching on purgatory, and performing infant baptism.[54] Less than two years later, Bernard set off for Toulouse to combat heresy on the ground. This time, we know that the heretic he was confronting was Henry of Lausanne. Bernard had left his own monastery and become a gyrovague in his attempts to stamp out heresy. All in all, this correspondence gives a sense of the seriousness with which Bernard, Peter the Venerable, and others approached the issue of stamping out heresy in the area, which resulted in preaching missions and attempts to rout heresy in the area of Languedoc and would continue by the Cistercians long after the Petrobrusian threat had faded. And Bernard established a pattern that other Cistercians would follow in coming generations, one in which the order, despite living an ascetic life on the edges of civilization, would actively fight against heresy.

Lasting Impact

Thinking about the difference in the twelfth century between heresy and doctrinal belief, we can say that the wandering preachers focused on the same concerns as the orthodox preachers but with an imprecision that led them into heresy.[55] There's a spectrum of principles, and the principles Henry preached could, in fact, be seen in the Gregorian reform and will continue to be seen in some of the new orders still to be created and receive official recognition within the church.[56] While the issue of doctrine and dualism might be part of it, there are two much larger issues at play in this first "widespread" medieval heresy. The first is the issue of popular spirituality threatening church power and authority by seeming to offer criticism of the way the church presented the sacraments and performed the liturgy. Asceticism was acceptable on an individual level or even on a corporate level when it was part of the structure of the church (such as in the officially recognized Cistercian men). But when asceticism was seen as a critique of the clergy, it became a much more dangerous issue. The second is that the lasting impact of this heresy seems to be the increasing severity of response, in large part determined not only by the church and its local leaders and allies but also by the orders. In the person of Bernard of Clairvaux was born an unflagging champion of orthodoxy. Finally, the church struggled with the question of what constitutes appropriate forms of lay fervor and how it can be kept within acceptable confines that can be controlled by the church, such as within the third orders of the mendicant orders.

One of the lasting impacts of the Petrobrusian heresy was that it inaugurated the mechanism of condemnation that would emerge. A number of notable people spoke against the heresy: Peter the Venerable, Bernard of Clairvaux, Peter Abelard, and Hildebert of Lavardin. Following these outspoken monks and academics, laws and regulations began to be enacted or established. The fighting of heresy, which had previously been the purview of bishops, was becoming the role of all clergy and orders within the church.[57] Canon 3 of the Council of Toulouse condemned a number of propositions the Petrobrusians had accepted, including rejecting the Eucharist, infant baptism, priesthood, and matrimony. In 1139, the Second Lateran Council under Pope Innocent II issued almost the same statement verbatim. Second Lateran would be the start of real anti-Petrobrusian activity, the beginning of a development not just of increasingly focused definitions of heresy but also of the mechanisms by which it would be dealt with. Throughout the Middle Ages, both local and ecumenical (church-wide) councils will deal with issues of heresy, with the tendency being for the Holy See to make more pronouncements that help to both define heresy and explain its punishments as the Middle Ages continue. The identification of heresy became one effect of the consolidation of power, and it would become entwined with the attempt to clearly regulate the acceptable forms of religious and lay life in the church.

Perhaps the greatest of repercussions for this time was that the Cistercian involvement in the detection and prevention of heresy will see several things happen. First, the Cistercians will be involved in the investigation and prosecution of a number of heresies that we will see over the following chapters. Second, the Cistercian work will become a forerunner of the work of both the Dominican order and eventually of the Inquisition, under the aegis of the Dominican and Franciscan orders. That the Cistercians saw church reform and the rebuttal of heresy to be interconnected was not surprising. One of the reasons this heresy seems larger than the two men who "founded" it is the response it garnered. The official church response will continue to escalate, particularly in this area and in response to the Cathars.

CHAPTER 2

The Cathars

The Turn to Force against Group Heresies

PERHAPS MORE THAN any other medieval heresy, the Cathars evoke images of an organized group of heretics brazenly attacking the church. It is no wonder we have this perception, given the ferocity with which the church attacked the Cathars and the violence it used to quash them. The church tried a new approach with the Cathars, one that asserted that military force worked better than preaching crusades.[1] It was the tenacious strength and influence of the Cathars that led the medieval inquisitorial machine to develop. Although there was some variation in how effective this new machinery actually was against the suppression of heresy, a series of heretic burnings occurred throughout the twelfth century: Soissons in 1120; Cologne in 1144 and 1163; and Vézelay in 1167 (the Dualists at Liège were almost burned in 1144 but were spared that fate).[2] Such suppressions would reach a climax at the massacre of Béziers in 1209, where the infamous rhetoric of the campaign was so vehement that a legend arose: the abbot of the monastery of Cîteaux, Arnaud Amaury, is claimed to have insisted on sparing no one, saying "Kill them all, God will know His own."[3] This massacre marked the start of the Albigensian Crusade (so known because it sought to correct or rout the Cathars, or Albigensians, around the town of Albi), a crusade against heretics within Christianity's own lands. It was a move that asserted, "In a society founded on community of religion, were heretics not foreigners?"[4] During the time of the Cathars, the idea that Christianity was under threat became commonplace.

The Cathars were not particularly organized until the thirteenth century, and the categorization of a Cathar set of beliefs and adherents was imposed on them by those who vowed to fight them.[5] The church followed this strategy to help define the enemy and make it possible to repress them, a job much more easily undertaken when the enemy could be identified. As such, this heresy represents a missed opportunity for reconciliation before heresy fully developed, a situation the church used "in order to establish the conditions for, and legitimation of, repression and persecution."[6] Like the preaching of Peter of Bruys and Henry of Lausanne, the Catharism of Languedoc found success in the same area and in the same sorts of communities: in the smaller towns surrounding cities and in villages strung along the hillsides. Catharism thrived in places where small workshops were the focus of the economy. Cathar growth highlighted shortcomings of the church: there were no standard procedures to address heresy, no penalties outlined, and no clear sense of who should prosecute heretics or how the accused should be examined. Nor was there a sense of how to deal with nobles who, while maybe not heretics themselves, supported heretics in an attempt to weaken church interests financially or politically. In reality, the Cathars, though more widespread than previous heresies, were hardly a majority. It is estimated that even in the most saturated areas, Cathars could not have been more than 10 percent of the population, and less than 10 percent of those were fully initiated Cathar perfects.[7]

It also became clear that whatever success Peter of Bruys and Henry of Lausanne had previously had in the same region, the Cathars eventually more became organized than either man could have dreamed of. That organization underscored the Cathars' real threat to the church. While secular and ecclesiastical power were being consolidated in other parts of Europe, including the northern parts of France, the Languedoc region was not nearly as controlled by feudalism as other regions. Culturally, Languedoc had a stronger lingering presence of the ideals of the Roman Empire. The lords and counts of the area could not depend on raising an army nearly as easily as their neighbors to the north, and they had to rely on mercenaries;[8] there was more of a spirit of independence and less of a sense of conformity required within the region. The Cathars could easily grow as one of several competing religious groups in this milieu. With this development comes a focus on a rival system of beliefs, practices, and social organization, which was a greater threat to the power of the Catholic Church than individuals. In the rise of the Cathars, we also see a shift from heresies that followed the charismatic ideas of an individual to ones that were more socially spread, whose dissemination relied on communities of believers and not a cult of personality. There was also a sense of various groups within the church finding new ways of life, new expressions of faith. But the lesser nobility could not construct grand monasteries. They sought something that appealed more to their personal piety and that inspired them.

Cathar Origins

Because the Cathars were such a widespread group, and the attack against them so violent, they have been subject to a lot of scholarly attention. The Cathars often called themselves "Good men," "Good women," or "Good Christians" but also took the name Cathars from the Greek *katharos*, meaning pure or innocent. They focused on the practice of asceticism, the reception of one sacrament, and the belief that salvation could be attained by all believers. The movement lasted for half a millennium and spread through southern Europe, from the area of Languedoc to the eastern Mediterranean.

The Cathars have long been assumed to have developed in conversation with other heretical groups from the eastern edges of Christianity, such as the Bogomils.[9] Thus, attempts have been made to trace the group's intellectual dissemination and genealogy of ideas, particularly the basis for its dualism, which was perhaps its strongest point of departure from Catholicism and one that hearkened back to an early church heresy, Manichaeanism. There was also a good reason for wanting to develop a genealogy, as the Bogomils believed that genealogies of spiritual authority determined if the sacrament of *consolamentum* (spiritual baptism) was efficacious, and scholarship on Cathars has inadvertently mimicked this belief.[10] It is easy to spend too much time focusing on origins and lose focus on the Cathars' views in and of themselves. Such genealogical accounts tend to minimize the distinctions and variances in doctrine and avoid infusing the ideas with the social milieus in which these groups lived.[11] Trying to construct a lineage reinforced the medieval notion that all heresies were part of the same tendency for Satan to mislead people to undermine and overcome the church, a viewpoint that adds nothing to our comprehension.[12]

The standard description of the Cathars states they were dualists who were the heirs of the Manichaeans from the late antique church, and this dualist framework was brought to the West by returning Crusaders who heard about it from the Bogomils of the East.[13] Alternatively, some describe the Cathars as a constructed foreign heresy in the midst of the Christian West, created by overlaying Augustine's anti-Manichaean writings on a contemporary heresy. Each description of the Cathar heresy defines it as distinct from Western Christianity, an important move in an era when the Western church was encountering Islam in the Crusades and in its expansion into the Iberian

Peninsula and Languedoc and recovering from the 1054 schism between the Western and Eastern Christian Empires.[14] For Western Europe, the twelfth and thirteenth centuries were a time of renewed contact with outsiders, especially the East and the Muslim world. The writings of al-Farabi, Avicenna, Averroes, Avicebrol, and Maimonides all entered the Western universities at this time, creating anxieties around this new, non-Christian knowledge.

Cathar beliefs were both sufficiently developed and sufficiently different from Catholic theological views to cause suspicions of their origins. One likely origin is Bogomil, the founder of a dualist sect in Bulgaria that bears his name. He was a reform-minded priest during the reign of Czar Peter (927–69). Our source for Bogomil's beliefs is Cosmas, a priest who argued against him: Bogomil believed that the devil created matter, that Christ did not have an ordinary material body, and that he therefore did not suffer and was not born of Mary. Bogomil identified the devil with Jehovah of the Old Testament, and he also denounced veneration of the cross as useless because material aids could not help spiritual prayer and were creations of the devil. The followers of Bogomil rejected the Christian church and all its sacraments. Bogomil religious communities had simple prayer practices, saying the Lord's Prayer four times during the day and four times at night. They also had group confessions. The group gained popularity and spread throughout the Balkans and into Asia Minor.

Cosmas described the Bogomils in tenth-century Bulgaria as simple people whose religion had an ascetic orientation that would have resonated with the Eastern Christian monastic tradition.[15] The Bogomils denounced procreation and were strict vegetarians because they believed meat was the product of procreation, as were eggs and milk. The group spread to the Greek areas of Byzantium in the eleventh century, and the church would continue to grow and organize. Euthymius Zigabenus, a scholar and monk who wrote on the Bogomil heresy at the request of Byzantine Emperor Alexius I in the early twelfth century, stated that the Bogomils separated their church members into hearers (people just entering the community) and members with full initiation. By this time, they had developed a liturgy, scriptures, and rules for exegesis of scripture.[16] They would come under condemnation, beginning with the Holy Synod of Constantinople in the reign of Michael II of Oxeia in 1140, which condemned them to burning.[17]

While the nature of contact between the Bogomils and the Cathars is not known, a few dates evidence when Cathar activity began to appear in the West. Everwin of Steinfeld penned a letter to Bernard of Clairvaux in the 1140s about a Greek heresy that shared some similarities with others in the West, namely a concern for apostolic life. He described a group that sprang up as a fully formed church in the Rhineland. By the next decade, the first condemnations in Cologne mentioned Cathars. Eckbert of Schönau wrote a series of sermons against this new Cathar heresy. In these sermons, he linked the Cathars with the Manichaeans, against whom Augustine had fought in the late antique church.[18] He also pointed out new and unique beliefs among these heretics, including that the souls of humans are the angels who have fallen from heaven, something not seen in either Manichaean or Christian theology.[19] In 1144, there were appearances of a dualist group in Liège. A report from Rheims in 1157 said Catharism existed in Flanders, especially among weavers and cloth merchants, occupations that required regular travel. At about the same time, reports of Cathars in north and central Italy started to emerge. Cathar missions to various areas in France, including Languedoc, would occur in the 1160s. The Cathars made it to southern Italy in the 1190s.[20] There is also evidence that from 1209 until the fourteenth century, Languedocian Cathars made their way in groups to Italy or were shepherded by Italian Cathar communities as the Albigensian Crusade continued to employ tactics ranging from direct assaults to starving Cathars out of their walled fortresses over winters.[21] This movement of people required the Cathars to develop a network of safe houses for those who would travel and to have knowledge of how to undertake travel, which was neither easy nor safe in those times.[22]

While the Cathars were most prominent in the Languedoc region, they also had considerable presence in Italy, such as in Orvieto and Viterbo, where local leaders opposed the papacy and, as such, permitted the Cathars' power. The Cathar ecclesiology in Italy would grow and shape itself into three administrative areas: the Albanenses, the Garatenses, and the Bagnolenses, each named after the areas in which they flourished. The Albaneses were located in the area around Lake Garda and had closest ties with the Bogomil church of Drugunthia, or Dragovitia, in the southeastern Balkans, the church from which Pope Nicetas hailed. The Garatenses were located near Milan and had ties to the Bulgarian Cathars. The Bognolenses were located around Bagnolo and had ties to the Bogomils of Sclavonia.

Cathar Growth and Development

Some of the most detailed records about the Cathars exist in the Languedoc inquisition trials.[23] These records show a very open movement that progressively became less public and more secretive as oppression continued. Other texts include the disputations of adversaries who engaged the Albigensians in debates; three rituals, one in Latin and two in Occitan, including *Rituel de Florence*; *Rituel de Lyon*; and *The Book of Two Principles*, attributed to John of Lugio—along with some troubadour writing.[24] The social history of the Albigensians explains their influence and the reasons for their growth and stubbornness to convert to Catholicism. The groups came to light as highly organized heretical churches that had social and ecclesiastical structures and clearly defined beliefs. Cathars and Catholics even shared church facilities in some areas of the Midi (southern France), giving the Cathars a sense of equality with Catholics and making it hard to distinguish between the groups in some towns. It is believed that Catharism was first introduced among the elite classes, possibly brought from the East via the trade routes, and that the ideas gradually filtered through the larger society.[25] As the Cathars became the focus of antiheretical campaigns, they moved to smaller towns and found support from rural peasants.[26] Apprentices would often work while listening to the perfects preach and discuss religious matters. Unlike the Petrobrusians and other heresies of the time, the Cathars were not practitioners of voluntary or apostolic poverty; instead, they were often situated along trade routes, used trade networks as part of the system for spreading Cathar influence, gathered and distributed large donations for the support of other Cathar houses, and actively participated in the Langedocian and Italian local economies.[27]

Cathar teaching and spiritual direction occurred within the same houses people used to learn trades. These houses were largely public in nature and served as social centers as well as places of religious instruction and craft learning; here the Cathar perfects helped instruct novices.[28] In the south of France, the primary organizational structure was the *castrum*, or a fortified village around the castle of an overlord. Because of the system of subdividing inheritances, many of the aristocracy lived among their subjects, and so persons of varying social classes lived side by side in the *castri*.[29] The Cathar houses in the north were more prosperous, as trade was more developed in these areas; in Languedoc, the nobles did not have the same financial distinction from other classes, were often involved in trades such as weaving, and would work with those of other social classes. The situation would follow in a similar but weaker fashion in Italy. The church of the Italian city-states was not strong enough to fight all the lay movements effectively, and the bishops of some areas and cities were not sufficiently connected to work together effectively.

The thirteenth century saw a continued strengthening of the Cathar organization. As the group became more established, it created a formal religious instruction in the Cathar faith. Its hierarchy of priests, perfects, believers, and hearers was reflected in the local networks it developed. A collection of houses of Cathar perfects developed, much like the networks of monastic houses in Christianity. These houses were the backbone that made the Cathar movement as strong as it was. Cathar houses of perfects were distinguished from Christian monasteries by both their openness to laity visiting and their dual purpose of vocational and religious instruction. This dual focus echoes the Benedictine vision of *ora et labora* (pray and work) punctuating the hours of the monastic day. Cathars allowed apprenticeships of young children similar to the practice of child oblation within Benedictine monastic houses. The Cathar houses allowed the free coming and going of all who wanted to visit, and they served as centers where people could buy goods or provide and receive services. In the later days of Catharism, these houses disappeared as the Cathar networks fell apart.[30]

Beliefs

The Cathar beliefs that clashed with the church can be categorized into three groups. First, there were issues related to Cathar ecclesiology (how the group's communities were organized and structured) as well as the education of certain individuals to higher levels within the community. Second, there were issues with the philosophical underpinnings of their theology, such as their dualism, the source of evil in the world, and the nature of Christ. Finally, there were derivative issues related to the sacraments.

Ecclesiology and Education

The Cathars developed a far stronger sense of ecclesiastical administration than other heretical groups. Once there were a number of Cathar communities across southern France, a synod was called in St. Félix-de-Caraman. The records of this meeting, held in 1167, list some of the Cathar leadership of the time, including Pope Nicetas, head of the Greek-speaking Bogomils of Constantinople and presiding member of the synod; Robert of Epernon, bishop of the northern French Cathars; and Mark, Cathar bishop of Lombardy.[31] The emphases of the synod were establishing a church structure, regulating beliefs across Catharism in the West, and professing to one form of Bogomil beliefs.[32] The assembly emphasized doctrinal consistency and ecclesiological organization. The development of a Cathar church required the development of both the ecclesiastical structure and regional dioceses. By the end of the twelfth century, there were at least six Cathar dioceses, which the group likened to the seven churches of Revelation; just like those churches, these Cathar one worked independently on behalf of their local followers and were loosely connected to each other in faith.[33]

The synod was the moment when the Western Cathars definitively adopted the dualism of the East; previously, the Cathars had followed Monarchianism, believing that God was in charge and that a lesser deity created the world. At this synod, Nicetas asked Mark to receive *consolamentum* again, saying that his earlier one was received from a Cathar bishop whose lineage left its efficacy under suspicion. The Western bishops aligned themselves with the Bogomil church and accepted the relationship between the two churches. Cathar bishops served primarily a pastoral role since it was a missionary church. Underneath each bishop was a *filius major*, who would take over after him, and a *filius minor*. There were also deacons who ministered to aristocratic families, undertook missionary activities, and tended to farther-flung communities. By the conclusion of this meeting, the hierarchy of the Cathar church was largely worked out and adhered to.[34]

The social structure of the Cathars differed from that of the Catholics. The Catholic Church held ideas of the distinct roles that men's and women's houses served in religious life, but the Cathar houses did not have such distinctions. Catholic houses placed more restrictions on women's houses, which were seen as a financial and spiritual burden. Both in the laity and among the perfects, women in Cathar communities had more responsibilities and religious opportunities. They could teach, preach, minister to others, preside over the sacrament, and serve as spiritual directors.[35] Men and women were not always treated identically, but women who received *consolamentum* often retired to quasi-monastic life, though they would still conduct the rites their status allowed.

As in the Catholic Church, persons to be received into the Cathar church underwent a period of instruction in the beliefs and culture of the community. People had different levels of spiritual attainment, reflected in differing roles within the Cathar community. In Cathar ecclesiology, the real distinction wasn't between laity and ordained but between the "perfect" (*perfecti*) and others. A novice who sought instruction would undergo a probationary period in which the perfect would observe them to see if they were capable of the strenuous demands of Cathar asceticism. This probation could last a year or more and might involve ascetic practices such as completing three fasts of forty days.[36] *Abstinentia* was the period in which a perfect mentored someone in the Cathar austerities. Given that apprentices received religious education as well as training in a trade, the Cathars had a natural way to network into other cities and regions.

The perfects were a small central group that had gone through rites after sufficient attainment of spiritual skills. They were the drawing power and the spiritual center of the Cathar movement, where the Holy Spirit could be channeled to the Cathar believers. They provided pastoral attention to believers (*credentes*), preached to convert new members, instructed novices, and administered *consolamentum*. It took a year's novitiate to be chosen to receive the status. Those who were initiates were chosen by the other perfects, but not all would complete the training. The perfects were ascetic in diet (pescatarian) and abstinent from sexual contact. Lifelong celibacy was required—if married, the couple would be permanently separated in preparation for receiving perfect status. However, their renunciation did not include financial renunciation.[37] Cathar initiation was based on the laying on of hands in the Scriptures. In the Cathar view, this action by a perfect could serve a number of functions, from ordination to confirmation to forgiveness of sins and viaticum.

While the process just described was the typical way to join the Cathars, there were other ways; one was *convensa*, an agreement that people could make to be received into the Cathar religion near the end of their lives. The inquisitor Bernardo Gui (noted in the bibliography under his Latin name, Bernardus Guidonis) complained about this practice because he feared that a dying person might not be able to affirm that they wanted to leave the church and be received into the Cathars. He further complained that the Cathars received the sick into their group even if they were too weak to make a full proclamation of faith, saying that the Cathars allowed the people around them to respond for them, which Bernardo did not consider adequate.[38] Another rite was *melioramentum*, a greeting in which one Cathar kneeled before another and asked for their intercessory prayers to God.

Cathar Theological Foundations

The Cathar rituals were a result of their distinct theological views. At the foundation of the Cathar view was a creation in which there were two opposing principles at work and a belief that Lucifer created both the material world and humans after his fall. The treatise *Interrogatio Iohannis* (*The Questions of John*) stated that the flesh was the prison of the soul. The world was created by a demiurge, just below God, but which was a malevolent force.[39] It explained, "There is another principle, one of evil, who is mighty in iniquity, from whom the power of Satan and of darkness and all other powers which are inimical to the true Lord God are exclusively and essentially derived."[40] One reason Catharism spread so well was that it appealed to those who saw in its dualism an explanation for good existing alongside evil and misery. In Cathar cosmology, humans were witnesses to the cosmic struggle between good and evil. As *The Book of Two Principles* explained, "There is another principle, one of evil, who works most wickedly against the true God and His creation; and this principle seems to move God against His own creation and the creation against its God, and causes God himself to wish for and desire that which in and of himself He could never wish for at all. Thus it is that through the compulsion of the evil enemy God yearns and is wearied, relents, is burdened, and is served by His own creatures."[41] The Cathars interpreted Scripture metaphorically when it talked about the creation being material: their theology reread the Scriptures in a way to retell the creation as a spiritual creation as well as a material one. The material one was of less consequence to them than the spiritual one.

This dualism drove the asceticism of the Cathar movement, insisting that those who would follow it should aim for the good principles and not be misled by focusing on material needs. As a result, the body was considered unnecessary and something that needed to be disciplined and put in place. Along with vegetarian fasts and sexual abstinence, Cathar asceticism also came with a rigorous moral code.[42] Gui noted that "they deny that the Lord Jesus Christ was incarnate of Mary ever virgin, maintaining that he did not have a real human body or real human flesh as other human beings do by their very nature, nor did he really suffer and die on the cross, nor did he rise from the dead or ascend into heaven in human bodily flesh, but that all this only seemed to take place."[43] The Cathars held the material world in enough contempt that they could not consider the incarnation possible.

Sacraments in the Cathar Church

In contrast to the Catholic practice of seven sacraments, the Cathars believed that the only sacrament necessary was the *consolamentum*. Marriage and the Eucharist were not sacraments, although the Cathars did share a nonsacramental act of breaking bread together. Their lack of sacraments was in large part due to the lack of accord given to the material world. Sacraments required material elements in the Catholic worldview, such as water for baptism or bread and wine for the Eucharist. Cathar dualism denied the possibility of material elements serving as a means for the sacraments. Because physical bread could not be considered good, it would not be a fitting vessel for the spiritual ideal of the Eucharistic celebration. Gui commented that the Cathar disdain for the Eucharist stemmed not only from their dualist tendencies but also from a literalness that they applied to their thought about the physical body of Christ; namely, it would need to be very large to be consumed by the vast numbers who desired to do so.[44]

Cathar beliefs focused on the rite of *consolamentum*, which had a number of purposes in the Cathar church. The perfects promised remission of sins through this rite if it was performed by someone who was worthy. This ability to escape from the material clutches was the driving force of the Cathar movement. At its heart, it was a rite recognizing the spiritual power that the perfects had and was the initiation ritual to that status, a spiritual baptism like Christ had said would replace baptism by water.[45] A postulant went through stages toward becoming a spiritual perfect. After they were judged ready, they were given the Lord's Prayer to say. Next, the person would be encouraged to keep studying and praying in order to someday receive *consolamentum*. After receiving it, the believer renounced the material world. The perfects, those who had received *consolamentum*, were to withdraw from the world and live in the single-sex Cathar houses, akin to monasteries. If a person committed a great sin after Cathar initiation, they lost the right to give or receive *consolamentum*.[46] At a perfect's death, their body would release their soul, to be freed forever from material restraints. Laity were encouraged to receive *consolamentum* at least once in their lives, and many would receive it near the end of their lives. The Cathars held up the possibility of universal salvation, encouraging individuals to seek it through *consolamentum*.

The Cathar rituals exist in a Latin and a Provençal version.[47] In each case, the texts include a collection of prayers and liturgical instructions that most likely represent a series of parts of services rather than the layout of one service. The prayers in both versions include a variety of rites, as well as explanations of what some prayers mean. For instance, the Our Father is explained, phrase by phrase, to help the believer to understand the prayer's significance. The ministration of the *consolamentum* has a detailed description of the order and type of different obeisance that a believer should offer. At the heart is the receiving of the Book "in which are written the commandments, the precepts, and the admonitions of Christ, so, spiritually, you must admit the law of Christ into the works of your soul, to keep it throughout your whole lifetime." Taking this up symbolizes receiving a spiritual baptism in Christ and reminds the receiver of all the powers this process entails: casting out of demons, forgiving sins (loosing and binding), discerning of spirits, and other gifts. As the ritual explains to the person who has just received the spiritual baptism, "Accordingly, you must understand that this is the reason for your presence here before the Church of Jesus Christ: It is the occasion of your receiving this holy baptism of the imposition of hands and receiving pardon for your sins by the examination of a good conscience which is made toward God by good Christians." It further describes the effect of this initiation: "Therefore, you should know that even as you are in the temporal sense in the presence of the Church of God, where spiritually you dwell the Father, the Son, and the Holy Spirit, so spiritually you should be with your soul in the presence of God, of Christ, and of the Holy Spirit, prepared to receive this holy consecration of Jesus Christ." It lastly leaves the initiation with instructions: "And even as you took into your hands the Book, in which are written the commandments, the precepts, and the admonitions of Christ, so, spiritually, you must admit the law of Christ into the works of your soul."[48] Those who had received the *consolamentum* were seen as hinge figures who dwelt spiritually with the Trinity and corporally with their neighbors. Although there is a dualism in this belief, there's also a recognition that the embodied state of humans must be attended to in some of their beliefs and practices. The *perfecti* needed to be well-principled people, for they practiced a spirituality that was ascetic like Catholic monastics, yet they did so while still in contact with the outside world. Services were ministered by one person with one assistant. Those who were to administer the *consolamentum* to a new postulant could be any Cathar member not in a state of sin, although the duty was usually carried out by the bishop or deacons. If they were not available, those who had lived in the Cathar community the longest would administer the rite. This information demonstrates that the Cathars were moving away from an exclusive sacerdotal role for ministers and toward a priesthood of all believers.

Opposition and Suppression

The suppression of the Cathars would take centuries, involve external forces, and be aided by internal disagreements.[49] In part because of their numbers and in part because of political struggles in the areas where they lived, the Cathars were the group among all others that had the greatest influence on the development of the medieval inquisitorial machinery.[50] Opposition to the Cathars took the widest variety of forms of any heresy during the Middle Ages. There were monastic preaching crusades against the Cathars, military crusades that routed entire towns, church councils condemning Cathar beliefs, and inquisitorial hearings. Some of the council meetings, such as the first (in Germany), condemned only a handful of individuals. Others involved great numbers of condemnations or targeted entire communities.

Opposition to heretics in the Midi was slow to develop, and the area was wary of outsiders who would target their neighbors. A church council at Toulouse in 1056 had excommunicated heretics, and although the records do not include much about the unspecified beliefs of those excommunicated, it is likely they were suspected Cathars.[51] In 1163, the Council of Tours, under the leadership of the exiled Pope Alexander III, focused on the conversion of Cathars, trying to discern how to bring lost sheep back into the fold of the church.[52] By the time of the Cathar Synod in 1167, the Cathars had been invited to a public debate, which was to include five southern bishops, seven abbots, and various other clergy from lower ranks, as well as prominent orthodox laypeople from Béziers and Toulouse. These church officials faced off against someone named Oliver, who with a few assistants had been chosen to represent the Cathars. The debate quickly turned into a shouting match, and the judges of the debate (all Catholics) declared the Cathars heretics.[53]

Also at play was the uneasy tension resulting from the pastoral mission of the church's clergy to reconcile the sinner with the congregation. Early attempts at addressing heresy encouraged finding ways to reintegrate a person within the larger orthodox community. This strategy would prove more difficult with the Cathars, whose workplace, trade contacts, and entire family were also Cathars; even when disavowing the beliefs, they were still in constant contact with Cathar members, short of a total relocation. Still, the earliest inquisitional records list the penances offered to heretics and show a consistency in the inquisitor's sense of being ministers first. These penances would evolve into attempts to remove heretics to new locations as a way of reinforcing the return to orthodoxy, which might be accomplished by physically separating the heretic, such as through imprisonment or pilgrimage to distant locations.[54] Travel was physically draining, dangerous, time-consuming, and expensive, and it would serve to temporarily locate a heretic in a new community to reinforce their move toward orthodoxy while traveling. Burnings, however, had the strongest influence and were a tactic employed strategically, as the punishment of a few heretics could have a profound effect on an entire community. It came to be the case that anything less than death by burning would be considered a penance.[55]

The church's first attempts at controlling the Cathar threat required a series of negotiations to secure additional supporters to help the church. In 1173, the archbishop of Narbonne wrote to King Louis VII, saying he was considering some type of forcible repression of the Cathars.[56] He felt his diocese was weakened, and in his message, he said he perceived the weakening of the local aristocracy as well and knew he could not count on secular help from the region. By 1177, Henry of Marcy, the abbot of Clairvaux, urged King Henry II of England and King Louis VII of France to fight the Languedoc heretics, but both were short of the necessary supplies. They suggested turning the problem over to another preaching crusade like Bernard of Clairvaux's. The idea was to use Bernard's approach, grounded in *caritas* (love), to persuade heretics to return to the fold.[57] The pope approved this move, and Peter of Pavia, the papal legate in France, led it with the assistance of the Cistercian Henry of Marcy and two English bishops. They arrived in Toulouse in December 1178. The Cathars took to jeering the group before they even entered the city.[58] The meetings would be a sham. The crusaders asked for a list of suspected heretics to be drawn up. While waiting for the names, they chose a Cathar spokesperson to debate with. A wealthy man, Peter Maurand, was offered; he presented them with a repudiation of the Cathar faith, and they accepted him back into the church. Emboldened, they went to look for more to convert. The next two they encountered, from Lavaur, were not successfully won back. They could not speak Latin, and the visiting clerics did not know *langue d'òc*. When the two men offered up a statement of their belief, it was creedally correct. They were taken to a nearby church, where laypeople swore the two men had preached dualist heresy. The men denied it, and they were ultimately judged to be excommunicated due to their obstinacy. They were granted safe passage from the city, and the count of Béziers granted them safety. The Catholics returned home; the tour hadn't accomplished much.

With nothing resolved, the church would make ever-increasing attempts to control and undermine the influence of the Cathars. At the Council of Verona in 1184, the foundations of the Inquisition were built. Previous councils of the century had made declarations of one type or another condemning heresy or stating how heretics were to be punished, including Toulouse in 1119, Second Lateran in 1139, Sens in 1140, Rheims in 1148, Tours in 1163, and Third Lateran in 1179. Verona was another on that long list, but it would also be a turning point. Pope Lucius III passed *Ad abolendam* (*Toward Abolishing*), which required archbishops, bishops, or their representatives to do twice-yearly checks into the state of belief in their dioceses. Those guilty of heresy were to be excommunicated and handed over to secular justice. Towns refusing to agree to these rules were to be put under interdict, which prevented the residents from participating in the liturgy or sacraments. This plan was a direct and serious attempt to ensure local bishops and clergy supported the church's efforts against heresy. The process for prosecuting heresy would evolve to have four steps: detection, arrest, trial, and punishment.[59] It would be solidified by Pope Innocent III at the Fourth Lateran Council in 1215. The trial model would change from the accusation model, in which a person stood to provide evidence that supposed an accusation against someone else, to an inquisitorial model, where the judge, acting on a plausible accusation, would ask the person to explain and defend themselves against the accusations. Questions would clarify if the person believed or acted in ways consistent with the accused heresy and would be used to guide the process by the inquisitors. Based on the person's answers, their guilt or innocence was decided.

Next, Innocent III added special papal legates for particularly concerning areas; they were to work alongside the archbishops and bishops. From 1184 onward, councils comprised of bishops and archbishops would conduct investigations into heresy. The first of these Episcopal inquisitions was held in Languedoc in 1184. A few years later, Innocent III confirmed *Ad abolendam* in his 1199 papal bull *Vergentis in senium* (*Inclining toward Decay*). Aimed at Viterbo, in northern Italy, it addressed the heretics and their protectors and stated that any sacred or secular authorities found to be protecting heretics would lose their ability to inherit or pass on property to their children. Heresy was, in his view, a form of treason against the church, so Innocent held those holding heretical views or protecting heretics to the same punishments as for civil treason. Although *Vergentis in senium* looked as if it relied on the local clergy, it also had some teeth in the event local support was not forthcoming by allowing the confiscation of any lands belonging to heretics. There was a legal basis for this action: the bulls related to the Holy Land Crusades promised the distribution of confiscated lands to those who fought on behalf of the church. This confiscation turned the attack on heresy into a land battle between the pope and the king of France. In 1230, the Episcopal inquisitions would morph into the centrally led papal inquisition. From that time, Pope Gregory IX would hand over most inquisitorial activities to the Dominicans and Franciscans; the Dominicans were quickly establishing a strong presence in the fledgling universities of Europe and showing their theological prowess.

Pope Innocent III ordered Raymond VI, count of Toulouse, to support his efforts against the Cathars, but Raymond refused to do so, feeling that the Cathars' independence would help to prevent other landholders from gaining more power than he had. In 1208, the papal legate Peter of Castelnau was assassinated, probably by Raymond or his associates. Peter had been in the area, on orders by the papacy to suppress the Cathars, but he had met with resistance from aristocrats such as Raymond. In response to the death, Innocent excommunicated Raymond and absolved his vassals from fealty to him. The crusade against the Cathars was declared, and the pope said that confiscated lands would go to those who conquered the Cathars. Raymond realized that to reconcile himself to the papacy and keep power, he needed to help lead the crusade. By 1209, the effort was under the command of Simon of Montfort, who would oversee Raymond's return to the church. The Albigensian Crusade would last from 1209 to 1229, effectively showing that force like that used in the Crusades against Muslims in the Holy Land could be used in Europe against heretics seen as foreigners to Christendom. A fair number of people joined the crusade, in part because unlike the Crusades in Jerusalem, which required a lengthy commitment—until either the Holy Sepulchre was freed or until the person was relieved of their duties—this crusade required only a forty-day commitment.[60]

With *Vergentis in senium*, the church had tried a legal approach; with the Cistercian preaching tour, it had tried an evangelical approach. Where both had come up short, force was the next approach. Under the leadership of Simon of Montfort, effective persecution "descended like a storm on the minority leading families and their supporters in Toulouse who had been involved with Catharism."[61] In 1209, at the start of the Albigensian Crusade, the Béziers Catholics had been ordered to turn over their Cathar neighbors or share the same death as them. The Catholics refused to do so, and the crusaders chose to slaughter the entire population of the town, with the (likely apocryphal) rallying cry quoted at the start of this chapter. In short order, the crusade moved from violence justified by heretics' outsider status to wholesale massacre. In Béziers, priests were killed alongside the laity, and all 20,000 inhabitants were put to the sword. While garnering the most attention, the Béziers massacre was but the beginning of two bloody decades in which the Cathars were systematically routed and destroyed.

During the years that Rome fought against the Cathars, a regularizing of the Inquisition took shape under Gregory IX. The Albigensian Crusade began as locally focused attacks and slowly moved outward, involving more areas.

In the midst of this crusade, the pope convened Lateran IV (1215), which dealt with the issue of conquered land and to whom it would be awarded. He passed the 1231 constitution *Excommunicamus et anathematisamus* (*We Excommunicate and Anathematize*), which regularized legal measures and sent heretics to secular justice for death by burning: it renewed the sentence of excommunication against Cathars, Patarines, and the Poor Men of Lyon; all convicted were to be denied public office, to the second generation. All who were convicted of heresy were to be denied Christian burial and were to suffer perpetual imprisonment as well as deprivation of civil rights.[62] The local papal inquisitors were to have power independent of local bishops, which would allow them to work directly for Rome and sidestep any local bishops protecting heretics, as had happened in Languedoc.

On the ground, the suppression gave way to short rallies in support of the declared heretics among the weakening regions of southern France. Languedoc submitted in 1211. Raymond was left with Toulouse and Montauban, while the rest of his territory was carved up. In 1215, the Battle of Muret saw Peter of Aragon, Raymond's son-in-law, killed. Simon of Montfort became the count of Toulouse, at least until the city revolted and he was killed. In 1222, Raymond's son succeeded his father. He regained most of his father's former territories, causing fear that the heresy would reemerge. By 1223, the crusaders had fled, leaving the area again to the heretics. In 1225, Louis VIII, the king of France, had gained Simon's rights to Toulouse. This turn led to a new crusade; now, Raymond VII offered to submit, but he was excommunicated anyway. By 1226, all was united under the ownership of the king of France. In 1229, at the signing of the Treaty of Paris, Raymond submitted to the king, ending two decades of war. Raymond retained his lands in Toulouse and Agenais. By 1233, he promulgated statutes for hunting heretics, and specialist inquisitors were introduced to the region. Toulousian society was destroyed, as was Catharism: the Albigensian Crusade destroyed precisely what it had hoped to save. The 1229 Treaty of Paris would bring the crusade to an end, but in the final move, many of the southern lands would be placed under the leadership of the French crown, uniting Languedoc with northern France and destroying its independence. Yet it did little to truly keep the peace; by 1242, two inquisitors would be murdered in Avignonet, once again leading to suppressions, a cycle of suspected heresy and response that was to continue for years to come.[63]

The Cathars

At the end of the Albigensian Crusade, the 1229 Canons of Toulouse extended the measures that could be undertaken in the fight against heresy. They included the power to search for heretics. Repentant ex-heretics were required to live in areas considered orthodox once they had repented and sought correction. This practice would dilute their influence and prevent them from reentering heretical networks. Former Cathars were to be marked with yellow crosses on their clothing. Suspected heretics could even be barred from some professions. In 1230, King Louis IX of France issued *cupientes*, a secular law allowing royal officials the authority to seek out suspected heretics in their jurisdictions. Although the Albigensian Crusade had been led by Cistercians, the inquisitions were mainly to fall under the control of the Dominicans in the future; this order had developed from its founder Dominic de Guzman's preaching against heretics.[64] The law also established a wider approach to the eradication of heresy, and not a regional approach. By the time the last Cathar perfect was killed in 1321, this new network could be sure that Catharism's grip had been eradicated.

In April of 1233, Pope Gregory IX empowered the Dominicans to conduct a general inquisition in Bordeaux, Bourges, Narbonne, and Auch. It would be followed by the Council of Albi in 1254, which offered monetary rewards to laypeople for each heretic turned in. Pope Clement V promulgated *Multorum querela* (*The Complaint of Many*) at the Council of Vienne in 1312, which stated that the bishops and papal inquisitors needed to work in common. The papal response to the Cathar threat was to treat it as a serious issue that needed to be addressed swiftly and in a manner that recognized that local authorities might try to either ignore or encourage heresy for their own power and financial benefits.

The inquisitors knew that the Cathars had not been completely eliminated. In 1245, Bernard of Caux and John of Saint-Pierre attempted a census of all adults in Toulouse and its surrounding area to ask about encounters with Cathars and about the respondents' beliefs. The answers showed a range of responses, from people who had believed Cathar teachings but were now orthodox to people who admitted still being involved.[65] Although the Cathar dissent had been dampened, it was not fully gone. While these attacks on the Cathars were taking place, the church was also actively addressing other groups, such as the Waldensians, who would begin to garner the majority of the church's attention.

Lasting Impact

It is in the moment when we see the strongly violent reaction against the heretic that we also see people praise the heretics most. The inquisitor Bernardo Gui reported what he heard said about the Cathars: "They declare that they are good Christians who do not swear, lie or curse anyone, that they kill neither humans nor animals nor anything that breathes, that they hold the faith of the Lord Jesus Christ and his gospel as he and his apostles taught it; that they themselves stand in the place of the apostles." This description is fully consistent with the outward actions a good Christian should strive for. He continued, noting that people say the Cathars would befall a fate of being persecuted for their faith, following the model of Christ, that the "prelates, clerks, religious and especially the inquisitors into heresy, persecute them, although they are good men and good Christians, just as the Pharisees used to persecute Christ and his apostles."[66] Their claim to be good Christians meant they identified as persecuted Christians when attacked. In Bernardo's comments, we also see the crux of the problems that existed between the Cathars and the Catholics: the Cathars both preach anticlerical ideas while also claiming a truer apostolic succession than the church leaders. In short, the Cathars claimed the authority that the Catholic Church also exclusively claimed, but the Cathars did so while espousing a very different theology. This position reinforced the idea in the Cathar minds that they were persecuted Christians. In another comparison, the Cathars saw themselves in a light similar to the new monastic traditions within Catholicism through the appeal that their strong asceticism provoked in followers. They were also adept at developing networks: an education network for new members, a network of houses of adepts, and a strong ecclesiastical network with multiple layers of governance. But all these points ignore the radically different theology underlying the Cathar position.

The Gregorian reform had drawn attention to the fact that a fair number of the clergy were short on needed abilities and were unworthy candidates; it highlighted a greater need in the populace, one that the Cathars were better at responding to than the Catholics were. Also, the Gregorian reform in Languedoc had not made as much headway as in other places because Archbishop Berengar of Narbonne was a cleric who was interested in the acquisition of wealth more than leadership. Another distinction was how the Albigenses and the Catholics recruited their clergy in areas such as the Midi. The Albigenses tended to create a clergy that was well educated, spiritually developed, and rigorously ascetic, as compared with the Catholic lower clergy, who were rural peasantry and had little or no formal education.

We saw a shift, in the combatting of the Cathars, from the previous century's choice to fight heretics head-to-head with reason and persuasion to fight them with force. In the previous century, Bernard preached against the Henricians, and Peter the Venerable wrote tracts refuting them. The Inquisition began by seeking to remedy the heresies by providing doctrinaire, well-taught preachers. It attacked the Cathars by assuming that if the people had good preaching, they would come to correct beliefs. But this course would be inconsequential. The shift toward taking forceful power over heretics would not come solely from the church but also from secular lords and lynch mobs.[67] And yet, for the turn to force, the Albigensian Crusade did not accomplish the routing of heresy. What it did accomplish was the end of Languedocian independence, placing these lands under royal rule. It also saw the beginnings of a shift from the church assuming that local law enforcement would handle the issue of local heretics' punishment to recognizing that the central church lacked the legislative/judicial structure and a developed punishment structure.[68] Beginning in 1231, Pope Gregory IX would oversee the development of the Inquisition as an institution and the codification of legislation concerning heresy. Although the attempt to eradicate heresy would continue to operate on various levels and would not become one institution, being seen instead as the province of various mendicant orders, locals, and the papacy, it did become more coordinated.[69] Force and a legal system newly focused on the Cathar threat reinforced the group's idea of being easily targeted.

As with the previous heresy, the Cathars garnered attention in the monasteries: a number of women monastics joined male monastics to write against the Cathar heresy. Elizabeth of Schönau teamed up with Hildegard of Bingen in writing against it.[70] Hildegard, a Benedictine abbess, was known for writing visionary treatises. In an unusual occurrence, she was even authorized to preach publicly against heresy and the clergy's failure to eradicate it. Through the influence of these two women, Elizabeth's brother Eckbert of Schönau, who was a Benedictine monk, wrote a number of sermons against the Cathar heresy as well. The Cathars can be said to have represented an unprecedented threat to the Catholics, at least since the time of Augustine, even if just by the size of the reaction they provoked. Perhaps what made the Cathars so fascinating to the monastics was the strong asceticism and the lives of the *perfecti*, who were the spiritual core of the movement, ideas that resonated well with how monasticism positioned itself within the larger church.

These first two heresies have taken place in overlapping areas in Languedoc. But although social structure plays a part in the spread of heresy, this area of southern France is not alone in attracting heresies; the political and economic power associated with land ownership, and who gets the spoils of heretical seizures, will be part of the strategy of the victors. Part of the march of this book will be an ever-widening range of locations where heresies are tracked and suppressed. As we progress further into the High Middle Ages, heresy will find new ways to flourish as it appears within the newly developing cities in Northern Europe. Heresy will also begin to spread easier, following routes of trade, rather than following wandering preachers and family ties between small towns.

CHAPTER 3

The Waldensians

Heresy and Reunion

THE WALDENSIAN HERESY is a complex phenomenon to summarize because the Waldensians survived and even thrived for centuries, the longest period among the heretical groups, and repeatedly came under both reproach and approval during the Middle Ages. Several Waldensian communities successfully integrated back into the medieval church, while other descendants of the Waldensians continue to live in parts of the Alps and to have their own church, now associated with the Methodist Church. They've been described as "the last and the most tenacious of the twelfth-century wandering-preacher movements."[1] The Waldensians serve as a good counterpoint to the Petrobrusians and Cathars, showing a startling diversity of heretical viewpoints and church responses, especially with their repeated desire to remain among the faithful.

The first references to the Waldensians appear in the late twelfth century as the Poor Men of Lyon. Here, the "poor" referred both to their voluntary poverty and to the charism of the Beatitude "Blessed are the poor in spirit."[2] Named after their founder, Peter Valdesius, the Waldensians were largely associated with the Piedmont region of Italy and the Cottian Alpine valleys located between France and Italy, although they extended as far as Languedoc, the Pyrenees, parts of Germany, and even to Sicily at various points in their history.[3] While some proliferation can be explained from Valdesius's connection to merchants, some areas where Waldensianism developed and thrived were cut off from such routes.[4] Recent discoveries have highlighted how periodic oppressions of Waldensians led to adherents becoming refugees, adding to the spread of the group and hindering understanding of their chronological development.[5] The sporadic oppressions the group would face also suggest networks among some Waldensians that allowed those facing oppression to find coreligionists in other areas who could provide asylum.[6]

There are three periods of Waldensian development: a first period to 1240, the inquisitorial period from the thirteenth to fifteenth century, and the Reformation of the sixteenth century.[7] Each period would have its own struggles, ways of understanding the group's goals and identity, and relationship with the Catholic Church. It should be a common observance by now that the Petrobrusians, Cathars, and others were more loosely affiliated than their detractors suggest. Constructing heresies as unified fronts certainly amped up the assumed threat; having an organized enemy would be an inquisitorial construct meant to help press upon Catholics the need for definitive action against the heretics. Considering the physical isolation of some Waldensians, it is not surprising that some groups were not well connected. Given the longevity of the group, their geographic spread, and the many who eventually settled in remote Alpine villages, defining the Waldensians is hard, but an overview will show their beliefs and appeal. For the purposes of this chapter, I will focus on the early Waldensians and the years in which they came into conflict with the medieval church, particularly around the time of the Fourth Lateran reforms.[8] The early sources consist of narratives, sermons, theological expositions, and antiheretical treatises against other heretical groups such as the Cathars.[9] The surviving documents are written in the languages of the local communities, and in the Middle Ages, that would have primarily been a peripheral version of *langue d'oc*.[10] But much of the information available still comes from the mouths of detractors who often lumped the Waldensians together with the Cathars in treatises that spoke against heresy.

As the movement faced opposition, groups retrenched to Alpine valleys, which were harder for outsiders to reach, and began to develop an ecclesiastical structure. It was based on family ties, which extended across valleys; this connection meant that once one family converted to Waldensianism, the whole family tended to convert, making it less likely that individuals would go back. Their relative isolation meant that Waldensians had a degree of privacy and that their comings and goings were less obvious to outsiders unfamiliar with the social structures of the region. The Alpine area also was not as subject to feudalism as most of Europe was.[11] In fact, the remoteness of the Waldensians meant that even the inquisitor Bernardo Gui had to base his descriptions of them on the account of a Dominican who talked to a priest who knew Valdesius. Gui based his questions for heretics on this third-hand account from the mid-thirteenth century.[12] The other inquisitor associated with the investigation and suppression of the Waldensians, Peter Zwicker, was even more removed than Gui.[13] The Waldensians will provide a couple of significant differences from the previous heresies: first, several groups among them will be reintegrated into the church; and second, they show that the inquisitors were unfamiliar with the people and were constructing an image of this heresy. The fact that some of the Waldensians later joined with reformers affirms that the heart of their dispute really was, as they claimed, the issue of whether the Roman church alone had the authority to decide issues such as who could preach.[14]

The Milieu and Growth of the Waldensians

The Waldensians spread more widely than any other heresy in the Middle Ages.[15] Yet this growth was not marked by an attempt to chronicle the movement; they saw themselves merely as a typical evangelical group within the Catholic Church. The lack of Waldensian sources meant that by the late Middle Ages, even the Waldensians were somewhat uncertain of their own origins.[16] To unpack the real development of the Waldensians, it is important to start with the figure of Peter Valdesius, whose name the group bears.

Peter Valdesius (ca. 1138–1218) arrived on the scene in what was the last great wave of wandering preachers. What these preachers shared was a zeal for church reform through a return to apostolic poverty and a strong asceticism shared by all the followers. Just as the Cistercian monastic order sought to impose a monastic set of values (including asceticism) first on the monks within the cloister, then on the clergy, and finally on the laity, these wandering preachers carried out a similar task outside the walls of the monastery.[17] As mentioned in the chapter on the Petrobrusians, some charismatic preachers such as Robert of Arbrissel eventually found their way into the church and founded monastic orders. Other groups, such as the young Carthusians, the mendicant Franciscans and Dominicans, and the ascetics who followed Peter Damian, were born of a similar desire, and all these found places within orthodoxy. Some wandering preachers found themselves outside of orthodoxy; the case of Henry of Lausanne and Peter of Bruys has already been discussed in length. Similarly, Eudes de l'Étoile from Brittany was condemned by the Council of Rheims in 1148. Although his followers were ascetic and austere in nature, they also attacked monasteries and hermitages, which was a good way to get one's movement condemned.[18]

It is into this world of religious possibilities that Peter Valdesius emerged as a wandering reformer.[19] In the early 1170s, Valdesius heard a jongleur singing the life of St. Alexis of Rome.[20] The song told how the young man, born into wealth, gave it up for a vocation of holy poverty until the Blessed Virgin Mary identified him as a holy man. To escape fame, he returned to Rome and went to live, unrecognized, under the stairs of his own parents' house. The story left Valdesius disoriented, whereupon he recalled the scriptural advice Jesus gave the rich man: sell everything and follow Jesus.[21] Valdesius wanted to learn more, so he went to the theologians and asked them for biblical passages in the vernacular and for some sentences from the church fathers.[22] Upon reflection, he began a program of giving away his assets. He "went to his wife and gave her the choice of keeping his personal property or his real estate, namely, what he had in ponds, groves and fields, houses, rents, vineyards, mills, and fishing rights."[23] She chose the real estate. Then, he established his daughters in Robert Arbrissel's house of Fontevrault. Next, Valdesius began giving away bread, soup, and meat every other day to those who asked for food. Eventually, he would scatter his money on the ground during the Feast of the Assumption, saying he could not serve both God and mammon. He explained his actions as an attempt to break the snares by which money had bound him. Like many medieval saints' lives, this account is more reliable for the trope of conversion to Christ than for its absolute truth in reporting. Following his decision to cast aside all his money, Valdesius found it necessary to beg from a former peer of his. His public begging angered his wife, who pointed out that he had not begged for food from her first. Archbishop Guichard of Lyon then ordered him to rely on his wife for alms. The story of his life navigates between a desire for monastic renunciation and the duties of married life. Valdesius sent off his daughters, providing for them so as to free himself from the burden of taking care of a family; his wife retained assets and very possibly gained new duties when he renounced his fortune. Guichard's request that Valdesius receive support from his wife essentially stated that divorce was not a valid option.[24] Valdesius was both a man who renounced the world and one who could not fully leave it.

From this conversion, Valdesius would acquire a group of followers who would practice voluntary poverty and atone for their sins and the sins of others.

Part of his fervor was to incite others to follow the same charism of voluntary poverty that he had decided to follow. Valdesius undertook biblical study and preaching and helped his followers learn as well. He wanted an orthodox training, even if he could read only in the vernacular, did not have any prior theological study, and thus could not be confirmed as knowing the writings of the fathers well. Between 1177 and 1179, these studies would develop into his preaching missions. During this time, Valdesius put his poverty and his conversion to a life of renunciation on display. Yet he lived at a time when the roles of clergy and laity were becoming more clearly separated and defined; when laypeople wanted to preach on moral issues, they needed to receive permission of the bishop, which he did not request.

During Valdesius's life, wandering preachers had fallen into disrepute, but as the mendicant orders emerged with their public preaching, this situation would begin to change. Valdesius and his followers made clear efforts to ensure that they separated themselves from identified heretics, in particular the Cathars.[25] Valdesius would soon discover this change when he presented himself at the Council of Lyon in 1180–81 to reaffirm his orthodoxy when it came into question. This council was summoned by Archbishop Guichard and presided over by the new papal legate and cardinal to France, Henry of Marcy, a Cistercian involved in fighting the Cathar heresy just a few years before. Guichard had also been involved in suppressing Cathars at Vézelay a decade earlier. All three who investigated Valdesius and accepted his profession of orthodoxy—Henry of Marcy; Archbishop Guichard, who was the former abbot of Pontigny; and Geoffrey of Auxerre, who was then abbot of Hautcombe—were Cistercians.[26] After Henry of Lausanne and Peter of Bruys, the Cistercian order continued to stay involved in attempts to identify and eliminate heterodoxy. Cistercians such as Geoffrey of Auxerre actually went further than Bernard of Clairvaux's generation; while Bernard believed the work against heresy was the work of all clergy and vowed religious, Geoffrey viewed suppressing heresy as the work of knights and the laity and anticipated that sharing the work of social exclusion and enacting civil penalties would help heretics decide to return to the fold.[27]

We have the text of Valdesius's profession of faith from this meeting; public confessions of faith were new developments in the second half of the twelfth century that helped to bring the laity under clerical control and also served to show correct doctrine to others.[28] The profession attributed to Valdesius stated that he accepted the Trinity, the creeds of the church, the divine origins of the Scriptures, the incarnation, and the sacraments, which were valid even when administered by a sinful priest.[29] This last point suggests the inquisitors wanted to ensure that his criticisms of the clergy's conduct didn't espouse Donatism, an early church heresy that stated a priest in a sinful state would be unable to perform the sacraments efficaciously. Similarly, Valdesius attested that the devil was made evil by an act of will rather than by nature (thus separating him from dualists like the Cathars), and he accepted that alms, Masses, and works could benefit the dead.[30] The confession of faith also affirmed support for the existing Catholic ecclesiastical structure, and it included denials of refusing to eat meat, an ascetic practice that was also associated with the Cathars.[31] His profession was crafted by those who interrogated him to distinguish him from the Cathar heretics with whom numerous councils had dealt over the last decade. He repudiated all those preachers whose teachings lay outside of the church. He was found not guilty of heresy but guilty of sacrilegious presumption (*de sacrilega praesumptione convictus*).[32] The questioning ended with a statement that all future Waldensian representatives would have to affirm the same profession of faith: "If it should happen that any people should ever come before you, claiming to be our representatives, if they have not this faith [i.e., the faith sworn to in this document], know for certain that they are not from us."[33] This statement set a foundation for Valdesius's followers to have a place in the church.

Following Valdesisus's profession, the next known Waldensian writing is by Durand of Huesca. He was a Spanish follower of Valdesius who had come under condemnation about the same time Valdesius was examined. Durand wrote his *Liber antihaeresis* (*Book Against Heresy*) (1210) that attacked Catharism and provided a statement of what the Waldensians believed and why they were justified in disobeying some of the requests they had received from Catholic authorities.[34] Durand wanted to distinguish the Catholic faith from the Cathar heresy. This book described much about the social life and beliefs of the early Waldensians.[35] In the first half, he addressed Cathar beliefs and rejected them, stating and reaffirming the Waldensian views and also defending the Catholic sacraments and incarnation. In the second half, he directly challenged the theology underlying Cathar views. He presented Valdesius as a person called by God to correct errors in the church. The freedom to preach and the willingness to abandon material goods voluntarily were intertwined in this story, and Valdesius served as an example that those who followed the Lord to be preachers should give up manual labor in favor of a life spent meditating on the meanings of Scripture.[36] The book portrayed the clergy of the Catholic Church as compromised in their abilities to defend itself against heresy; groups like the Waldensians needed to step up and defend the church. This view was not Donatism in that this moral weakness of the clergy did not affect the efficacy of the sacraments, but the Waldensians did believe that moral failings left the clergy incapable of pastoral and administrative efficacy.

Originally, the Waldensians centered in towns, cities, and smaller villages. The Waldensian attraction cut across class lines from their inception. What made Waldensianism so convincing to many people was not that it required a new faith or a new set of practices but that it merely asked people to be better Christians.[37] In addition to medieval peasants, village artisans (including cobblers, tailors, farmers, and millers), and some learned men, the group attracted former nuns and monks and also received some support from nobility.[38] The Waldensian ideal spread via family, community, and locality, as well as though affiliations such as trades. For the first half-century of the movement, Waldensians of both sexes would gather to listen to wandering preachers when they traveled through towns, and the people would take on works of austerity. Unlike the Cathar houses, these Waldensian preachers were itinerant and not embedded within communities, so instruction and pastoral care in between visits was sparse.[39] As oppression increased, the Waldensians went underground and developed a more formal structure, one that was increasingly male. Care would be taken to try to keep ministers on regular circuits so that they saw the same communities and established a pastoral relationship with them. Confession to the wandering preachers became a central tenet to show one's continued affirmation of Waldensian beliefs.

As the Waldensians grew, each community in different geographical areas developed somewhat independently of others, so they began to pursue different practices and beliefs. At first, the inquisitorial tendency was to remove heretics from their home communities and send them to places where they had no connections, but in time, it was acknowledged that this practice helped aid the spread of heresy further afield. To combat this problem, inquisitors replaced expulsion with civil citation by the early thirteenth century. Their penalties ranged from penances for those who repented to death for those who had fallen back into heresy or who refused to acknowledge the error of their ways.[40] As Waldensianism continued northward and eastward, a mix of missionaries would go into new communities, and in areas where their message was well received, entire communities could form bases for further expansion. By the fifteenth century, expansion slowed, but Waldensian communities that were already converted held strong. In Germany, they were up against a system in which the lower clergy—the parish clergy—were both undereducated and understaffed, leading to clerical shortages and a sense that the church was inadequate for the people it served. The Waldensians must have seemed far more pastoral.[41] The *Passau Anonymous*, a chronicle written by a cleric in the 1260s described the Austrian Waldensians. The book distinctly declared the Waldensians to be heretics and attempted to explain why; the list was exhaustive and quite overblown in some of its claims, but interestingly, the *Passau Anonymous* directly acknowledged that the Waldensians were successful because the church was too corrupt to be respected and too understaffed to be effective. By this time, the Waldensians had also begun to separate their followers, intentionally or not, into a counterclergy and a simple faithful.

The Evolution of Waldensian Beliefs
Ecclesiology

Waldensian ecclesiology would develop as the communities moved into new areas. We know that as the group grew and spread, the Waldensians had roles within their membership; there were people who held positions that ministered or preached to others, heard confessions, and taught. Administrative roles would develop to organize the regions, determine who would be trained, and make sure all circuits were covered. Administrators would also communicate with Waldensian groups in other areas, especially when trying to work with each other, clarifying group beliefs and practices, or even when reconciling with Rome.

The Waldensians did not see themselves as trying to establish a new church at first, so they spent little time thinking about the organization or leadership of their group until they had to. Voluntary poverty was the main focus of asceticism within their communities, but it was interpreted differently in various groups. Among the French Waldensians, the preachers denounced laboring for wages once they reached this position. In the Italian communities, the Waldensians founded many schools. The communities in the Italian north generally fared better economically. There were other types of denials or asceticism among the groups; for example, they believed that the swearing of oaths was forbidden. This prohibition derived from their literal reading of Matthew 5:24, in which Christ tells his followers not to swear when making a promise. Other beliefs, such as opposition to capital punishment and war, similarly arose from a literal interpretation of Scripture.

The Waldensians held one or two general chapters every year in an appointed town, meeting as secretly as they could in a house that one or more believers had previously rented as if they were traders. In these chapters, the most senior person present arranged and decided which preachers would go to different districts and regions to visit believers and friends, hear confessions, and collect alms; this senior person would hear and receive details of income and expenses.[42] In part, the loose Waldensian ecclesiology aided in the group's success: it led to relative cohesion, with priests who exercised a sacramental power similar to that of Roman priests but who claimed to be closer to the imitation of Christ, inspiring greater devotion. It did not ask for adherents to leave Roman churches; it merely offered an improved experience. The Waldensians also introduced an idea that would blossom in the later Middle Ages: a traceable apostolic history that would define what is the "true church" and what is not. This focus on historical continuity was over and against the spiritualizing influences of groups such as the Cathars, who saw neither Christ's life nor body as having historical significance or reality. It also meant that for the Waldensians, the imitation of Christ took on a focused metaphysical significance that pointed both to the past and to the future. Other later groups, such as the Spiritual Franciscans, Lollards, and Hussites, would echo this idea of continuing an apostolic church in their own groups.

Preaching and Interpreting the Scriptures

At the heart of Waldensian ecclesiology was the practice of lay preaching, and at the heart of their doctrines were many of the same things as the church but with an emphasis on personal will and a conviction that individual community members could serve as religious leaders. The Waldensian approach to preaching was based on the commissioning of the disciples by Jesus in Mark 16:15

to go preach the gospel to all creation. They claimed that as the inheritors of such a commission, evangelism was commanded of all Christians and therefore no church authority needed to be asked for permission. This assertion would be the crux of their clash with the church authorities. Although literacy was unusual among the laity in the early and High Middle Ages, the Waldensians were particularly known for encouraging their supporters to become—if not literate—at least quite familiar with the Scriptures, memorizing the Gospels and parts of other books of the Bible.[43]

The Waldensian preachers went forth two by two, owning nothing. Their preaching circuits did not respect traditional diocesan boundaries. The chronicler Burchard of Ursperg wrote in the 1212 *Chronicon Urspergense* (*Ursperger Chronicle*) that "they wandered through town and country, stoutly affirming that they, imitating the life of the apostles, wanted to have neither possessions nor a place of their own." He continued by stating they'd already been rejected by the church authorities for pretending to be members of religious orders: "The Lord Pope objected to them because their conversation revealed certain superstitious usages, viz., they cut off the tops of their shoes and went about nearly barefoot; though they dressed as if they were members of a religious order, they would not cut their hair except after the fashion of laymen."[44] His complaints would also take on a sexual nature. "It seemed scandalous, moreover, that their men and women appeared together in the street, often staying together in the same house, and—it is rumored—sometimes occupying the same bed; all of which they claim has come down from the apostles."[45] Although his accusation here is mild, sexual license and indecency would repeatedly appear in inquisitorial accusations and records for all the groups henceforth and become a trope of heretical accusations. But by the time the inquisitor Bernardo Gui began to attack the Waldensians of the fourteenth century, he was convinced their primary heresy was not believing in the authority of Catholic clergy.

Early Waldensian preachers were simply selected when they met another wandering preacher and wanted to help preach. The preachers made up much of the structure in the early Waldensian communities and were usually called a variety of titles, such as *pauperes spiritu* (poor in spirit), *fratres* (brothers, brethren), or *sorores* (sisters). In Italy, teaching of the laity was done by wandering preachers known as *barba* (uncles) or *magistri* (masters), who would make yearly trips on a set route, visiting different communities, sharing Bibles in the vernacular, and teaching people. They eventually settled into locations and built up religious houses for men as well as for women.[46] In early Waldensian history, there was no official ordination for a preacher, and the Waldensians allowed women to preach. Those who responded to the preaching by seeking counsel with the preachers might, after a novitiate of the newly converted (*nuper conversi*), be sent into missions. There were also supporters who, while not preachers, assisted the preachers when they entered their towns. These friends (*amici*) stayed in the world but were supportive of the Waldensians, helping them avoid detection and providing food, shelter, and other things as needed.

By the fourteenth and fifteenth centuries, the training of preachers and masters showed the different geographies and situations of Waldensian communities. In fourteenth-century France, the training for a preacher might take five or six years. In Italy, it was shorter, usually no more than two years, but there was a more official school system used by the Waldensians in Lombardy.[47] In Germany, as Waldensian preaching roles separated from the laity, the training became more formal and a Waldensian minister's role might have started at about age fourteen.[48] There, the would-be minister became disciple to a master, traveling with them as they met with new and old communities. This master would repeatedly teach the disciple about the New Testament. Waldensian ministers were not necessarily learned; traveling with a master, they would be able to pick up the Scriptures through listening to the master preach day in and day out and being quizzed repeatedly on the Bible. Scriptures would have been memorized in the vernacular for the area in which the preacher traveled. Preaching consisted of leading worshippers through exhortation, acknowledgement and renunciation of their sins, and repentance. This training period could last ten to twelve years. When the disciple was ready, a group of masters would examine them, and when approved, the new master would be given their own circuit that would take them four to six months to visit, allowing them to visit each town or village two or three times a year.[49] While on their circuits, these new masters might also undertake new conversions in other nearby villages. This model led to the development of a laity that saw itself as empowered to undertake the work of salvation without the need for Catholic priests.

Criticisms of Catholic Clerics

The Waldensian theology of the sacraments broke from Catholic belief. The Waldensians de-emphasized Rome's sacraments but not because of an outright belief that sacraments were wrong or due to disparaging the material elements in favor of the spiritual form. After Fourth Lateran decreed in 1215 that people should receive absolution and the Eucharist at least once a year, the Waldensians sought to meet that requirement though their own preachers' yearly circuit visits. They were concerned that Rome had—through corruption—lost its ability to be a spiritual guide to the faithful and, by extension, its ability to perform the sacraments efficaciously. This concern was reminiscent of the early church heresy of Donatism, which posited that if a priest was in a state of sin, they could not perform the sacraments effectively, and the sacraments would not be valid. Not all Waldensian communities were Donatist, although at times in their history (especially later) some of their clerical criticisms were close to or outright Donatist. Yet the primary theological text we have from the same time, Durand of Huesca's *Liber antihaeresis*, does not endorse Donatism, but it does assert that sinful clergy might not have to be listened to on some matters if their sin clouds their ability to teach or lead effectively. This softer position, which limits moral, not sacramental, power, also explains why the Waldensians believed they could avoid receiving permission to preach.

More extreme Waldensians would say that the impact of Rome's whoring meant that its followers were not merely receiving inefficacious sacraments but that the anathemas Rome promulgated had no bite to them and papal decrees were useless.[50] Waldensians who believed this notion traced it back to the Donation of Constantine, when Pope Sylvester I accepted property from Emperor Constantine.[51] The Waldensians believed they were "the true apostolic church whereas the church of Rome was the *ecclesia malignantium* (*Church of people of ill-will*). Through its betrayal of Christ's teachings on apostolic simplicity the Roman church had become the whore of Babylon and lost its sacramental powers."[52] Later in their rhetoric, the Waldensians would refer to themselves as "*Kunden*," or "those known to God," and the Catholics were "*Fremden*," or "outsiders and foreigners."[53] Waldensians saw themselves as a Christianity that demanded not a new belief but a deeper belief.[54] The Waldensians, even when they went too far in attacking the worthiness of Rome's sacraments, never abandoned them.

Sacraments and Worship

Questioning Rome's authority led to a breakdown in the belief in the historicity and necessity of some of the Catholic rituals; the Waldensians saw some of them as human inventions and not as divinely mandated actions. Ultimately, this view would lead to a disavowal of many of the nonbiblical elements of the liturgical year, including feasts and fasts, pilgrimages, benedictions, singing, and other layers of ceremony that the church had developed throughout its history.[55] The Waldensians did not harbor a dislike of matter like the Cathars did when they denied some of these elements, nor did they denigrate the earthly life of Christ. In stripping away aggregate layers of church ritual, the Waldensians were not all that different from many of the ascetic reforms seen within monasticism, such as the Cistercians (and of some Protestant movements as well).

The Waldensians prayed several times a day. They would kneel, "bend forward and lean on some bench or other suitable piece of furniture, and thus with bent knees and stooping towards the ground they all remain in silent prayer for as long as it would take to repeat the Lord's Prayer thirty or forty times, or sometimes longer. The physical posture was one of supplication." The act of praying was the primary way of invoking and interacting with God, and it could be done individually. "They did this regularly every day when they were on their own with their believers and supporters, no strangers present, before and after dinner, before and after supper, at night when going to bed, before lying down, in the morning after getting out of bed, and at several other times, both morning and afternoon."[56] The regular rituals of prayers, individual or group, punctuated Waldensian daily life. This simplicity of prayer and church community could be seen in how communities welcomed the itinerant preachers. When a preacher would visit a Waldensian home, everyone would come together to have a meal. Afterward, they would share Scripture, and the preacher would spend time preaching, then hear confessions, and offer absolution. In places like Germany, there would be dedicated meeting places that were used throughout the thirteenth century. It appears that at least some areas were not inclined to act against the Waldensians. Elsewhere, evidence suggests they blended in with the Catholics by also attending local Catholic services.

Many Waldensian beliefs and practices were similar to Catholic ones, except they stressed the ability of many to lead others in belief and practices and, by doing so, blurred the line between clergy and laity. In the Catholic communities, the clergy were separated from the laity and had additional restrictions put on them, such as forbidding them concubines or wives. Clergy were also among the few who were literate and, as such, served to mediate all things scriptural and religious. The Waldensians sought to engage laity through functions that included reading Scripture, explaining and preaching it, and hearing confessions. The inquisitor Bernardo Gui noted that the Waldensians taught the seven articles of faith, the Ten Commandments and the seven works of mercy, although he said they did so "in a manner of their own."[57] This phrase referred to who oversaw the prayers or performed the sacraments. The Waldensians confessed to one another, absolved each another, and gave penances, meaning that laypeople did tasks that were the reserve of Catholic clergy. The Waldensians also taught that young children could not be saved by baptism because a child was not yet old enough to assent to belief.[58]

There were aspects of church practices that the Waldensians disagreed with. The *Passau Anonymous* recorded that they did not believe in the efficacy of indulgences.[59] Several Waldensian groups believed that purgatory did not exist due to its not being mentioned in the Bible; thus, prayers for the dead, almsgiving, and works of piety for the dead had no efficacy.[60] A disagreement arose between French and Italian Waldensians on the location of Peter Valdesius after his death: Catholic doctrine and one Waldensian group said he was in purgatory, expiating his sins. Another group said he was in heaven, an answer that negated the belief that everyone born of sin must spend time in purgatory. For those Waldensians, a person went either straight to hell or straight to heaven after death, without purgatory first. The practice of praying for those in purgatory, however, drove many Catholic devotional practices and had economic impact: payments for indulgences and prayers for the dead completed by monasteries helped fund these establishments and the papacy.

Opposition and Identification as a Heresy

Given that the Waldensians were not as militantly opposed to the church as were the other groups discussed already and that they viewed themselves as Catholics but better, the question remains why the Waldensians were declared heretics and why the Inquisition steadily turned against them. They didn't attempt to loot and burn churches as Peter's and Henry's followers did, didn't set up rival diocesan structure and alternative churches as the Cathars did, and didn't attack the sacraments. In fact, the Waldensians came to church councils to profess their intent to remain part of the church. They were against Catholic teachings on the issue of the worthiness of Catholic hierarchy and how it affected the ability of clerics to do parts of their jobs, but for much of their history and in most locations, they held a position that wasn't fully Donatist. The mechanism by which the church suppressed the Waldensians was slow to develop and involved a series of pendulum swings between papal attempts to reunite the group with the Catholic Church and statements of condemnation.[61] Since the first condemnations came early in their history and mention only disapproval of their preaching, it would be easy to say that their identity as heretics pivoted on the issue of refusing to give up preaching. But that would be a too-simplistic view. At the heart, there were at least four issues: (1) who preached, when, and about what and the speed with which their message was able to be spread; (2) their rejection of the authority of Catholic bishops to decide who was able to preach and their pseudo-Donatist tendencies to mistrust the administrative authority of Catholic clergy; (3) the vernacular translations of the Scriptures that the Waldensians shared in their communities; and (4) their literal interpretations of the Scriptures, which led to them rejecting various practices of the church, such as prayers for the dead. The identification of the Waldensians as a heretical group came only after long and inconsistent attempts to reconcile them to the church.

As early as 1179, Valdesius sought out an audience with the pope, seeking approval for his preaching. He had found support hard to come by locally, especially for his preaching, since he was not trained clergy or a vowed religious. His representatives were questioned to show their fitness to preach, and the results were mixed. Their voluntary poverty was deemed acceptable and could continue. But the approval depended on the Waldensians receiving local bishop approval for preaching, which Valdesius did not seek after his meeting with the pope. It was a test: Would the Waldensians fall into order with the papacy? It was also, intentionally or not, a trap; local support proved difficult to obtain, and Valdesius regularly avoided seeking it. Yet he did not give up preaching, which was a direct attack on the church's authority. Although the Waldensians had received conditional approval from Pope Alexander III in 1179 at the Third Lateran Council, they would find themselves condemned just a few years later for failure to receive local support. Thereafter, the condemnations began growing more detailed. Geoffrey of Auxerre would complain that the Waldensians not only did not seek approval to preach, but they also allowed laypeople to preach when only clergy and vowed monastics could. He added that the Waldensians let women preach despite them being unable to seek approval.[62] The act of preaching itself, regardless of the content of the message, was the issue. In 1182, Archbishop Jean des Bellesmains of Lyon excommunicated the Waldensians and expelled Valdesius and his followers because they did not receive permission to preach. Unexpectedly, this decision would help further the Waldensian movement, as the expulsion from the diocese helped them to spread geographically.

In 1184, Pope Lucius III's decree *Ad abolendam* condemned a number of heretical groups, including the Waldensians, Humiliati, Arnoldists, and the Patarines.[63] This decree was then supported by Emperor Frederick I. It was also the first effort to deal with a heresy that wasn't on a diocesan level but on a level that transcended territories. This anathematizing attempted to encourage bishops to pursue heresy rather than ignore it case by case; it made bishops responsible for visiting any parishes with suspected heresy once or twice a year. They would impose an oath on locals and require them to report any known heresy. The bishops were to receive secular support for this program, and ignoring these precepts would bring about both secular and ecclesiastical penalties. Requests for help also came in from local bishops.

Ad abolendam was not successful everywhere; in places such as the south of France, where there was no strong complaint against heresy, few reports came in. The bull was not clear about the process of examining heretics, including who was to perform the examinations, and did not attempt to classify heretics. It offered only vague names and descriptions of some heretical characteristics, such as unauthorized preaching and false doctrine. The archbishop of Narbonne inquired into the Waldensians and issued a condemnation in the few years just after *Ad abolendam*. But in Languedoc, the population supported the Waldensian penitential life and their preachers continued to move about freely. There were spots where the anti-Waldensian counterattack was more solid: Count William VIII of Montpellier saw that the Waldensians were brought to attention, and in Aragon, Alfonso II and Pedro II also attacked them, eventually establishing the death penalty due to their obstinacy.[64] After these condemnations, many Waldensians scattered to the east and north.

Availing himself of the support promised in *Ad abolendam*, the bishop of Metz asked for help with the Waldensians in 1199. His concerns centered on the translations of the Scriptures, lay preaching, refusals to desist preaching, and the exclusivity of the sect.[65] Urging caution and asking the bishop if the reason the people wanted vernacular translations could be determined—noting that the church should not be quashing religious enthusiasm but should be making sure the laity was keeping in line with the expectations of its station and also not moving into heresy—Pope Innocent III sent Cistercian abbots to Metz to consider the vernacular texts the Waldensians had been using. Innocent asked about the tenor of the translations and for more information about the followers: if they were studying the Bible, they could not be entirely unlearned. The abbots sent were from Cîteaux, Morimund, and La Crête. They declared the followers to be heretics, named them as Waldensians, and burned their translation of Scripture. Yet Innocent continued to exercise restraint in dealing with them. He acknowledged that the Waldensians held unwarranted meetings and practiced unlicensed preaching, but he did not condemn them until their beliefs and behaviors had been investigated. He understood that an overly rigid attitude of church could drive the laity into heresy.[66]

During this time, the Waldensians who had been condemned found a champion in the Spanish theologian Durand of Huesca, whose *Liber antihaeresis* was designed to refute the Cathar heresy and also support the Waldensian view, showing it was supporting of Rome and distinct from the Cathar heresy.[67] The Waldensians did regularly express interest in staying within the church and were ridiculed by other heretics; the Cathars attacked them in Languedoc, saying that they were not truly following the apostolic life, as the Cathars were, for they did not have an ecclesiastical hierarchy—including bishops, priests, and deacons—like the Cathars had. In short, the Catholics could see that the Waldensians viewed themselves as a group within the church, trying to live out an authentic version of apostolic life based on the gospel, even if it meant overstepping one aspect of canon law about preaching. If the message was correct, the Waldensians thought, should it matter who delivered it?

There were, around the start of the thirteenth century, a number of attempts to reconcile the Waldensians, group by group. How these fared varied considerably. Two of the largest factors were geography and variety of theological views. Church officials were less willing to deal with Waldensians from areas that had historically been hotbeds of heresy, such as those from parts of southern France. The Italian communities fared better. In dealing with the Humiliati of Lombardy in 1201, Innocent distinguished between moral and dogmatic preaching.[68] The condition of the Waldensian reintegration was to follow a set rule that was chosen for them and allowed them to keep their own charism. There were no models within the church that looked similar; Innocent focused on trying to reintegrate people who had strayed. Again, the fate of the Waldensians seemed to hinge on the people who were talking to one another. At Pamiers, there was a conference that included Bishop Fulk of Toulouse and Bishop Navarrus of Couserans, among others. Yet the rigorous nature of some Waldensian groups left them less willing to negotiate for places within the church or limited their options for reintegration. But in the early years of the thirteenth century, leading up to Fourth Lateran, a number were reconciled successfully, although all the groups eventually died out or lost their unique character within a generation or two.

After Valdesius died in 1205, Durand also sought to be integrated and found favor in 1207.[69] In 1207–8, the Poor Catholics in the Narbonne area, whom Durand had left, were reconciled. They had accepted a confession that was almost identical to Valdesius's. It stressed needing to receive permission to preach and contained anti-Donatist language meant to reinforce that they would not attack clergy based on their perceived moral shortcomings and that these failings did not affect the sacraments they performed. The reconciliation happened during the years that saw the development of the mendicants, the wandering preachers in the Dominicans and Franciscans; they served as a model for apostolic preaching within the church. Innocent allowed Durand's group both itinerant preaching and building conventicles, which Alexander III had forbidden.[70] Durand received permission for some Waldensians under his leadership to live under a rule.[71] While part of the difference may have been in the two popes, part of it was simply that the time had come when itinerant preaching was recognized within orders in the hierarchical church and therefore need not be looked at as unsanctioned or dangerous. But the Poor Catholics, as the group was known, had to submit to hierarchy and offer regular professions to assert their orthodoxy and compromise on some issues, such as oaths.[72] It was allowed to retain its ability to preach for at least a while. In 1247, it would be ordered to join other orders, and by 1256, the remaining Poor Catholics would be absorbed into the Hermits of Saint Augustine as part of its Grand Union, where several smaller orders and fringe groups were taken under the order of the Augustinians.

In the same year, Innocent began talks with another Waldensian group from Milan that would later become known as the Lombard Reconciled Poor. The local archbishop had destroyed the Waldensians' schools and seized the land. The members wanted the land back if they were to be reconciled. In early 1210, they formally began the process. This group would be required to profess a longer reconciliation statement; it had been accused of more positions that diverged from Catholic practices, including allowing righteous laity to consecrate the Eucharist, hear confessions, and offer absolution. The men of this group agreed to live in a community with voluntary poverty and study and preach against heresies. They could do manual labor, and they retained at least eight of the schools they had owned. This reconciliation largely met with the goals of the early Lombardian Waldensians in terms of division of labor (prayer, teaching, and manual labor) and formal recognition by the church. However, with their evangelical missions decreased, their numbers declined as well, both by death and by some members leaving for other orders.

In 1215, the Fourth Lateran Council would declare all who preached without permission heretics.[73] From this condemnation, some of the Waldensian groups, whose exact relationship to each other is not known, started to take stronger stances against various church practices, such as the swearing of oaths, war, and capital punishment.[74] These positions would put them at odds with those conducting the Albigensian Crusade, leading to complaints that the Waldensians were undermining their efforts.[75]

In 1218, the Council of Bergamo facilitated meetings between representatives of the Lombardian and Languedocian communities of Waldensians to find common ground. At stake was the question of whether the traditions of Valdesius were meant to be set in stone or could be adapted for culture and the times. Manual labor was one of the topics both groups wanted to discuss. The doctrine of purgatory was also contentious: the French Waldensians insisted that Valdesius and his companion Vivetas were in heaven, while the Italians rejected knowing their location with certainty. Last was the question of whether a sinful priest was worthy of celebrating the sacraments. The Italians tended toward Donatism, and the French believed that any prayers or sacraments performed by a validly ordained priest were efficacious. They never fully reconciled these differences, though the two groups remained in contact.

In slightly different circumstances, the ideals and actions of Peter Valdesius and his followers might have been easily integrated into the church, making the identification of this heresy feel like an accident of time and circumstances where new ideas repeatedly came under suspicion. Indeed, the case of Saint Francis shows that someone holding very similar evangelical tendencies could find his order accepted within the church. Parallels between Francis and Peter Valdesius are striking.[76] Francis was a merchant's son, whereas Peter was a merchant himself. When both converted, they were following the imprecations from Matthew's Gospel. Francis, a century later and in Umbria rather than in Lyon, found the apostolic life of poverty and the evangelical perfection to hold the same appeal as Valdesius did. Both also held their followers to minimal constraints: follow evangelical ideals. Both journeyed to Rome, but each met with different receptions. Pope Alexander III was willing to approve the way of life for Valdesius, but he could not approve the preaching. Pope Innocent III, on the other hand, balked at granting the strict ideal of poverty that Francis advocated, but he and his brothers were granted status as an order and allowed to preach.[77]

In other times, the Waldensians might have been seen as faithful believers. And at least with some Waldensians, it would wind up being the case, as several groups were restored to the church by Pope Innocent III and others.[78] Some would be rather straightforward, whereas others were more complicated. The case of the Dauphiné Waldensians involved a heretical inquisition that would take over two decades and reach its peak in 1501–9 in a complicated legal battle involving multiple questions of jurisdiction and enforcement. The judgments against them were ultimately voided for legal reasons. The reintegrations, when theologically oriented, continued to focus on the issue of preaching. But others would simply become legal battles over the issue of land confiscation.

Lasting Impact

The legacy of the Waldensians is still not entirely understood. New works of the Waldensians continue to be discovered among archives, often mixed in with other types of records.[79] Many scholars have seen them as proto-Protestants (as it is common to see several other groups in this book, such as the Lollards and Hussites). But this reading is based mostly on two issues: it looks at late medieval Waldensians, who continued to thrive in smaller individual communities into the time of the Reformation, and it relies on the fact that some Waldensians have joined the United Methodist Church since the

Reformation. It also rests on modern stereotypes that Protestants read the Bible and Catholics do not; in the medieval church, the Bible was officially in Latin for everyone—what was at issue was unapproved translation into new languages that were at risk of being inaccurate.

Unlike several of the heresies in this book, the Waldensians didn't have large doctrinal clashes with the church. Starting in 1526, having heard about the inroads the Reformation was making, the Waldensians sent delegates from Italy to meet with heads of Protestant churches and learn more about the situation. There were certainly some shared concerns. The French Waldensians would begin meeting with Reformers in 1530. And some Waldensians would move closer to joining the Reformation through the Synod of Chanforan, which met in the fall of 1532. This synod would pass the Resolutions of Chanforan, which stated that those gathered agreed to print the Bible in French, to be paid for by the Waldensian churches as their contribution to the ongoing Reformation efforts.[80] In the Reformers, especially the French, the Waldensians found similar beliefs, including a rejection of papal institutions such as the Mass, prayers to the saints, purgatory, priestly celibacy, and prayers for the dead.

Would the Waldensians have lasted? Even if they had been successfully reintegrated, history suggests no. This answer is best explained through an analogous situation with another group: the Catholic Poor came under challenge at the local level frequently, with local bishops suspecting they had lapsed back into heresy. Innocent's approach to reconciling the groups was also gentle toward those who challenged people as heretics. Innocent stated that the church had two goals: to protect the faithful, which he identified as the most important aspect, and to lead the wayward back.[81] He replied to the bishops that they should treat the Waldensians and Catholic Poor as gently as the newly won for the church, but he also cautioned Durand to be true to the statements made to the church and to use only experienced preachers when going to unreconciled heretics.[82] The suspicion was always there, even when unwarranted, and continued to weigh on the group, limiting its future.

The attempt to bring the Catholic Poor back into the fold stands in contrast with some of the strong-arm tactics seen in the previous chapter. And it shows just how capricious the decision one was condemned or approved could be. Part of this variance may have been location: the Waldensians thrived in an area less accessible than Languedoc and in one of less political concern.

Part of the lingering legacy of this group was its geographic dispersal. The Waldensians became separated from the original location and had little contact with each other, which limited the impact of each group. They were a sect of small groups, loosely connected, that spread wide among the Alps and surrounding regions. They were sometimes in contact to sort out differences in doctrine among the followers; for example, in the later Middle Ages, as some in Strasbourg and Switzerland fell into persecution, contact with the Czech Waldensians helped move the persecuted to safety into Hussite Bavaria.

Waldensianism was a movement that was not based primarily on the charismatic nature of the leader. Compared to the early Franciscans' focus on their founder's personality, Valdesius's role in the Waldensians seems practically effaced. His strong commitment to having laity in the organization and to their role in teaching, preaching, and learning the gospel—rather than wanting an order solely of friars—seems to have been at issue. The Waldensians just did not look like any other religious organization in terms of structure or membership, which meant there were no models for wholesale reintegration, even with a willing pope.

CHAPTER 4

The Beguines and Beghards
The Rhetoric of Defining a Heresy

AN ENDURING VISION of the heretic is the lonely figure, condemned to die beside their book on an auto-da-fé pyre stoked by the church. Chief among those who met that fate are the beguines, condemned as Free Spirit heretics. They were religious women living solitary or community lives, often in cities, who spent time both working to support their community and praying the liturgy of the hours; the beghards were their male counterparts. They were not official religious orders but local communities with shared goals. Another view of the beguines provides a contrast, one that recognizes and appreciates the extant texts of these individuals, still read today as fonts of holy wisdom and records of truly extraordinary mystical experiences. The Free Spirit heresy was defined into existence with both of these contradictory elements: the individual ardor that was focused on living as authentic a life as possible, following Christ in simple work and prayer, to experience God's presence and the institutional paranoia that these groups misled laity into believing humans could live independently of God. The High Middle Ages were both a time of new forms of religious life and a time in which many forms of religious life, such as beguinages, were curtailed and actively repressed, often in very dramatic ways. Marguerite Porete sought a widespread audience for her *Mirror of Simple Souls*, believing that its mystical treatises expressed an authentic way to experience God. After her book's condemnation, she was publicly burned alongside it. Yet its dissemination continued anyway. And she was far from being a singular case. Unlike other groups we've seen thus far, this "heresy of the Free Spirit" was a construct used as an excuse to persecute laity and was not based on any self-identified group.

Defining a Heresy

The umbrella term *heresy of the Free Spirit* has now been shown to be an invention created by a papal council and university scholars to describe the beguines and the German Rhineland mystics;[1] no one went around calling themselves a Free Spirit. Ecclesiastical identification of the so-called heresy under which the beguines and beghards were condemned would appear in two documents from the 1311–12 Council of Vienne and be based on one condemnation, from ideas extrapolated from the writings of Marguerite Porete.[2] What was labelled the heresy of the Free Spirit was part of a larger development in lay piety that occurred in a number of places throughout continental western Europe at roughly the same time but wasn't seen as heresy by those who wrote its texts and certainly wasn't an organized movement. The reaction shows a widespread distrust and dislike of lay piety on the part of church leaders.

During their early stages, the beguines attracted negative attention from people such as Phillip the Chancellor, who preached against them, was worried that their unregulated way of life was licentious, and claimed that consorting with other heretics made beguine women fall pregnant.[3] Others such as Caesarius of Heisterbach and Robert of Sorbon condemned them because the beguines and beghards were in fact too pious.[4] Yet others complained that the groups were hypocritical: while they made a big show of praying and practicing asceticism in public, they led rather scandalous lives of sexual immorality, lack of temperance, and luxury.[5] In the 1270s, the Dominican scholar Albertus Magnus, known best as the teacher of the formidable scholastic theologian St. Thomas Aquinas, compiled a list of concerns about the beliefs of the beguines. This collection, called *Compilatio de novo spiritu* (*Compilation of the New Spirit*), focused on the beguines and beghards of the Rhineland areas where Albertus lived. He identified several unifying beliefs of these potential heretics. Among them was a belief that God and the perfected soul are one. This metaphysics denied the ontological distinction between God and fallen creation. The groups also believed that to a perfected soul, the sacraments were no longer needed as they were earthly, material aids that the perfected soul had surpassed. This view insinuated that the groups did not need the church, its ministers, or intercessory prayers on their behalf; by contrast, the church considered moving beyond needing these aids, impossible in this lifetime. Further, they believed themselves beyond sin after union with God. These ideas would form the background of discussions about the beguines up to the time of the Council of Vienne. Additionally, the new, urban, unenclosed lifestyles of the beguines would vex the church so much it would push for them to be transitioned into more recognizable forms of religious life. A growing number of papal orders saw the beguine houses fall under the responsibility of the Dominicans and Franciscans between 1220 and 1260.[6]

The beguine and beghard lifestyle came under official investigation in 1274 at the Second Council of Lyon. Before the council, three tracts were solicited to discuss the beguines. Bishop Bruno of Olmütz wrote one of them, in which he complained not of heresy but that beguines lacked being under the discipline of an official order yet conducted themselves in dress and behavior as if they were. He complained that laypeople of both sexes dressed and acted like vowed religious while they displayed no discipline. He did state that there did not seem to be heresy among those he was complaining about, but the lack of a recognized and approved discipline was the troubling aspect for him.[7] The Dominican Humbert of Romans wrote that the only women who should be allowed to live in such circumstances were those who had the means to support themselves; he explained that he was opposed to lay piety that involved begging and wandering, so the beguines were, in his view, not to be permitted. At the heart of his complaint was a belief that women did not belong within the mendicant life but should be cloistered; activities such as preaching, selling goods, teaching, and tending to the sick and poor took the women out of the cloister and should be forbidden. Gilbert of Tournai, a Franciscan, was the most condemnatory. He stated that the beguines had vernacular translations of the Bible, which they studied and read in public, and that these books contained many heresies. The Second Council of Lyon restated the thirteenth canon of Fourth Lateran Council: no new orders were to be formed and any that had arisen since 1215 had to be dissolved. Thus, the beguines could not be officially recognized as a religious order. But the Second Council didn't condemn them as heretics. It was concerned with their way of life, but the idea that heretical beliefs were associated with the movement would not yet find footing. This period was one of burgeoning lay piety, which could not all be funneled into the extant orders, so the council did not actually address the tensions at hand. In its wake, how beguines fared also depended on where they lived. Trials appeared in waves. One occurred simultaneously with the absorption of communities between 1220 and 1260; a later round would occur between 1310 and 1325. There would then be a lull until 1359.

Condemnation would officially occur at the Council of Vienne in 1311–12; according to the bull *Ad nostrum* (*In Our Time*), the Free Spirit heretics were identified by the church as "an abominable sect of wicked men, commonly called beghards, and of faithless women, commonly called Beguines" found primarily in the Rhineland areas of Germany.[8] This heresy would be defined partly by a way of life, focusing on those living outside of traditional religious orders and those not living under religious vows as being most suspect (but being in orders didn't fully absolve one from suspicion, as in the case of Meister Eckhart). Condemnation of the Free Spirit heretics also focused on the spirituality in the beguine writings, which aimed at reaching a state of experience of God, usually through contemplative prayer, reflection on the Scriptures, and ascetic practices. Beliefs identified as questionable or heretical included, foremost, statements about the soul achieving either perfection or a state of union with God. Many of the statements that would be defining claims about the beliefs of the heresy of the Free Spirit would come from *Ad nostrum*'s overview of the created heresy, which began, "first, that a person in this present life can acquire a degree of perfection which renders him utterly impeccable and unable to make further progress in grace."[9] Other charges would be that the soul did not need the virtues, intelligence, or penitential practices once it achieved perfection through union with God. Another stated that such heretics believed that to leave the heights of contemplation to observe the consecrated host being elevated at the altar was to show imperfection and to be less pure.[10] The beguines and beghards would eventually be accused of significant doctrinal errors, including beliefs that humans could become God and that there was no free will.

Beguine Origins

The beguines and beghards are first attested to in the twelfth century around the area of Liège. Despite levels of persecution and condemnation, some communities lasted over half a millennium, gradually declining through the time of the French Revolution but with a few communities lasting into the modern age.[11] Beguines sought to live the apostolic life through poverty, manual labor, and preaching. This goal was the same spiritual emphasis that spurred on the monastic as well as mendicant orders and their lay associations. A beguinage could be a small house where women lived together, but as this form of religious life grew, beguine communities became larger with more services: communal beguinages were enclosed communities within the larger city, consisting of "streets, gardens, churches, even cemeteries."[12] Beguinages were soon found in many cities, such as Bruges, Ghent, Paris, Amsterdam, Valenciennes, Cambrai, Norwich, Brussels, Antwerp, Leuven, Marseilles, and Liège. At their peak, they were found in dozens of cities across Europe. While some could be small, housing an apostolic dozen women, others like the one in Paris could house hundreds or, as in the case of Ghent's beguinage, over a thousand. Beguine communities attracted adult women and would usually not accept any members under the age of sixteen. In 1215, the Fourth Lateran Council had stopped the creation of new religious orders, so these new communities had two options: find religious orders willing to take on the financial and spiritual requirements of administering new women's houses or exist independently and unofficially.

Larger beguine communities developed in cities and served as educational centers and work opportunities for women. Beguinages especially flourished in the southern Low Countries, where cultural forces such as cross-pollination between French speakers and Dutch speakers and advanced urbanization worked to bolster the beguine movement. Prior to the beguines, the model for women's religious communities was the cloister, where inmates came with dowries and gifts as well as political and ecclesiastical connections. These gifts supported the running of the monasteries, and connections helped to keep them safe when conflicts broke out. But this practice limited potential members—these communities took recruits only from families with resources and connections. In beguine communities, the women provided for each other by the work of their hands, and their ability to work within large urban centers in profitable trades made their communities economically viable.

Authorities were concerned with who would oversee and direct the unregulated, unincorporated beguine communities. Each established its own rules or regulations and sought out pastoral guidance from anyone available to offer it. Orders had a structure and oversight that helped ensure ecclesiastical control. Being part of an order would mean they followed an approved, set charism and rule and that they had a clear chain of authority that they would submit to. Furthermore, without the networking that belonging to an order provided, beguines had to work to secure ecclesiastical protectors, lest they come under suspicion for their autonomy.

Women's Beguine Communities

Key to understanding the beguines is the development of lay piety, especially women's piety, in the urban centers of Northern Europe. The beguines were part of an ongoing development of a wide movement of women's extrareligious communities. Scholars today tend to unite their terminology, using *mulieres religiosae* to cover all such women's groups.[13] Among the counterparts of the beguines of the Low Countries, Rhineland, and northern France were the *beatas* of Spain, the *bizzoche* of Italy, and the *anchorites* of Northern Europe and England. These terms refer to women with similar goals living a spiritual life but in very different circumstances. Such a multiplication of forms of life would be paralleled within the ranks of the church as well when new orders came into existence in the twelfth and early thirteenth centuries to follow different charisms and to respond to different needs of the church militant.

Increasing limitations on women's options for religious life helped spur the *mulieres religiosae*. Some orders did not allow women to join at all, seeing them as a drain that took time and financial resources from the pastoral work of men. Others stopped allowing women's houses; the Premonstratensians withdrew from women's spiritual development by 1200. The Cistercians backtracked on the issue of incorporating women from 1212 onward.[14] In 1206, Southern European women from Cathar houses converted by the preaching of Diego were sent to Dominican houses, straining the Dominicans' ability to accept any women who weren't reformed heretics into the order and substantially decreasing their willingness to admit further women.[15] Still other communities lived a liminal existence; women's communities that lost their affiliations with their orders continued to live as religious communities, but the houses were no longer under official guidance and might not receive regular spiritual direction. Other times, women's houses were nominally Benedictine but in reality followed various customs, especially Cistercian ones, before the Cistercian order officially allowed the incorporation of houses of women. These women were often of the lower nobility and, as such, lacked the ties to the wealth and power of many women previously living in these houses, rendering them both less useful to orders and more vulnerable to others who wished to control their daily lives and activities. This situation also made their communities less attractive to men's communities, which were needed by the women's for sacramental duties and spiritual guidance. In short, religious opportunities for women were far smaller than the interest in joining such communities. Into this vacuum grew communities of women who found ways to support themselves within the cities' networks of trade and guilds. The monastic theology of the day stressed that the cloister was an imitation of Jerusalem and that the lives of the monks and nuns who lived there presented a guide for the way of life needed to enter into the heavenly city.[16] Many of the larger beguinages in the cities would adapt this theology to a quasi-monastic life that contributed to the urban trade and livelihood.

As they evolved, the communities of the beguines exhibited four distinct periods of growth. The first groups started around individual women who showed spiritual or ecstatic gifts that were believed to demonstrate their connection with God.[17] Marie d'Oignies (1177–1213), often cited as the first beguine, convinced her husband to let her live as a solitary near a religious community in Oignies. Her works of charity and spiritual advice became well known, and other women sought out her guidance. Marie also received various mystical visions and engaged in strict fasts, which her confessor Jacques de Vitry (ca. 1160–1240) wrote about in his *Life* of her. At the time, the newly formed bourgeoisie challenged the feudal hierarchy and exerted its own power and authority. Among this social upheaval, the beguines found niches, such as the textile trade, in which to work. What separated these women from previous communities was that they did not live behind cloistered convent walls. Many of the houses unofficially used the customs or rules of other orders but were not incorporated into them or did not want to be subjected to their full administrative charters. The women took vows of chastity and lived in houses that eventually became known as beguinages. While women were central to this movement, men had their own communities too. Some of the men even lived in or near the convents, serving the sisters.

The beguines were not simply poor women who could not marry. In the urban social environment, marriage often occurred in women's midtwenties and a noticeable number of women decided never to marry.[18] The women seeking communities renounced the wealth of their parents and rejected marriage opportunities.[19] These actions paralleled the renunciation of wealth that accompanied many forms of intensification of religious feeling, particularly in the Franciscans, Humiliati, Waldensians, and other penitential groups. In Liège, Thomas de Cantimpré wrote hagiographic lives of several of the holy women living in his diocese, including Christina Mirabilis (Christina the Astonishing, ca. 1150–1224), Margerite d'Ypres (1216–37), Lutgard of Aywières (1182–1246), and Marie d'Oignies.[20] One notices that the women who tended to be identified as spiritual as opposed to heretical often lived where there was strong spiritual support and confessors or church leaders who would advocate for them.

The second stage in the development of beguine communities began in the thirteenth century as the women organized themselves into congregations that coalesced around shared work and devotional practices. In this stage, groups submitted to a female leader acting as a de facto abbess or prioress. It was at this time, as the women began to plan communities together, that the church sought to control the process, insisting that if women were going to found brick-and-mortar communities, they must be under the direction of an established order. Officially, this requirement was a way of making sure that new communities had the spiritual direction of a group that was approved by the church. Such a simple life did find supporters; Jacques de Vitry was a canon regular who later became a bishop and then cardinal. He would eventually become spokesperson for these women, and his power as a cardinal would help beguine communities receive papal consent to self-regulate.[21] Ultimately, these communities would increasingly come under not just the spiritual direction of the orders but also the direct control of local bishops, all in the name of proleptically preventing heretical ideas among the women.

In the third stage, the communities focused on their work integration and how it shaped the beguinages. The different works of each community—whether in the woolen trade, leper hospitals, lacemaking, or domestic work—were meant to serve the needs of its local city. This integration also meant the beguinages could be a variety of different sizes, often relatively small, and fit into the community as typical houses of people. Different communities had different expectations of stability, and while many insisted on members not moving between communities, some thought that the ability to move could have apostolic benefits through setting examples of holiness and thus influencing others.

Court beguinages, large communities with a Dominican or clergy from another religious community as a director, developed at this time.[22] Dominicans helped erect court beguinages in Douai, Lille, and Antwerp when heresy was suspected among communities and the laity there, as a way of helping to protect them.[23] These communities were to be self-supporting and required property to join, and the sisters would also do labor within the beguinage.[24] But the self-regulated communities still challenged both civil and religious authorities who wanted them to be under the control of either bishops or orders. These women yielded important social and spiritual power in the cities, largely through their reputations for holiness. The women were also a visible presence, in part because of some of the work they did, such as caring for the sick and the dying.

In the final stage, beguine communities were required to be enclosed, and their work was limited to certain trades, such as lacework and health care. The beguinages became almost cities unto themselves. They would contain all the resources and facilities needed to support the community of women. The mendicants, especially the Dominicans, took over their spiritual care. The Dominican friars were chosen for this task because they were known as the keepers of orthodoxy through their roles in preaching and in the Inquisition. They helped to make sure that the women were on the right path for their stated goal: the *vita apostolica* for the beguines was not just a path of becoming like Christ but a path that would lead the follower to be one with Christ.[25] But this aim was also the goal of much thirteenth-century mysticism, even within orthodox convents. After all, *unus spiritus cum deo* (becoming one spirit with God) was the Cistercian motto guiding spiritual attainment.

Women's Mystical Literature

While the monastic exhortation of *ora et labora*—pray and work—structured the day-to-day lives of the beguines, these women demonstrated a characteristic piety that focused on both experience of God and on the effect that it had on the human. They left the largest body of writings out of all the groups covered in this book, which may partly be explained by the era in which they lived; other mystics of the time, including Bernard of Clairvaux, Hildegarde of Bingen, and Julian of Norwich also wrote mystical treatises. The literature of the beguines includes texts from both men and women and lives from their confessors. It comes from a wide range of areas, including Germany, the Low Countries, and France, and it features writings in a number of different genres, from spiritual treatises to hagiographic lives to poems. There were spiritual dialogues, such as *The Mirror of Simple Souls*; the love poetry of Hadewijch of Brabant; the *Life* of Marie d'Oignies; and the sermons of Meister Eckhart. The development of mystical literature was an outgrowth of lay spirituality's focus on personal experience of God. The beguine writers largely wrote in vernacular languages, which could cause problems; the theology of how humans can talk about human union with God was very regulated within Latin and was the subject of debate in the universities. Those linguistic boundaries were unclear in the vernacular languages, which displayed none of the scholastic intricacies of theological distinctions.

The spirit of seeking direct experience of God can be seen clearly in the early beguine Christina the Astonishing, a woman from Belgium. A shepherdess, she had a massive seizure while attending her animals and was presumed dead. She reanimated during her funeral service, flew up to the church rafters, and began a new phase of life as a holy woman. During her "death," she had seen purgatory, heaven, and hell; afterward, she could smell sin on people. What she saw convinced her to turn her life around and live in service of praying for the dead and working to save the living. In her case, the direct experience of the divine caused a radical reorientation of the purpose and outward acts of her life. She was called "the astonishing" because her body could withstand all sorts of painful situations, including extreme fasting and punishments such as entering burning furnaces or jumping into an icy cold river. Unusual feats of the physical body were an outward manifestation of divine gifts. Christina also had a sense of "shame and embarrassment" over the actions God prompted her to perform.[26] Other supernatural bodily manifestations of divine favor would be seen in the stigmata of Christina von Stemmeln, a beguine in Cologne a generation after Christina the Astonishing.

Christina the Astonishing's confessor and advocate, Thomas de Cantimpré, explained that although Christina caught the attention of clergy several times in her life, God used her as a tool to admonish clergy not living up to their station: "She would admonish sinning priests or clerics lest they blaspheme the good name of Christ through their public excesses, but she did so in great secrecy and with a wondrous reverence and as sweetly as if they were her own father."[27] Although such an action could cause her to be a target, having an advocate like Thomas seems to have helped her; she would be recognized as a holy woman. Thomas, the writer of her *Life*, stated that "God granted that she endure purgatory in the world while still living in the body."[28] When telling her story, he makes sure to root it and her bodily mortifications in her desire to return to contemplation of the divine. That continual focus on God gives her all the outwardly astonishing abilities. As he noted, "When the time approached that she be held fast in the sickness of death, she was overtaken by such an unbroken grace of contemplation that she found it very difficult to direct the attention of her mind anywhere else."[29] Thomas said that the reason for writing her life down is that just as she inspired people to amend their ways during her lifetime, writing down her acts and miracles encouraged the reader to do penance for their sins after her death.[30] This personal experience of God, shared with others, was to be a central organizing aspect of beguine writing.

Douceline (ca. 1215–74) was another beguine from Hyères, Provence, and founded the beguinage of Marseilles. She represents a less sensational form of beguine spirituality. Growing up a pious child and teen who focused on the care of the poor and sick, she had a conversion experience at age twenty in which she took a vow before her brother, Franciscan, and established a beguine community in the city. She eventually founded a second house there as well. About 1250, she established a third beguinage in Marseilles, just outside the city walls. Her communities followed a blend of the beguine and the new Franciscan way of life, although she did not impose a requirement of poverty on the community.[31] She would spend the last twenty-five years of her life in Marseilles. Douceline had family connections to church leaders that would help to ensure her convents remained unmolested by inquisitors during her lifetime, and her convents were attended by women with aristocratic connections. Just like *The Life of Christina the Astonishing*, *The Life of Douceline* narrated the life a woman who is very much in the world and sought out by locals to help heal and bless them. It began with short descriptions of her childhood, then focused on the community she established and how it was structured. Next, it described her humility, obedience, and austerity, and how these qualities led to favors from God, which established her authority among outsiders, who could see the fruits of her holiness. In so telling, it focused on her virtues, how they helped her to have a strong contemplative life, and how this life aided the people around her by allowing her to heal people and perform charitable acts for the good of the community. It was the story of a woman who constantly sought the presence of God through contemplative ecstasies and whose ecstasies inspired piety in others, helped her to cure people, and offered her an opportunity to pray for the people who entrusted themselves to her prayers more effectively. Though the ecstasies were the focus of her spirituality, the miracles were the outward manifestations that reinforced the beguinal idea of being a religious community within the world.

Beguine writing can be difficult to fully appreciate because it is so varied. There were multiple traditions that influenced it, although the affective piety of people such as Anselm of Canterbury, Bernard of Clairvaux, and Francis of Assisi is perhaps the most noticeable influence. Affective theology focused its meditation on a particular material object (such as a painting or a crucifix) or written or spoken story (or even biblical tableau) as if the one praying was present in the original moment depicted. The person gives themselves over to an emotional response that frees them from overrationalizing and allows them to unite to the divine by just experiencing God. It was also something that didn't require enormous amounts of theological training to accomplish.

One specific element that we see in several beguines was a focused type of affective mysticism known as *Brautmystik*, or bridal mysticism. It fully flourished in the thirteenth century but had its origins in twelfth-century monasticism. Writers such as Bernard of Clairvaux preached and wrote extensively on the *Song of Songs*, which was interpreted as a marriage song between God and the human soul. From the opening words of "Let him kiss me with the kisses of his mouth," Bernard sought to interpret the sexual language of the book's verses in a way that instructed the person on how to attain union with God. Bridal mysticism would be the main form of expression in writers such as Hadewijch of Brabant and Mechthild of Magdeburg. But just as the beguines were of the world as well as contemplative, here they joined theological and secular traditions to new effect. To the *Brautmystik*, they coupled tropes from courtly romances with the troubadour and trouvère traditions.

Complicating everything was the fact that the beguines were writing about theological ideas in decidedly nontheological vernacular languages and genres rather than Latin, and much of their work was influenced not by the genres of literature open to men (theological treatises, sermons, and tractates) but those that women could read or write (poems, letters, narrative stories, and spiritual autobiographies, as well as accounts of mystical visions). These works used the images of Scripture and vernacular literature but in a spiritualized manner. So a love poem to the beloved could become one addressed to the bridegroom Christ when written by the beguine's hand. The language became metaphorical, not literal, and the transposition of such ideas to fit new types of writing opened up places where women's writings could be misunderstood, either intentionally or unintentionally. Writing in the vernacular also put the ability to interpret Scripture—a task usually set aside for clerics—into the hands of the writer and reader. Furthermore, the expression of the soul's ascent to God was usually written in terms that were born out of courtly love and courtship; to write in highly metaphorical ways invited scrutiny that asked if the underlying doctrine could be misunderstood. The masters who would investigate beguine writings were experts in theology, not in vernacular literature, and would find the language and imagery used to express love between the human and God to be quite different and unorthodox compared to the language used by theologians.

This difference underscores the fact that not all beguines were accepted by the church; Marguerite Porete is perhaps the best case study on how women could be labeled heretics when associated with the beguine life and spirituality. Her book *The Mirror of Simple Souls* was written between 1296 and 1306. Although some bishops who read it lauded it as orthodox and sublime, others did not find it to be orthodox, and ultimately it was condemned and burned in her presence. She was warned not to continue disseminating her ideas, a warning she ignored. She believed the book was orthodox and stood with those who agreed. As a woman, she had no right to a theological education and could not make the case for her book's orthodoxy; she had to rely on those who were by position entitled to make such judgments. She was brought before Philip of Marcigny and the inquisitor of Lorraine. There, she was accused of sending her book to John, the bishop of Châlons-sur-Marne, as well as propagating it among beguine and beghard communities in Hainault. Late in 1308, she was taken into custody. Two years later, on May 30, 1310, Marguerite was declared a lapsed heretic and handed to the provost of Paris for secular justice, which was execution. The issue was not that she was a beguine but her dogged insistence that her book contained divine truth and her attempts to get church officials to recognize it as orthodox. Her condemnation was a turning point, for it marked the start of authorities taking more serious actions against the beguines.

Marguerite Porete's book was condemned for theological inaccuracies related to the perfection of the soul and the idea that human obedience to the church, the sacraments, and the virtues were unnecessary for perfected souls. These condemnations would be the line of reasoning through the ideas in *Ad nostrum*, which attempted to suppress the beguines a couple of years later. *The Mirror of Simple Souls* is written in Old French and divided into two parts. The first part comprises about 80 percent of the text and is an allegorical dialogue between Love, Reason, and the Soul, along with other allegorical characters. Such dialogues were common in the literature of her time, both in Latin, such as Boethius's *Consolation of Philosophy*, and in the vernacular in Guillaume de Lorris and Jean de Meun's *Roman de la Rose* (*Romance of the Rose*). The second part of the book is much shorter and is written with a more personal, narratorial voice that seems to give voice to Marguerite herself.

In the larger first section of *The Mirror of Simple Souls*, the soul moves through seven levels of spiritual ascent toward eternal union with God.[32] Schemata of spiritual ascent in which the soul would finally come to rest in God were common, especially among writers in the monastic traditions. It was an inheritance from the Neoplatonic tradition, which saw the soul gradually cleanse itself of the material and become more spiritual; Bernard of Clairvaux and William of St-Thierry in the Cistercian tradition are two such examples. But here is where Marguerite seems to have gone too far; namely, in overstating both the nature of this union and how it removes the creature from needing material aids. As the soul ascends, it leaves behind earthly devotions and the virtues, and in the seventh stage, the soul is annihilated in God. Marguerite explains this last stage: "This Soul . . . is totally dissolved, melted and drawn, joined and united to the most high Trinity. And she cannot will except the divine will through the divine work of the whole Trinity. And a ravishing Spark and Light joins her and holds her very close."[33] Marguerite also explains that the annihilated soul cannot possess its own will.[34] The creature wants to will the will of God, which God has given her, but is too small in her creaturehood to do it. So, "God wills that she would will this, and that she would possess such a will. Such a will is the divine will, which gives being to a free creature. This divine will, which God makes her will, courses through her veins of divine understanding and the marrow of divine love and the union of divine praise."[35] Such quotations could be read as both an imprecise human language approximating the experience of the divine—perfectly orthodox, as all human language is imprecise when trying to describe divine things—or as heretical misinformation that denied human free will. Marguerite's legacy would be one where her book would continue to circulate as a spiritual treatise and where she and the book would be burned at an auto-da-fé.

The Heresy of the Free Spirit and Women's Persecution

If it is possible to see Marguerite Porete as the first condemned Free Spirit, then it raises the question of why her individual condemnation becomes an identification of an entire sect.[36] The Second Council of Lyon restated Fourth Lateran's declaration that there were to be no new orders, effectively preventing the beguines from being recognized unless individual communities could be accepted into existing orders. But it didn't condemn the beguines as heretics. This declaration occurred in the midst of a number of other synods that discussed the issue of women's spirituality, including Fritzlar (1259), Mainz (1261), Eichstatt (1282), and Béziers (1299). It would be almost forty years later that the Council of Vienne once again pressed the issue of the beguines when it met in 1311–12 and suppression began.

The Council of Vienne explicitly stated that women were not to follow the beguinal way of life, though penitential women could live in communal houses whether or not they were under a rule of life. Beguines were explicitly distinguished from other groups of women and came under more scrutiny, but the council gave no direction on who had to decide what to do with houses of women, who would figure out how to distinguish good houses from bad houses, or how to determine explicitly what constituted a beguinal house as opposed to other forms of religious life. It would put forth two decrees that linked the beguines and heresy. The first document from the council, *Cum de quibusdam mulieribus* (*Concerning Certain Women*), focused on women who were not regulars (did not live under a rule or take vows) and who did not give up private ownership of property. Some of the complaints were behavioral, such as wearing a habit, and some were doctrinal, such as saying they believed things inconsistent with the faith and leading other laity into error. For this reason, the decree forbid women from following the way of life of the beguine. But it did allow for pious women to live, with or without vows, in communal houses. This document also had an escape clause: it said that houses of women in which there were no misdoings were to be left alone. It didn't give a clear set of instructions on how to make such assessments.

The second bull, *Ad nostrum*, looked directly at the theological ideas associated with the beguines. It condemned eight errors of the beguines' and beghards' beliefs:

1. A person could achieve such perfection in this lifetime that they were incapable of sin.
2. This person achieving perfection does not need to pray or fast, for the senses are already subjected to reason.
3. The beguines are not subject to human obedience to the law of the church because "where the spirit of the Lord is, there is liberty."[37]
4. A person could attain final beatitude just as much here as in heaven.
5. The groups did not need the light of glory to be elevated to the vision of God.
6. Only imperfect humans needed acts of virtue; the perfect soul did not need to act virtuously.
7. Sex was not sinful when demanded by nature.
8. One did not need to show reverence to the consecrated host; to do so was to descend from the lofty heights of contemplation of God.

Ad nostrum also confirmed the beguines and beghards were a danger to other humans.[38] This list of supposed errors is an amalgam of beliefs culled from beguine writings (particularly from *The Mirror of Simple Souls*) and are presented without textual or community context. Like inquisitor's questions for suspected heretics, they read as a list formed to be applied as a test. And that is largely what would happen: the council drew up a list of beliefs and deputized local authorities to investigate if anyone believed some of them.

Ultimately, this list would create suspicion about how beguines worshipped, how they viewed human nature and original sin, and whether they downplayed the necessity of receiving the sacraments. Therefore, *Ad nostrum* called for routing and punishing the sect's members. This document served as "the birth certificate of the heresy of the Free Spirit since, technically speaking, heresy is defined by the pope and the decree referred explicitly to heretics who spoke of their 'spirit of liberty.'"[39] In short, this heresy was not defined by the believers, who saw themselves as churchgoing mystics seeking union with God. Nor was it defined by any collection of people who acted as a group, as the beguines throughout Europe didn't view themselves as part of an organized movement—they focused on their local communities. Rather, it was a heresy only as defined by the magisterium, which saw the beguines trying to achieve spiritual union with God in too free a manner. And this view partly explains why the fates of beguines would vary so widely, depending on whether they could find allies within their local church hierarchy to advocate for their holiness.

The Council of Vienne was dismissed in May 1312, before it had set all its decrees into final form. Pope Clement V, who presided at Vienne, intended to polish and circulate them to the universities but was unable to do so before his death in 1314. They were not to be officially published until October of 1317, under Pope John XXII. It was at this point that *Cum de quibusdam mulieribus* began to be used to forcibly close beguine houses. This church action became too enthusiastic. The next year, the pope issued *Ratio recta* (*Correct Reasoning*), "which ordered the clergy to protect all beguines who led stable lives and refrained from disputing about the Trinity, divine essence, or sacraments."[40] In it, he admitted that the term *beguines* was often used to describe many women who lived a pious life and obeyed local clergy. The clarification spoke directly to bishops, telling them not to bother such pious women. Yet the clarification did not slow the persecution, which would continue under the guise of enforcing the Fourth Lateran Council decree regarding no new orders: those that were not recognized as one of the extant orders were to be suppressed. Strictly speaking, Fourth Lateran's ban on new religious orders applied only to men, so it should have been possible for these women's communities to find a home in the church if the papacy wanted to allow it. In reality, the ruling was never applied the way it was written. Beguines had an intermediary status at best—they were not officially recognized, but many communities were under ecclesiastical supervision and open to those who accepted the community vision. They might have had postulants take vows, but since they were not officially recognized orders, the vows were not seen as official by the church, and the leadership felt that such an omission implied lack of serious purpose.

The persecutions would continue in waves across various parts of Europe, especially in the Rhineland valley. In a later wave, on June 6, 1366, the inquisitor Henry of Agro executed Metza of Westhoven, who had been found guilty of being a lapsed beguine. She had recanted fifty years prior in the trial of John of Duerbheim. Strangely, she was the only one executed, and by this time, she was an old woman. There is no record of the charges against her. In 1374, yet another campaign began against the beguines. Bishop Lambert of Burn accused the beguines of ignoring the precepts of the Council of Vienne. The Dominicans would answer the allegations on behalf of women under their care. Scholars have noted that the persecutions were often associated with waves of persecutions against others, such as the Waldensians, suggesting that the seriousness with which the beguines were attacked was in part colored by more organized or larger groups because, in the mind of the church, all heresy sprung from a similar impulse.

Arguably, persecution of the Free Spirit heresy was aimed primarily at women. As these waves of persecution started, the accusations against the beguines became more pointed and detailed. The Franciscan Gilbert of Tournai, who would take a large place in the condemnation of Marguerite Porete, claimed that beguines read vernacular copies and commentaries of the Scriptures in public squares, rather than at home in private. That caused two problems for Gilbert: (1) Latin was the only officially recognized version of the Scriptures at the time, and (2) reading them aloud was tantamount to preaching, an activity reserved for men and that required episcopal approval. This view points to the zeitgeist and its feeling that there was a need for social control. The mendicant orders were espousing the *vita apostolica* at the same time that the beghards and beguines were being condemned for it. This attempt at suppression actually served to make the beguines and beghards more fervent in their piety, initiating a cycle in which they would then face charges of heresy because of their zeal.

Beghards and Persecution

Although women were disproportionately the target of Free Spirit heretic investigations, the persecution of the heresy wasn't only one of women. Men's groups that were interested in following the same way of life as the beguines probably date back to about the same time as women's, the 1220s.[41] Some of the oldest men's communities include Diest, founded in the 1250s, and Sint-Truiden, founded in 1270. Other communities of men existed throughout the Low Countries, including towns such as Maastricht,

Leuven, Antwerp, Tournai, and Zoutleeuw.[42] Men's communities worked in the wool trade, as some of the women's communities did, and supported their communities by copying manuscripts.

Men were not targeted as heretics as frequently as women were but not for the reasons we might expect. Many of the men associated with the movement were not from beghard communities but were simply in contact with it through women's houses and wanted to support it; these men were usually members of existing orders of monastics, canons, or mendicants. Those who supported the movement from these positions probably helped it in three ways. First, they were less likely to come under suspicion, being attached to a recognized and approved order. Any questions would be dealt with internally within their order. Second, they had access to theological education, especially in the mendicant orders, and thus were less likely to accidentally make theological misunderstandings. Finally, they usually wrote and preached in Latin, a language with a vocabulary used for theology. But there were several men whose theology became known as emblematic of the heresy. Chief among them was Meister Eckhart, a Dominican from the Rhineland who was incorrectly credited with writing the *Sister Catherine Treatise*. Another example is Jan von Ruusbroec, who was both accused of heresy (but not condemned) and accused others.

Meister Eckhart was an immensely popular and learned preacher who wrote and preached in both Latin and the vernacular of his area, Middle High German, depending on his audience. He studied in Cologne and was appointed to be a master at the University of Paris twice, a rare honor. Eckhart regularly preached sermons to the beguines of the area and provided spiritual direction. The rediscovery of Plato and Aristotle, and their influence on theology à la Aquinas in the early thirteenth century, meant that Neoplatonic ideas were being adopted among the theologians and filtering to the public. Among the common elements of Eckhart's sermons are some ideas seen in the *Ad nostrum* condemnations. Liberty of spirit, one of his key doctrines, contrasted with the idea of Christ the teacher. The liberty of spirit made a person perfect and was the operation of grace within the soul. Eckhart also spoke about the birth of the word in the soul, another way of talking about the growing presence of grace in the human who sought God. His point was that a person became freer the more closely united with the will of God that they became. Eckhart denied the possibility of human perfection in this life, but he did believe that as a person became perfected, they did not need to listen to the church or civil authorities. Arguably, this state couldn't happen in this life, although nowhere does he explicitly say it only happens afterward.

Cologne Archbishop Henry of Virneburg asked Nicholas of Strasburg, the Dominican papal visitor, to investigate Meister Eckhart. He was declared free of heresy, but this conclusion was not enough to satisfy the archbishop; he would continue to lead a campaign against Eckhart. After 1306, Henry promulgated a series of synodal decisions aimed against the beguines and beghards. He based his complaints on the ban against new orders, noting that the beghard lifestyle was a new pursuit of the apostolic life under a new guise. He also complained that the beghards, whom he took as illiterate, disrupted the sermons of licensed mendicants and challenged them to public dispute, undercutting their authority. But he went further and accused the beghards of heresy, saying that the group stated that those who did not follow them could not be saved. They also supposedly declared that they were not subject to the law if they had the Spirit of God.[43] The archbishop also accused the beguines of saying fornication wasn't a sin. But his decrees contradicted his point, stating the beghards believed that a man could send away his wife in order to join the group, suggesting that its members preferred asceticism to wanton sexual fulfillment.

Being accused of heresy, especially in an intellectual setting, was not necessarily unusual. Theologians at universities experienced condemnations during the same periods, such as condemnations associated with Aristotelianism and Averroism; the Paris and Oxford condemnations of 1277 contained nearly 250 propositions.[44] Among them were ones found in the works of prominent University of Paris theologians such as Thomas Aquinas. Also condemned at that time was Andreas Capellanus's work *De amore* (*A Treatise on Courtly Love*). In the case of Eckhart, several factors were at play. First was the issue that his vernacular sermons were rarely about one topic only, and they assumed that the audience could make connections to previous sermons. Second, the idea of the birth of the word in the soul was easily misinterpreted to suggest a comingling of the divine and human natures, through a literal interpretation of Eckhart's words. His exegetical method favored the spiritual senses of Scripture as the key to understanding them. Similar issues were raised concerning his idea of the nobility of the soul, which said that the powers of the human soul were related to God. He also talked about the soul's divine nature: "The

Father gives birth to his Son in eternity, equal to himself... Yet I say more: He has given birth to him in my soul. Not only is the soul with him, and he equal with it, he is in it, and the Father gives his Son birth in the soul in the same way as he gives him birth in eternity, and not otherwise."[45] While there are orthodox ways to parse this statement (such as saying the soul is made in the image of God), Eckhart didn't clarify his meaning, leaving his detractors free to think he believed the divine nature was part of the human soul.

Third, like others from contemplative traditions, Eckhart was interested in the nature of human union with God and especially how it affected the person in this life who strove wholeheartedly for it. In explaining how a person must put God first, Eckhart talks about a person needing to abandon themselves in order to allow God to fill them with Godself. While the language of emptying oneself can be understood in the orthodox idea of humility, the language of annihilating and abandoning oneself for God is not. Eckhart preached, "An authority says: 'All things that are alike love one another and unite with one another, and all things that are unlike flee from one another and hate one another.'... I say the same about the man who has annihilated himself in himself and in God and in all created things; this man has taken possession of the lowest place, and God must pour the whole of himself into this man, or else he is not God." Later he adds, "he must pour all of it fruitfully into the man who has abandoned himself for God."[46] Finally, inquisitors were concerned with his claims of the divine as the ground for each person's existence. While most of these ideas could be rehabilitated or clarified rather easily within the Neoplatonism of the universities, the expressions in his vernacular sermons were the challenge for inquisitors; the way he expressed the ideas, for an audience without theological training, raised concerns.

Under the request of the archbishop of Cologne, forty-nine articles culled from Eckhart's writings were presented as being doctrinally questionable, and Eckhart was called by inquisitors to answer for them in 1326. His reply was not politic, saying he refused to recognize their authority as he was a Dominican and therefore not under the archbishop's authority but responsible only to the pope. He also questioned the morality of the examining committee members.[47] In response, Eckhart received a new list of fifty-nine articles to answer for. He was brought before the judges on January 24, 1327, to answer the charge of heresy. He died just before the final verdict of the trial in 1329. The papal bull *In Agro Dominico* (*In the Lord's Field*) condemned twenty-eight propositions of Eckhart's, seventeen as heretical and eleven as suspect. Despite this finding, Eckhart's students and fellow Rhineland mystics John Tauler and Henry Suso found acceptance for their ideas.[48]

Another example of a condemned treatise is the *Sister Catherine Treatise*. One challenge of reading medieval texts is that their authors are sometimes incorrectly identified. In this case, the book was incorrectly ascribed to Meister Eckhart, probably because someone thought it sounded like him. The *Sister Catherine Treatise* was comprised of a series of dialogues between Sister Catherine and her confessor. In the beginning, the confessor directed her to live a sinless life and to seek God. The confessor advised her that hell is "nothing other than a mode of being. Whatever your mode of being is here on earth, it will be the same eternally—that is hell."[49] The treatise also made claims about who could be saved, for instance, stating that women had to become men to enter heaven.[50] The treatise was a mix of the typical Christian exhortations, reminders to follow her confessor's advice (which she rebelled against early on in the text). After a while, she returned to her confessor, who did not recognize her. Seeing she was now a spiritually superior being to him, he endeavored to learn from her, but she fell into a trance. Following several years of spiritual practice, Sister Catherine had several experiences of God and would fall into a deathlike state for several days. She did so again in front of her confessor.

Like much of what we read in Marguerite Porete's book, the *Sister Catherine Treatise* said that the human and divine join in union and God becomes the person's being: "In the same manner the ones who do not let anything else but God reside in their being retain their being as is. God becomes their being and remains their being eternally."[51] Sister Catherine had prayed to experience as much suffering as she could bear and described her experience of being in a state of emptiness and having experienced the superabundance of God.[52] When talking about the virtues and sin, it is revealed that she no longer needs the virtues and has entered a sinless state. After explaining to her confessor how the seven deadly sins were driven out of her, she continued to explain that if Christ had revealed himself to the disciples completely, they would not have been able to withstand it. The confessor fainted; Sister Catherine's explications on the nature of the Son have led the confessor to ecstatic union with God.[53] Texts that lead a person to experience God through mystical union would continue to be a popular form of writing for centuries to come; we see the beginnings of this phenomenon formulated for the laity and quasi-religious in the beguines.

Lasting Impact

Although some high-profile beguines and beghards were found guilty of heresy, the overwhelming majority lived out quiet, dedicated lives within their communities, often with the support of local clergy and sometimes with the support of popes. There were a number of clerics, both individual priests and friars, as well as some bishops, who kept a pastoral eye on the beguinages in their areas. Marie d'Oignies's confessor was Jacques de Vitry. He received permission from Pope Honorius III (1150–1227) to direct pious laywomen in Liège, France, and Germany.[54] The pope said that the women should preach or exhort to one another within their communities.[55] Some cities encouraged large houses of women; in Belgium, there were self-centered communities, but in the Rhineland, the beguines lived in individual houses. Cologne and Strasbourg were the largest centers.[56] There were other singular supporters as well. Robert Grosseteste, the bishop of Lincoln, proclaimed that the beguine life was a higher form of perfection and Christian poverty because its practitioners did not live off alms but their own labor.[57] Robert de Sorbon said the beguines in Paris were more likely to survive the last judgment than those at the University of Paris.[58] A community couldn't count on individual support, knowing that bishops were moved among cities and the life spans of supporting clergy and popes were shorter than the lives of communities, but it provides a counterpoint to the well-publicized trials of Free Spirit heretics and suggests that the association of the movement with heresy was based on a few spectacular situations.

A prevailing sense of orthodoxy characterized the medieval church. Heresy required both an orthodoxy and a body strong enough to enforce it. Heresy implied an opposition to authority. What is curious about the Free Spirit heresy is the disjunct between the unilateral condemnation at the Council of Vienne and the other, sporadic condemnations. The beguines and beghards were merely striving for what other religious—both orthodox and heretical—strove for: spiritual renewal and a reawakening of evangelical principles.[59] The beguines and beghards might not have been condemned at all in a different social milieu, for their religious life followed accepted forms, though new expressions were limited in their particular era.

One of the popular complaints against the beguines was that they vacillated between following the examples of Mary and Martha (as opposed to contemplative nuns, who followed the example of Mary strictly).[60] And this practice was a challenge for a church that was trying to uphold previously decided boxes for each order; the mendicants had already challenged the Mary/Martha divide. But the post–Fourth Lateran church tried not to allow new interpretations of the religious life. Interestingly, with the case of the beguines, we see a change in the way that the monastic orders handle the issue of this heresy. The Cistercians waged an anemic battle against the group. In general, though, they refused to admit women and refused to deal with issues of informal women's communities that followed Cistercian customs. They did not manage as fully vehement an attack on the Free Spirit heresy as they did against the first three heresies we've investigated. One of the ironies of the Free Spirit persecutions is that the very inquisitors who were asked to condemn them were from the same order that was asked to provide spiritual guidance to the unordered women. This heresy is associated with mendicancy, for both its support and propagation. And some of this situation might be tied to the Mary/Martha divide. Meister Eckhart stated that both women came from the same place and had the same end, a good way of describing all that the beguine life contained:

> It is actually the same thing, for we take only from the same ground of contemplation and make it fruitful in works, and thus the object of contemplation is achieved. Though there is motion, yet it is all one; it comes from one end, which is God, and returns to the same, as if I were to go from one end of this house to the other; that would indeed be motion, but only of one in the same. Thus too, in this activity, we remain in a state of contemplation in God. The one rests in the other, and perfects the other. For God's purpose in the union of contemplation is fruitfulness in works: for in contemplation you serve yourself alone, but in works of charity you serve the many.[61]

Traditionally, preachers interpreted the story of Mary and Martha to indicate that the contemplative life—the one Mary chose—was better than the one Martha chose as she bustled about. Eckhart's reading elevates the work of those in the world to the same level as the contemplatives, raising not merely the dock worker, the merchant, and the baker but the beguine and beghard as well. And that rereading resonated with the mendicants and other worldly orders but also challenged the supposed superiority of the monastics.

CHAPTER 5

The Templars
Power, Publicity, and Authority in Heresy

KNIGHTS, CRUSADES, AND the conquest of foreign lands all for the sake of glory is a large part of the mythology of the Middle Ages. And the Knights Templar were a pinnacle of both the chivalrous and the churchly ideal of knighthood. Yet perhaps no heretical movement has caused as much sensational speculation of conspiracy as that of the Templars. They are forever associated in the popular imagination with shadowy political intrigue, crusades and war, and the type of power and wealth that defied all forms of church or political control in the Middle Ages. But the change of fortunes—from the group being a military-spiritual arm of the church to being its most prosecuted heretical enemy—was one that turned on a quick series of events, largely motivated by finances and temporal power, and was not based on church doctrine. When the Templars fell from grace, they fell quickly and inspired the first comprehensive set of medieval multinational repressions. These repressions and the ferocity with which the secular powers went after the group, as well as the dramatic accusations against them that led to their names being associated with heresy and antichurch activities, make this heresy unique. The content of these accusations illuminates the other associations the church made with heretics beyond doctrinal concerns. While there were claims of sexual misdoings among the Waldensians and the beguines, from the time of the Templars onward, a standard catalogue of sexual misdeeds would form part of the stock accusations against heretics.

The Templars were set up to be condemned, and their condemnation was a result of political wrangling that perceived them as a threat to the political power of the secular leaders, first and foremost, and of the Roman See. Yet the outward reasons given for the condemnation of the Templars were wrapped in the rhetoric of heresy, showing that it was by now a default category for exclusion and raising yet more questions for us about heresy as a reliable charge. Indeed, their fall from grace shows how the banner of heresy could be raised as a specter of fear rather than merely of condemnation of viewpoints. Heresy became a weapon to gain power over a group and to cow others into obedience. The Templar "heresy" tells us not how a heresy unfolded or how it encompassed new ideas, but rather it shows us that the specter of heresy had become a category that justified immediate, extreme force as a new form of social and economic control.[1]

Background and Foundation

The Templars' original goal was to protect pilgrims and the borders of Outremer (the lands conquered by the Crusaders, which comprised four Crusader-states) against Muslim incursions and, eventually, to fight against Muslims when they retook some of these lands. Once Jerusalem was captured by the Christians, it became a pilgrim's destination. Pilgrimage was a popular undertaking, both by an individual's choosing and as a penance given by a priest. One condition of pilgrimage was that the pilgrim had to be unarmed as they traveled toward their destination. Jerusalem, Santiago de Compostela, and Rome were among the most popular sites in the High Middle Ages. The First Crusade was preached in 1095 and began in 1096. It recaptured Jerusalem by 1099. In the wake of this result, Hugh of Payens asked Warmund, the patriarch of Jerusalem, and King Baldwin II to allow for a new order to protect the city and the returning pilgrims. Pilgrim recollections reported Muslims and bandits lurking in caves along the route from the coast to Jerusalem.[2] Protecting future pilgrims and the pilgrimage routes was the first goal of the Templars.

The Templars' second goal was to protect the Christian boundaries of land reclaimed as a result of the Crusades. Whereas in the early church, there was a strong sense that the church should abhor violence, the late eleventh century's preaching of a crusade, coupled with the prior admission of the warlike Germanic tribes into the church in the early Middle Ages, meant that church opinion about the use of violence was shifting. Not all church leaders found the concept of a military order easy to swallow. There were other military orders established in the same century: the Knights Hospitaller (founded 1113) oversaw the hospital in Jerusalem, and the Order of Saint James (founded 1170) helped escort pilgrims to the shrine of St. James of Compostela. Each military order had a particular protective goal. The Hospitallers were mainly dedicated to dispensing charity, originally at a hospice dedicated to sick and injured pilgrims. Some leaders, such as Peter the Venerable from the Abbey of Cluny, had expressed misgivings about the Templars. Of the newly formed military orders, the Poor Fellow-Soldiers of Christ and the Temple of Solomon (founded 1118), known as the Templars, were by far the most aggressively focused on knighthood.

The medieval history of the Templars, written by William of Tyre in 1184, dated the founding of the Templars to 1118.[3] William wrote that Hugh of Payens and Godfrey of Saint-Omer were the first two men to take vows of poverty, chastity, and obedience; they professed their vows to Patriarch Warmund. King Baldwin II of Jerusalem gave them permission to use part of his palace as their base of operations, near the Temple of the Lord. Hence, they were known as the Canons of the Temple of the Lord. They were granted several benefices, the income from which helped support their activities. The Templars adopted their role of protecting pilgrims as a type of ongoing penitential lifestyle; thus, they were meant as a complement to the Hospitallers, who provided shelter and care to those on pilgrimage. In 1120, the Templars went to the Council of Nablus to ask for permission to become an order. Baldwin granted them the Temple of Solomon, the former al-Aqsa Mosque, next to the Holy Sepulchre. With this grant, they were formally tied to the protection of the Holy Land.

These new orders were unique in that they combined religious life with a military mission. Yet while Peter the Venerable expressed his disagreement with the idea of military orders in the church, the Templars found an unexpected source of support in the Cistercian Bernard of Clairvaux. Bernard's writings, in fact, came to be foundational documents for the order, helping to frame its understanding of its vocation. His work *De laude novae militie* (*In Praise of the New Knighthood*) was a reply to the Templar Hugh of Payens, who had asked Bernard three times for guidance. This text, the *Rule of the Templars*, and the letter of "Hugo peccator" were often copied together and viewed as guidance for the fledgling order.[4] As a result, Bernard—whose Cistercian order was a reform of the monastic tradition—helped lend support and credibility to a very different sort of enterprise through the Templar order. In a letter to Hugh of Champagne, Bernard offered his support of his friend's vocation with the Templars and implicitly offered support of the charism of the new order.

Bernard's letter shows the closeness and affection he had for Hugh when he wrote of his friend's vocation:

> If it is for God's sake that you from being a count have become a simple soldier, from being a rich man have become poor, then it is right that I should congratulate you, and glorify God in you, seeing in this a "change of the right hand of the Most High." ... How can I forget your long-standing affection and generosity to this house? ... How willingly would I provide for your soul and body were it but granted to us to live in the company of each other! But because this is not to be, because I may not have you ever present as I should like, it only remains for me always to pray for you absent.[5]

Bernard's personal history with Hugh and his previous benevolence in helping to establish the monastery give the abbot a context in which to understand Hugh's current endeavors. Having a friend so well connected was an auspicious beginning for the new military order.

Knightly culture was not new, but it had previously been associated with courtly love and with the fighting of battles rather than with the monastic tradition. The Knights of the Temple attempted to combine into a meaningful pattern two very distinct parts of medieval culture that previously had not been conjoined. It was a novel way of uniting secular traditions with the church and of connecting the ecclesiastic and political consolidation of power in the wake of the Crusades. We already saw how the Cathar heresy was tentatively linked to the returning Crusaders, and their suppression repurposed the forces of the Crusades; the Templars were tied to the Crusades, particularly to the Crusaders who remained in the Holy Land after the First Crusade. One ongoing concern of church leaders was how returning knights fit back within the order of the church. After the initial takeover of Jerusalem, the Crusaders were happy to return home, taking their spoils with them. Within a year of Jerusalem's capture, only 300 infantry and 300 knights remained in the city. The Templars were meant to be a military wing for a church that needed military force against heretics and infidels and to help channel the military desires of noble young men returning from crusading: it was a radical acknowledgment of the changing role of the church in the world. Although the church had long contended with wars and barbarian tribes in Europe, the creation of military orders acknowledged that it had a political role of preserving Christian holy places and attacking those considered hostile to Christianity. But this role meant that the Templars had to justify their own understanding of how to navigate between the traditional monastic focus on stability and the contemplative, inner life with a more active lifestyle.

We know Bernard of Clairvaux helped provide influence and support for the fledgling Templar order, but not much else about its early history and founding is well documented. This situation isn't surprising, as new orders often sought to tie their work to earlier traditions, making their organizations look older and more established than they were or making them look as if they were outgrowths of previous movements in the church. For the Templars, the lack of documentation was in part because they attracted men infatuated with knightly honor rather than with university learning: "Many were craftsmen, or people who performed ordinary agricultural tasks such as herding sheep or cattle."[6] They did not sit around writing documents about how the order would run, nor did they have the political ties needed to navigate diplomacy within the church. They had little participation in the theological discussions of the time and do not appear to have written down their own history.

The Templars were approved as an order at the Council of Troyes in January 1129. William of Tyre noted that the initial years of the Templars were not wholly profitable, and at the council, they had only nine official members. They were quite destitute and could dress themselves only in the clothes that had been donated to them, even though the work of the order leading up to the council had included a large-scale recruitment and donations campaign.[7] By 1128, the Templars' mission had expanded to include the defense of Jerusalem as well as fighting Muslims in Syria.[8] In 1135, Pope Innocent II promulgated the papal bull *Omne Datum Optimum* (*Every Perfect Gift*), which approved the *Rule of the Templars* and declared that the Templars were responsible only to the pope. The bull gave all spoils of war with Muslims to the order. The order very quickly managed to become yoked to the central authority in the church, exempt from local political powers and local bishops; for example, Templars could build their own churches without needing to seek the approval of local bishops and would not be expected to pay tithes. This freedom allowed them to pursue what they considered their mission without local or temporal interference. In 1144, Pope Celestine II announced the papal bull *Milites Templi* (*Soldiers of the Temple*), which further asked the local clergy to protect and support the Knights Templar and allowed them to take up collections once a year in all their locations. A year later, Pope Eugene III would promulgate *Militia Dei* (*Soldiers of God*), which sought to consolidate the previous papal announcements about Templar freedoms. It declared that they could travel around Europe freely, could take tithes and burial fees, could bury their own dead in their own cemeteries, and were free from obedience to local clerical administration. This independence would prove to create the tension that would undermine them. With added responsibilities came more recruits and more gifts to support the order. By 1180, the Templars numbered at least 300 in Jerusalem; the order would grow to over 7,000 within the next seventy-five years.

The order attracted a number of noticeable patrons. Fulk V, Count of Anjou, came into contact with the Templars during his pilgrimage, thereafter granting them an annual payment, an example that was copied by a number of nobles in France. As the order grew in wealth and scale, they gained property not only in the Levant but also throughout Europe, especially in France, England, and Spain. They became good at moving gold and other valuables around and were involved in banking and finance as a result. The Templars even counted among their patrons Eleanor of Aquitaine. When Alfonso I of Aragon died, he willed everything to be split equally between the Canons of the Holy Sepulchre, the Hospitallers, and the Templars.[9] Although the contested will would never be fulfilled, the Templars gained landholdings in Western Europe by agreeing to renounce their inheritance. While the fashion of deeding property to the Templars helped them to build a fortune, it brought them into conflict; money and landholdings meant power, which was a threat to the local leaders and the local bishops, who held no power over the Templars. The order increasingly focused less on their duties in Jerusalem in order to administer their far-flung properties.

Because their various missions meant the Templars had to be in many places, often without reliable communications, the order focused on logistical development to help support its far-flung work during its early years. Additionally, the recruitment of financial support from a large number of nobles and clerical leaders meant that the structure needed to be strong enough to not be swayed by any one set of outside desires. The Templars recruited differently than many orders: many men joined because they had been on crusades or joined as an act of penance or out of fear for their souls. Admission into the Templars was also given as a secular punishment for crimes. For instance, "in 1224, Pope Honorius III told the Master of the Temple to receive a knight, Bertran, who had killed a bishop, into the Order for seven years to do penance for his crime."[10] Because of such cases, the order attracted men without a common background or goal, whom it needed to form into a cohesive unit. Admission of brothers generally required only that they prove that they were free to join: not married, not belonging to anyone, and no legal or financial obligations.

As the order grew, fewer and fewer brothers could even claim to have had crusading duties within the order: by the early fourteenth century, few had been to the Holy Land, and being sent there was even seen as a punishment by some.[11] As a reminder of how little we truly know about the inner workings of the order, the regulations are silent on the matter of how the Templars determined jobs for recruits.

An Unlikely Ally
Bernard of Clairvaux

Bernard of Clairvaux's imprint on the order far exceeded his friendship with its founder, Hugh; his keen spiritual and theological mind would help to shape the foundational documents in an order that did not naturally attract people of learning and reflection. After being asked three times to write an affirmation of the Templars' vocation, Bernard finally did so, presenting a defense of the order that both praised the new knighthood as combining the military and monastic vocations while damning the secular knighthood as ephemeral and effeminate. His answer seems both somewhat standard—Bernard would go on to preach the Second Crusade—and rather shocking, boldly stating that killing is necessary. The key to this position lies in his use of Scripture, where he began with a literal reading and said that it provides for this new type of order. Bernard then moved into interpretation, using the spiritual modes. He noted that without the spiritual understanding, there was no benefit. But without the literal, he could not answer the request that had sought him out.

Bernard's response focused on the apparent alignment and clash between the temporal and the spiritual. The abbot talked about the spiritual topography of the Holy Land based around the death and life of Christ. The Templars' physical presence in these places was tied to the need to protect them because of their spiritual importance. In his defense of the order, Bernard wrote of its being a military order based on the spiritual warfare against evil, which extended into the physical world. Bernard acknowledged the Templar task of protecting the Holy Land:

> Of all the Holy and wondrous places, somehow the holy sepulcher hold[s] place of pride. I do not know why people feel a greater devotion at the place where he lay dead than at the places where he did things while alive, or are more moved by the remembrance of his death than of his life. I suppose that one is regarded as more desolate, and the other more pleasant; or that the peace of his repose fascinates human weakness more than does the hard toil of his way of life; the security of his death more than the righteousness of his life.[12]

Bernard of Clairvaux saw the Templars as a fulfillment of biblical prophecy. He ultimately placed the Templar mission in a line with the temporal defense of the new affective spirituality, particularly as it regarded the death of Christ. Two issues arose: the sudden and astounding return of the Holy Land into Christian hands, which Bernard noted was quickly told throughout Europe, and the request for a defense of the new Knights of the Temple way of life.[13] He found himself having to justify the literal way of life, to fit it within a monastic milieu that emphasized the spiritual aspects of life and placed the contemplative over the physical. The task was conflicted with itself, and Bernard knew he had to make a strong case on both fronts, taking each seriously, but his argument must ultimately conclude the spiritual was the higher calling. He placed his writing within the debate of the secular versus the spiritual, talking of secular knights versus the Templars, who fought for a spiritual cause. He felt that he must defend the Templars against charges of being sinful in their mission and place them within the recent history, the ideals of the Crusades, and an eschatological history emphasizing that the earthly Jerusalem was subsidiary to the heavenly one. Bernard's book ended with a catalogue of spiritual places, where he explained that the tomb of the sepulchre wasn't important because of its physical location but because of its connection to the spiritual; Bernard even expressed his wonder that people find it a place more sublime than others. Ultimately, Jerusalem was an important place, as the spiritual elements that these physical locations pointed to. This idea would be especially important for defending the order's charism after Christians no longer controlled Jerusalem—the Templars' work would point not toward the mere physical location but to the heavenly Jerusalem, the more important location.

In his defense, Bernard explicitly focused on the lives and characters of the men who were in the Templar order because it was based on the secular knighthood and held different values from vowed religious. Bernard offered a number of statements on the characters of the men in the order, well beyond what he would have had a way of knowing. His spirited defense of the Templars stated that "discipline is in no way lacking, and obedience is never despised.... They come and go at the bidding of their superior."[14] He added that the Templars "live in cheerful community and sober company, without wives and without children." This description set up a difference between mere Crusaders and Templars. Now Bernard could not have seen many or any frontline Templars in their day-to-day activities. And certainly, the ones closer to his home administered large granges, outlying farmholdings that provided a revenue for the religious community and were worked by laity. Almost certainly, he had the *Templar Rule* in front of him when he sat down to write *De Laude Novae Militiae* (*In Praise of the New Knighthood*).[15] Bernard carefully set the Templars apart from regular knights, showing the contrast as "when a battle is at hand, they arm themselves interiorly with faith and exteriorly with steel rather than with gold. Thus armed and not embellished, they strike fear rather than incite greed in the enemy... They set their minds on fighting to win rather than on parading for show. They take no thought for glory but seek to be formidable rather than flamboyant."[16] The picture is formed of a knight who was quite different from the traditional, secular knight: "Thus in an astounding and unique manner they appear gentler than lambs, yet fiercer than lions. Consequently, I do not know if it would be more appropriate to refer to them as monks or as soldiers, or whether it would perhaps be better to recognize them as being both, for they lack neither monastic meekness nor military might."[17] Here Bernard of Clairvaux tries to establish the contemplative cast of these warriors, seeing them as formed in monastic meekness while displaying military strength. His early approval of the order would serve them well as this new type of religious order had to explain their place in the Church.

The Documentary Development of the Templars

So far, the historical record that has been presented has come from William of Tyre, a chronicler who disliked the Templars, and a Cistercian abbot, Bernard of Clairvaux, who helped to promote the order and gave them a document confirming their spiritual role in the church. The men leading the Templars rarely focused on documenting the development of the order, and much of the history of the order is obscured. Like many of the monastic reform orders, such as the Cistercians, the Templars recruited only among adults and did not accept child oblates except in extenuating circumstances; in such cases, the children were raised in Templar houses but did not join the order officially until adulthood.

Whereas Bernard's founding documents gave the philosophy and theology behind the validity of the Templar order, the *Rule of the Templars* outlined how the order organized its members. There were four ranks: knights, sergeants, squires, and chaplains. The *Rule* included details of daily life, such as how many horses Templars of different ranks could have: "Each knight brother may have three horses and no more without the permission of the Master, because of the great poverty which exists at the present time in the house of God and of the Temple of Solomon. To each knight brother we grant three horses and one squire, and if that squire willingly serves charity, the brother should not beat him for any sin he commits."[18] The idea of a religious "order" is that there is an *ordum*, or structure that directs people in their exact roles within the community.

Medieval society was a highly structured society, and feudalism told people their exact place and to whom they owed loyalty, taxes, and tithes. Similarly, Templar life was carefully structured with different types of roles overseeing others; these details being laid out were especially useful as the structures among people could vary from culture to culture. The *Rule* described the different members of the order and their training and responsibilities. The Templar living situations varied according to where in the world they were. In the West, the Templars lived in houses like mendicant orders and canons and, like these clergy, were not under enclosure. In the East and in places where the Templars were actively on military campaign, they lived in fortified buildings, often castles. Much of the Outremer operations were not self-supporting but relied on supplies that came in from the West. Templar days were punctuated with prayer, as in the traditional monastic life; in between periods of prayer, they were engaged in tasks such as looking after horses, mending armor, and fixing weapons if they were on the front, while in Europe, they oversaw granges and other holdings, so they would engage in typical agricultural tasks.

With the Templar *Rule*, the order became clearer as a religious order. Before the Council of Troyes, the brothers in the order were following the *Rule of Saint Augustine*.[19] At the council (in 1129), this practice changed; the *Rule of the Templars* was based on existing practices of the Templars when it was drawn up by Hugh of Payens in accordance with the council and received approval. Just as Bernard reflected on the contemplative cast of this type of knighthood, the *Rule of the Templars* borrowed extensively from the *Rule of Benedict*, adding a monastic and contemplative cast to the punctuation of the day with prayers.[20] The *Rule of the Templars* had seven parts:

1. *Primitive Rule* covered a wide variety of issues of membership: who can be admitted, what the customs of the order were, what members wear, and what the grounds for excommunication from the order were.
2. *Hierarchical Statutes* were probably composed around 1165 and no later than 1187. This section set out the various offices of the order and gave the administrative structure of roles from the master downward. It itemized provisions and possessions, all the tools and consumables that the knights held in common. It gave instructions on how to set up camp, how to move when on military campaigns, and how to guard the True Cross.[21]
3. *Penances*, which would be further developed in later years with new sections on the same topics, addressed the sorts of infringements that a brother could be charged with and offered the judgments that could be given, from acquittal to expulsion from the order.
4. *Conventual Life* covered regulations governing the day-to-day brothers, such as meals, saying of the offices, discipline within the houses, and fasting.

5. *Holding of Ordinary Chapters*— the meetings where the Templars would hear about rule infractions and members would confess to such acts—was the order's penal code and included a list of potential judgments.
6. *Further Details on the Penances* were written between 1257 and 1267 and demonstrated the application of the rules in the hearing of ordinary chapters, showing how it worked in practice.
7. *Reception into the Order* included the ceremony of admittance into the Knights Templar.

All in all, the *Rule*, with its additions and aggregations, sought to lay out the day-to-day operations and spiritual expectations of the knights.

The focus of Templar spirituality was on the readiness to die for the Christian cause rather than on the killing of enemies.[22] Unlike most orders, the Templars allowed people to join for a set period; temporary members were mentioned in the 1130 clauses added to the Templar *Rule* by the patriarch of Jerusalem. The *Rule* did acknowledge both the necessity of killing, though, and the many different roles the brothers might take when it noted that "this armed company of knights may kill the enemies of the cross without sinning. For this reason we judge you to be rightly called knights of the Temple, with the double merit and beauty of probity, and that you may have lands and keep men, villeins and fiends and govern them justly, and take your right to them as it is specifically established."[23] This group was to be one of men whose religious life did not make them leave the secular aspects of feudal society, even while imitating the monastic ideal.

Running Afoul

Not everyone was charitably predisposed to military orders. Writing in the thirteenth century, Thomas Aquinas stated: "These religious orders are established for the purpose of military service aim more directly at shedding the enemy's blood than at shedding their own, this latter is more properly competent to martyrs. Yet there is no reason why religious of this description should not acquire the merit of martyrdom in certain cases, and in this respect stand higher than other religious; even as in some cases the works of the active life take precedence of contemplation."[24] Aquinas questioned both whether the aim of the Templars wasn't perhaps to kill, and he called into question their commitment to contemplation. By saying that they might become martyrs, he assumed it was the only way to turn the Templar work into something that would benefit the individual's salvation. It was even suggested that the Templars were borrowing the monks' idea of spiritual warfare but focusing on the literal reading of that metaphorical phrase.[25] Critics questioned the idea of the Templar's charism, and the cries became louder over the course of their existence. The worsening results of the Crusades just helped to embolden the order's critics.

The attempts to structure the order show what a complex beast it was. The unruly monster appeared completely unregulated and out of control to outsiders, which to some extent was true: the order had simply grown too strong, too fast. By 1300, it included "a network of at least 870 castles, preceptories, and subsidiary houses, examples of which could be found in almost every country in western Christendom" and probably numbered "as many as 7,000 knights, sergeants and serving brothers, and priests, while its associate members, pensioners, officials, and subjects numbered many times that figure."[26] Additionally, the order was extranational and, as such, served as financial agents to both the pope and kings because of its capital, expertise, and ability to move money safely from region to region. It was perceived as holding vast fortunes outside of any regulation and unable to govern itself. The wealth, spread as it was throughout Western Christendom, seemed to draw the efforts of the Templars away from the area where their energy should be: the Holy Land. Rapid growth had diluted their purpose.

Among the sentiments leading up to the trials was the predominant concern that the Templars had lost the way of their crusading spirit. When Acre fell in 1291 and the Crusaders were forced to leave the Holy Land, there was no longer any clear reason for the order. There was disappointment at the loss of Jerusalem and at the inability of the Crusaders to recover what had been lost—the Templars became a scapegoat. When the Holy Land fell, the Templars retrenched to Cyprus and Western Europe, forsaking the original goal of protecting pilgrims. The Hospitallers, who were also affected by the fall of the Holy Land, sought out small but necessary tasks: in September 1306, they began their campaign to conquer Rhodes that would find success by 1310. Their role in this part of the world would transform into helping to protect merchants and travelers from pirates. Their strategy would be part of what saved the Hospitallers from the same fate as the Templars in the coming years. It was also a time when Rome was consolidating power and its own wealth, much to the chagrin of the French king, who was trying to consolidate power over the nobility. The Templars, rich but secretive, did not need to seek the support of the local bishops or clergy, based on the bulls that founded the order, which drove local levels of church leadership to support the monarchy's cause against them.

It was in these years following the expulsion from the Holy Land that the grumbling against the Templars erupted; the charges were wrapped up in secular-vs-papal politics and in the rhetoric of heresy, sorcery, and sexual misdeeds. King Philip II and Pope Boniface VIII had been previously locked in political wrangling that had led to Philip's minister accusing the pope of heresy toward the end of his life. Philip would continue to try to exert control over the papacy through the accusations against and arrests of the Templars. The Templar trials began on October 13, 1307, with the roundup of all French members by the king's officials. A month before, Philip had sent secret orders to arrest the Templars. The trials ended on March 18, 1314, with a final auto-da-fé. Between 1308 and 1311, Templars were arrested in England, Germany, Italy, Castile, Aragon, and Cyprus. The forces that supported the attack on the order included the French crown and political allies. The trials in France led the way; they were nowhere else as successful, in part because the secular leadership of other realms was not attempting to take over the wealth and status of the Templars and papacy as trenchantly as in France. Other charges and trials would follow in England and elsewhere. In Cyprus there were better reasons for trying the Templars: in 1306, they were involved in a coup against Henry II. The king returned to power in 1310 and, in the wake of reestablishing his power, imprisoned the leading Templars. Outrage against the Templars seemed to come from those in power, not from among the people in general.[27] Those presiding over the heresy trials that followed would be well aware of the spoils of wealth, land, and power to be distributed after the Templars' demise.

The Trials of 1307

After the fall of Acre and the return of the Holy Land to the Muslims in 1291, the Templars lacked a purpose for their order, since they could not oversee pilgrims going to the Holy Land or protect the historically important Christian sites. More significantly, the fall of the Holy Land made it look as if they had failed to live up to their role of serving the church. The Teutonic order moved its work to Europe, especially to the Baltic areas. The Hospitallers regrouped in the eastern Mediterranean, as did the Templars on Cyprus. The Templars hoped to start a new crusade, and in 1306, Pope Clement V would call both the Templar and the Hospitaller leaders—Jacques de Molay and Fulk Villaret, respectively—to Avignon to discuss it. The meeting also broached the papal idea of the two orders combining, but Jacques was set against that idea. After the meeting, he would remain in France for a provincial meeting and to drum up support for another crusade.

The year 1307 would be one of many important changes. England's King Edward I, who had been a supporter of the Templars and a new crusade, died on July 7. On August 18, King Denis of Portugal began legal proceedings to recover Templar lands in his country, claiming that they had been misappropriated by the order. A week later, on August 24, Pope Clement V wrote King Philip II of France to say that the Templars had asked him to investigate the charges being made against them and that he was in the process of doing so. Three weeks later, on September 14, Philip sent secret instructions to French officials across the realm to arrest all Templars on October 13 and to seize their property. The charges would be heresy and sodomy.

This move would be where the inquisitional model, with its highly calibrated machinery, shone because the Templars were an order in multiple locations. While the Inquisition used inquisitors who worked locally and handed people over to local justice, the arrest of the Templars would challenge how to end a so-called heresy involving most localities in Europe and even farther abroad. The coordination of the arrests across France would show the power of inquisitorial networks. The time that followed would produce the most documentation about the Templars in their history: "papal bulls, letters, speeches, diplomatic reports, propaganda tracts, letters of convocation for the French Estates, consultations with university masters, and, most conspicuously, the proceedings of the actual trial, at the core of which were the depositions of the brothers themselves."[28] Yet despite all this material—or perhaps because of it—there are so many things we still do not understand.

Jacques of Molay was the last leader of the Templars, and it is on his shoulders that the trials fell. He had been living in the eastern half of the Roman Empire and was not well adapted to the social and political forces he would face in Western Europe. He found it hard to talk up his order to people who no longer understood or were not amenable to the crusading mentality. Originally, when he traveled to Europe in 1307, his mission was to meet with the pope about a potential upcoming crusade and then conduct a tour like Hugh of Payens had, drumming up support for the order and the new crusade. But his time there would be focused instead on the rumors surrounding the order's immorality and heresy. Most of the Templars were caught by surprise on the morning of October 13, 1307, when the arrests of the French Templars occurred. The move was initially treated with shock, but through 1308, similar Templar arrests occurred across England, Scotland, Ireland, Cyrpus, the Low Countries, Italy, and the Iberian Peninsula.[29] The arrest warrants listed charges including secrecy, sexual perversions, idolatry, and antisacerdotalism. The order for the arrests declared, "When they enter the Order and make their profession, they are confronted with [Jesus's] image, and their miserable or rather pitiful blindness makes them deny Him three times and spit in His face three times."[30] Jacques de Molay confessed to having spit on the crucifix.[31] The Templars were compared to Peter, who denied Christ three times, but were seen as true traitors. The charges continue, "Afterwards, they remove the clothes they wore in the secular world, and naked in the presence of the Visitor or his deputy, who receives their profession, they are kissed by him first on the lower part of the dorsal spine, secondly on the naval and finally on the mouth, in accordance with the profane rite of their Order but to the disgrace of the dignity of the human race."[32] The rite described is the perversion of another rite: removing secular clothes and donning the religious habit was commonplace when becoming a novice. But the sexualized behavior in the allegation is not in the typical rite. Esquieu of Floyran's letter to King James II of Aragon states that "they make them swear to be chaste as regards women and they are enjoined by their preceptors that when the desires of the flesh assail them they shall live with one another in carnal lust." Elsewhere, Geoffrey of Charney's (the preceptor of Normandy) deposition notes that the brothers were told it was better to have sex with each other than to give in to lust with women.[33] It's worth remembering the way inquisitions worked: inquisitors would have a list of questions, written in advance and based on what they knew about the suspected heresy, to ask each suspected heretic. Reading confession after confession of the Templars, the responses sound identical because the inquisitorial process asked about specific acts and supplied specific details.

It shaped the information that an inquisition could discover by limiting the scope of questioning. Elsewhere, the Templars were accused of worshipping "a certain cat that appeared amongst them," an accusation that foreshadows the accusations against witches.[34] And in a more banal fashion, the Templars were accused of seeking to increase the wealth of the order "by any means at their disposal, whether licit or illicit."[35] These charges ran the gamut, from illicit financial gains to sorcery and sexual misconduct.

When arrested in France, the Templars were told the same thing many accused heretics before them had been told: if they confessed and repented, they'd be treated better. If they refused, they'd continue to be tortured until they confessed. If they held on long enough and kept denying the charges, they'd eventually go to trial; if they denied the charges and were found guilty, they'd be burned to death. Many confessed. Thirty-six died of torture from the initial arrests, and their testimonies did not get recorded. The testimonies of 138 were recorded on October and November of 1307, and all but 4 of them confessed.[36] Jacques of Molay was brought before William of Paris, the inquisitor, on October 24, 1307, and confessed. A couple of weeks later, Hugh of Payens would too. The list of charges was drawn up and presented on August 13, 1308. In its fullest version, it listed 127 articles. But the Templars were not the richest order of the time; both the Hospitallers and the Cistercians were wealthier.[37] What the Templars were, however, was weakly strung throughout Western Europe, with a base in Cyprus, and without a clear sense of purpose after the fall of Acre. This tenuous network would have made them the optimal group for the secular authorities to go after in a land and wealth grab.

One of the big questions that endures today is the exact motivation for the sudden declaration that the Templar order was infested with heresy at that time. It was a complex economic and political situation. France and England were at war. King Philip IV of France had borrowed considerable money from the Templars and needed even more cash. A charge of heresy, if proved, would mean confiscation of Templar land and assets, providing more cash and erasing the king's debt to the order. A year prior, in 1306, Philip had arrested the French Jews and confiscated their property to be used to fund the war.[38] He was insatiable: he not only wanted the French Templars to be found guilty of heresy, but he also wanted the entire order to be suppressed by the papacy so they could not expand back into France. It was a delicate situation because the Templars reported to the pope, were an order with wide landholdings and extensive cash, and were located across Europe, with a headquarters in Cyprus. Heresy trials tended to be local and regional affairs. Suppressing an order also located outside of France would be complicated and could not be conducted by the French courts alone. France needed to move first to secure guilty verdicts before they could be found innocent abroad and needed to move fast before the pope could intervene on the Templars' behalf.

Jacques of Molay would retract his confession about a month after his initial admission.[39] The Templars asked for the papacy to intervene. Clement would seek out ways to exert control over the proceedings. King Philip had acrimonious relations with Rome. He had abducted Pope Boniface VIII from the city, who died about a month later. Benedict XI, the next pope, died the next year; rumors swirled that he had been poisoned by one of Philip's men. Clement's options for handling the French king were limited. But the pope could not ignore the arrests, especially considering the large number of quick confessions that resulted. From June 28 to July 1, a group of seventy-two Templars were brought to Poitiers to be investigated by a special commission. These Templars gave testimony that they spit on the cross and were required to deny Christ during the initiation ceremony. The pope didn't think the confessions indicated beliefs and behavior that rose to the level of heresy. Instead, it looked to be merely apostasy (the renunciation of religious belief), which, while serious, was not subject to punishments as severe as heresy was. The next day, a papal consistory, a special meeting of the College of Cardinals, met to pronounce sentence, where the pope gave his absolution to the Templars.

At the same time, Clement drew up the papal bull *Faciens misericordiam* (*Granting Forgiveness*) on August 8, 1308, and read it aloud to the College of Cardinals on August 12, calling for an ecumenical council to be held in Poitiers in 1310. It outlined how to collect depositions from the Templars across the order (not just the French) and named a commission and its members who would oversee this process. The commission was to look at other issues facing Christendom, including the potential for a new crusade. A few days later, the pope issued the bull *Regnans in coelis* (*Reigning in Heaven*), which provided more details about the ecumenical council. The council would be delayed a year due to a variety of factors and would eventually be convened as the Council of Vienne. In August, the pope sent his representatives to Chinon, where the Templar leaders were, and absolved them as well; the testimony of the leaders and their absolution are recorded in the Chinon Parchment, which was dated August 13–20, 1308. In it, Pope Clement V absolved Jacques de Molay and other Templar leadership. Papal absolution was not to end the trials, however, as they would continue in the French courts.[40]

On March 14, 1310, the French trials began anew; they contained accusations that were commonly held against heretics and were intended to undermine popular confidence in the Templars and play against its secrecy. The defense would be led by Peter of Bologna and Renaud de Provins answering the 127 charges made against the Templars. These charges included those mentioned previously as well as denying Christ, rejecting the cross, kissing their receptor's backside, teaching that homosexuality was lawful, engaging in sodomy when other Templars requested it, practicing idolatry, and refusing to consecrate the host during Mass. Other accusations included praying to an idol of Baphomet, denying the sacraments, and believing the grand master and other leaders could hear confessions even when those positions were filled by laypeople.[41] The accusations had led to Templars being tortured and then "confessing" to heresies and subversive actions that provided evidence for an ever-widening circle of suspicions against others.

For over three more years, the trial in France dragged on, moving forward in fits and starts until Philip forced its hand by getting Sens, a provincial council, to condemn fifty-four Templars as relapsed heretics; they had originally traveled to France to defend their order and were burned at the stake on May 12, 1310. A few days later, nine more were also burned. It was clear throughout the trial that Jacques de Molay was working in a political realm he didn't comprehend, stuck in the middle of a battle between the king of France and the pope.

Although the French trials were by far the most sensational, the Templars also faced trial in England. Following the arrests in France and the confessions they coerced, the pope sent orders on November 22, 1307, to various other European kings to arrest Templars in their lands and investigate. He sent such letters to Albert I of Habsburg, James II of Aragon, and Edward II in England. Charges there were slower to gain traction, and Edward II was slow to act until receiving the bull *Pastoralis praeeminentiae* (*Pastoral Preeminence*), with its demand once again to arrest the Templars. The Templars had a strong record of service in England, and the tide of public opinion wasn't against them. In late 1307, the order was sent around England for sheriffs to choose twenty-four

Templars to be brought forward. A survey of the order's possessions was also to be completed. The arrests did not take place until January, and by this time, the Templars were aware of what had happened in France. When the arrests occurred, 153 Templars in England, 2 in Scotland, and 15 in Ireland were apprehended. Even more seem to have been on open arrest, allowed to continue with their work in their localities.[42] Between the time of the arrests and the time of keepers arriving to safeguard their property and inventories, a good deal of the property went missing. In 1309, the king ordered the rearrest of all Templars set free and the inquisitors from the continent arrived to investigate. None of the British Templars confessed; therefore, the trial had to rely not on confessions of men from the order, as in France, but on hostile witnesses against the Templars.[43] Eventually, a few brothers would capitulate and offer confessions against the Templars, saying that they'd been part of dual good-and-bad initiations to the order. The good ceremony was a normal reception ceremony, and the bad one, primarily held before the leadership of Jacques de Molay, was where they would spit on an image of Christ and deny him. The Templars who confessed were then absolved, offered a penance, given a pension, and sent to monasteries. Almost all Templars chose this option as their end. Only two would refuse to submit and would die in prison.

The Council of Vienne (1311–12) dissolved the order through the bull *Vox in excelso* (*A Voice from on High*). Pope Clement expressed the belief that the evidence collected wasn't definitive and explained why judicial condemnation did not follow, but in the bull he explained the charges directed against the Templars and recognized that the order's reputation had been damaged too significantly to recover and that the suppression of the order "to protect its property... and advance the interests of the Holy Land" was the natural end.[44] The sheer fact that its leaders had been imprisoned for the last five years and would continue to be imprisoned dealt a blow to the organization and functioning of the order, whose landholdings spanned as far as Christianity did in those days. Yet even after dissolution, houses of Templars remained in some areas where there were lords sympathetic to the Templar cause; these houses gradually ended as the Templars died off. On May 2, 1312, Clement assigned the order's property to the Knights Hospitaller through the bull *Ad providam* (*To Provide*), except for lands and movables in Castile, Aragon, Portugal, and Majorca, which were reserved for future action."[45] A few days later, on May 6, he issued *Considerantes dudum* (*Considering Time*), which provided guidelines for provincial councils in dealing with Templars in their jurisdictions.

On March, 18, 1314, sentence was passed on the leaders of the Templars. The cardinals Nicolas of Freauville, Arnold of Auch, and Arnold Nouvel presided. The tribune condemned the four leaders to life imprisonment. Hugh of Payens and Geoffrey of Gonneville accepted the sentence, but Jacques of Molay and Geoffrey of Charney didn't. Heretics were condemned by the church and lived life in prison; the obstinate were sent to secular justice for burning.[46] Life imprisonment was a relatively new phenomenon; it was known in some monastic orders for crimes such as killing a brother, and from the thirteenth century, there was a gradual development among monastic and mendicant orders of the necessity for prison-building to mete out longer-term punishments for members who had committed serious offenses. The Templar penances stated that imprisonment was a known penance for certain crimes within the order from around 1165 onward.[47] Jacques and Geoffrey were burnt at the stake on the same day as their sentence. All remaining holdings of the Templars were to be transferred to the Knights Hospitaller. Trials would follow in England, Scotland, Ireland, Cyprus, Roussillon, Spain, and several Italian cities. The Order of Montessa was founded in 1319 and received the former Templar landholdings in Valencia. In Portugal, the Order of Christ was established and received the former Templar holdings there.

Lasting Impact

The Templars were not an order that leant itself to heresy or to accusations of immorality until its very last days. The order was based on strong support, but unfortunately, its charism was hamstrung by events in the Holy Land, and unlike the Hospitallers, the Templars were either not savvy enough to change their sense of direction or did not think it important enough to do so. It may well have been the case that the order felt maintaining their properties and wealth was a big enough job in the wake of the Christian expulsion from the Holy Land. That wasn't what the secular leaders or the church expected from the order, however. A change of direction for the Hospitallers meant that they were able to continue as an order past this point and, in fact, were the intended beneficiaries of the seized holdings of the Templars.

What stands out here is the way the charges of sexual immorality overtook the rest of the inquisitorial process. There had been some whispers of sorcery and sexual immorality with the Cathars and Waldensians but nothing that became a main accusation. Charges such as not believing in sacraments, not consecrating the host, not having license to preach, and not recognizing the authority of Rome were the sorts of charges that heretics had previously faced. Engaging in homoerotic acts during the profession of a novice is a new type of charge; perhaps it was because this heresy is the first in the Middle Ages to involve an order, one that was almost exclusively male at that. Sexual accusations would continue to play a part in heretical accusations through late medieval witchcraft.

The Templar trials show the tensions between secular and church power. This clash was a big concern, for heretical trials usually handed lapsed heretics over to secular justice to serve out their sentences (usually death). What this trial shows was that secular justice—in this case, the king of France—wanted to have a piece of the power pie as well and would not be subservient to the Rome. The reforms that had created a strong, centralized Papacy with a well-oiled machinery of canon law and heretical inquisitions were now using similar structures displayed against the Holy See. It shouldn't be surprising that the secular rulers' will to power would follow the same track as the Papacy's, and yet it took the Papacy by surprise. The sheer difference in the fates of the English and French Templars highlights how heresy was becoming a continental concern, but hysteria about heresy had not fully infected all of Europe. The trials also show that the inquisitorial process has come to be its own worst enemy by this point: the inquisitorial process essentially molded the deposition and trial process in such a way as to guarantee its results and made it abundantly clear this process was no longer about finding truth (if it ever was) but was solely about "proving" the accusations.

CHAPTER 6

The Spiritual Franciscans
Apocalyptic Literature and Claims to Authority in Heresy

DURING THE HIGH Middle Ages, Italian religion was increasingly inundated with lay religious movements, and the spirituality of the people intersected in multiple ways, formal and informal, with the mendicants, since they welcomed the task of preaching to the laity. The mendicant orders each had a first order of preachers (Dominicans) or friars (Franciscans), a second order of vowed sisters who lived an enclosed life, and finally, a third order of laity who wanted to follow the Franciscan charism and lifestyle but who were ineligible to take vows (such as if they were married). This third-order laity would live and work in the world. Some, such as Angela of Foligno, a Franciscan penitent, lived out individual lives that became models of pious behavior; Catherine of Siena, a third-order Dominican, took up far more precocious tasks, becoming an advisor to the pope. Other lay spirituality groups were treated as suspect and subject to limitations, such as the *bizzoche*. Whether their powers, charisms, and followers could be subsumed into the centralized power structure of an order usually determined whether a group or individual would be found acceptable.

The Spiritual Franciscans show how lay spirituality could alter the trajectory of an approved order within the church. From its founding, the Franciscan order attracted interested laypeople; but the Franciscans faced a challenge among its friars about the nature of how the order was to observe the notion of poverty, which would spill into its lay followers as well. The Spiritual Franciscans were a faction seeking a more stringent poverty and asceticism that became associated with both the Joachite heretical mystical tradition and a popular lay movement that followed the renowned Franciscan preacher and exegete, Peter of John Olivi (also known as Peter Olivi). He was a strong supporter of poverty among the Franciscans and wrote apocalyptic theology about the near end times. With these interlocking pieces, the

Spiritual Franciscan issue created a complex phenomenon of disagreements within the Franciscan order, including the effects of apocalyptic spiritualty and the enthusiastic following of a preacher, and would become labeled a heresy. It was a clunky amalgam of people seeking radical evangelical poverty, preparing themselves to face God, and fostering a spirituality of apostolic poverty in the face of what appeared to be a clamping down on the order's autonomy. Such a set of disagreements would challenge the resources of the papacy and local bishops as multiple leaders attempted to find an effective way to investigate and resolve disputes within the order and to mitigate popular sentiment in Languedoc, an area familiar with heretical uprisings.

The Franciscan order was the last of the orders to be created from the twelfth-century Evangelical Awakening and used the apostolic life as a model. It had its foundation in the person of Francis of Assisi (1181–1226), the son of a rich cloth merchant who spent much of his youth pursuing frivolous entertainments and hoping to be a knight until he had a stunning conversion experience. This conversion resulted in the foundation of the Franciscan order, a mendicant order that combined voluntary poverty—which he parsed to mean owning nothing individually or communally—with preaching the gospel. Francis's vision rooted the apostolic life ultimately in the imitation of Christ. All followers of Francis would strive to be Christlike in their poverty.[1] While founded with the loftiest of goals, the order began to fracture under the weight of such ideals during Francis's life. The mendicant orders were reforming orders organized against particular threats to the church: the Dominicans were founded as a preaching order in response to the Albigensian heresy; the Franciscans preached primarily in Italian cities, focusing on poverty and humility in the wake of a burgeoning middle class focused on wealth and materialism. After his conversion, Francis appeared at the court of Pope Innocent III, who recognized Francis from a dream he'd had, in which a ragged man held up the church. He granted approval to the order, probably in the hope that the Franciscans would not end up in heresy like the Waldensians of a generation before.[2] Like the Dominicans, the Franciscans went to the places where their preaching was needed.

Part of becoming an order required submitting a rule and administrative documents showing how it would be structured and governed. Although Francis was a charismatic preacher, the day-to-day operations and administration of the order were neither a strength nor interest of his. After Francis and the order failed to resolve lingering issues around everyday leadership and poverty, the papacy intervened in the internal affairs of the Franciscans, declaring how they were to organize their houses, how much property they were to own, and how they should support themselves. This intervention would lead to factions within the order, as some brothers supported the practical Papal guidelines, while others supported Francis's more lofty ideals. In his *Testament*, dictated at the end of his life, Francis exhorted his brothers to follow his *Rule* literally and not to seek papal dispensations from it and stated that it was acceptable to disobey superiors whose pronouncements went against the friars' personal beliefs.[3] Francis was seeking to support the more evangelical friars within the order after his passing.

In discussing the Spiritual Franciscans, there are two particular lay sects we'll focus on: one in Languedoc and one in the Italian peninsula. Both grow out of the "spiritual" interpretation of Francis's teachings, the interpretation that took poverty more literally. Each group emphasized slightly different issues, but by 1270, there was evidence of the two countries' adherents talking to one another.[4] In Languedoc, the first towns that supported the Spirituals are ones we have seen already in other chapters: Narbonne, Béziers, and Carcassonne. Sometimes the Franciscans within this movement are referred to as the Spiritual Franciscans; other times, they are called Fraticelli in Italy and—confusingly—Béguins in Languedoc. (They were not related to the beguines of the Low Countries, although at least one pope requested that it be investigated that they were not part of the Free Spirit movement).[5] These lay followers believed in Peter Olivi's radical interpretation of poverty and in his apocalypticism that said the end times were nigh. What began as an intellectual disagreement by those within the Franciscan order and the papacy turned into a popular movement when one side turned to the populace for support, disseminating these ideas.

Usus pauper and the Franciscan Charism

By the time of Francis's death, the order was faced with a two-forked path of irreconcilable ideals. On the one hand, the order numbered in the thousands, and it had attracted a large number of learned men; these friars had made the order a formidable one that had presences in many of the nascent universities. It was an order that saw its mission was to preach to the urban laity. It needed to be able to adapt to the variety of different locales in which the friars worked. On the other hand, Francis's ideal was one of a small, eremitic order: it held an ideal of absolute poverty, with no possessions. Franciscan theologians from the beginning of the order would identify perfection as being the observance of divine counsels that constitute their religious life. For vowed religious, this life would be following the vows of poverty, chastity, and obedience. Poverty was to be both imitated by owning nothing and to be experienced as sharing Christ's poverty and renunciations.[6] Obviously, the ability of the order to both administer the lives of so many friars and continue its intellectual and evangelical prowess was difficult to maintain with the eremitic ideal of absolute poverty.[7] Owning properties and having a coffer of available money to support provincial houses would help to ensure smooth administration of the order; relying on daily begging for alms was not a viable economic plan.

Even late in Francis's life, the fault lines were already drawn: the Spiritual Franciscans believed that Francis's desire that they should own nothing either individually or communally was still a defining aspect of who the Franciscans were. The other side, which would later take the name the Conventuals, held that individual friars in the order should not own anything, but corporate ownership of things like houses would support longer-term security of the order. In a stricter interpretation of the Spiritual side, people such as Olivi contended that the Franciscan vow of poverty demanded that the friars own nothing; what tools they needed should belong to someone else, and they should only be *used* by them. It is this idea that is at the heart of the *usus pauper* (*poor use*) controversy, and Olivi took it to the point of insisting that this poor use derived from the friars' vow of poverty.

Those who took the idea of poverty literally thought that it was against the spirit of their founder to hold any property, whether it be a bed to sleep in or a pot to make soup in. They did not want the order to hold property, nor did they even want it to store up goods of any sort, whether they be extra habits, libraries of books, or church decorations. But the order had grown since its establishment, and the friars now served a variety of roles, which seemed to require possessions. Some were university masters and needed books. Some were on preaching missions and needed transportation and supplies. Additionally, property gave a certain stability to the order: it allowed consistency of training, provided places for older friars to live out their retirement, and allowed a place for the sick to be tended to. Owning property, with houses in strategic locations, gave the friars a sense of regularity that the Papacy was striving for across all orders in the High Middle Ages. Eventually, the papacy became involved and instituted and oversaw a series of changes to the Franciscans, requiring that the order hold property and not adhere to strict poverty. This requirement was part of a larger set of institutional involvement in the order, which included giving a rule to the female Franciscans.

Apocalyptic Literature and Joachim of Fiore

Before the Franciscans were formed, there was a Calabrian abbot named Joachim of Fiore (ca. 1135–1202) whose apocalyptic writings created a stir. Apocalyptic literature is a type of spiritual writing that gets its name from the Greek word for Revelation. It is one of many related types of literature and spirituality, including works that look at eschatology (experience of the afterlife or the end of human history), prophecy (supernatural messages that predict the future), and mysticism (experiences of God). Apocalyptic spirituality gives voice to the anxieties of the age and attempts to find a resolution for these anxieties, be it a solution, a description of a new world in which people's wrongs will be righted, or the provision of a system for understanding the underlying significance of trials and tribulations. In the early Middle Ages, apocalyptic literature mainly looked at the outsider as the source of assault and reinforced a sense of collective Christian identity, but by the High to late Middle Ages, Christianity identified not outsiders but insiders as the greater risk; these insiders might be heretics, evil leaders, or false prophets.

Thus, apocalyptic literature gives voice to both anxiety and hope. It attempts to deal with anxiety over the current history by placing it in a context of a divine history with eschatological significance; it gives meaning to the trials and tribulations that individuals and communities presently face; and it tempers them through hope for a resolution. Apocalyptic systems view the human soul living on earth not just within a human timeline but within a divine timeline, which has consequences both for the individual and for their community as a whole. In this way, it doesn't merely console the persecuted but strengthens and encourages the reader to persist and keep fighting. At issue for the creator of apocalyptic literature is how these two intersect and how to interpret current history, or even perhaps how to hasten next stages. If one is living near the end of the human timeline, then one must prepare to enter the divine timeline. But one must know how to read the signs to know the end is near.

While on pilgrimage to Jerusalem, Joachim had a conversion experience that caused him to seek out the religious life. At first, he was a hermit, then he became a wandering preacher, and next he sought out life as a lay Cistercian brother, where he preached despite not taking vows. He was encouraged in his prophecy by three popes during his lifetime: Lucius III, Urban III, and Clement III, although he would only truly become noticed a generation after his death. In his prophecies concerning the end of the world, Joachim took St. Augustine's seventh day out of the ecclesiastical time of Revelation and placed it within historical time. He saw that time was split into two epochs, corresponding to the Old and New Testaments. It was also divided into three ages.

Joachim wrote that there were ages of the world that corresponded to the three persons of the Trinity and that the third age, that of the Holy Spirit, was to be introduced soon (in 1260). His books focused on the concordance of the Old and New Testaments, the exegesis of Revelation, and the Age of the Holy Spirit to come. It was a future-looking system, full of numerology and symbolism. In his three ages, the first began with creation; the second era began just before the incarnation with the rise of messianic hope and lasted through his time.[8] Humans were about to move into the Age of the Holy Spirit. In this third age, an angelic pope would lead and do away with all the corruption of previous and contemporary church leadership. Monasticism would play a key role in leading the people into this age of universal spirituality, which no longer needed the institutional church. Joachim was the inheritor of two other models for sacred history: Revelation's seven seals and Augustine's idea of seven stages, corresponding to the seven days of creation. Joachim's view of history as working toward an eschatological end based on Revelation and a reforming order having a particular role resonated with those who took poverty more literally. Just as the Franciscans, with their ideal of poverty, were to inherit debates about poverty, the order attracted some thinkers who possessed apocalyptic overtones. The Franciscan order's interest in Joachim seems to have been independent of how fanatical or conservative its leadership was; the apocalyptic element was embraced widely, and even the moderate Franciscan Bonaventura connected Francis to the sixth seal in his *Legenda Major* (*Life of St Francis*), giving official nod to apocalyptic readings of history as part of the order's lore.[9]

Peter of John Olivi

The person who would pick up the mantle of apocalyptic thought and combine it with Franciscan spirituality would be Peter of John Olivi (1248–98), writing a century after Joachim of Fiore. He was a Franciscan who would also wade into the *usus pauper* controversy on the side of the Spirituals. Peter Olivi entered the Franciscan order at age twelve. He was a Franciscan friar and theologian who had studied at the University of Paris and taught at a number of Franciscan houses, at the order's provincial school in Florence, and at the University of Montpellier. His works influenced the Spiritual Franciscan cause in three ways. First, he wrote supporting the idea that the *usus pauper* was part of the Franciscan vow of poverty, supporting the Spirituals. Second, he wrote about Revelation using the ideas of Joachim as a base for his interpretations, creating a position that would attack church leaders and have special roles for outcasts, heretics, and laity, something the Spiritual Franciscans welcomed given the papal meddling in the order's administration. Joachim's writings had already attracted the attention of several writers after his death; Olivi's use of them would bring them fully into the Franciscan orbit. Third, he acted as a spiritual director in his final years to both Spirituals and lay Béguins.

When Olivi weighed in on the *usus pauper* controversy, he argued that the poor use of items was not just following the *Rule* but was part of their vow of poverty, increasing the stakes in the controversy. In his Matthew commentary, he probed the interrelated nature of the Franciscan ideal of poverty and the apostolic calling in that Gospel. The process of entering into apostlehood was approximated through the process of becoming a Franciscan: first hearing about the order (or hearing about Christ), then becoming a novice (the apostles experienced the life of following Christ), and then becoming a vowed religious (parallel to the vows Peter, Andrew, James, and John made in Matthew 4), symbolically leaving behind one's nets.[10] Absolute poverty of possessions became the identity of the apostles for Olivi. And the idea of the apostles' identity is based on their imitation of Christ.

When he began to write about the *usus pauper* controversy, Olivi was stepping into a half-century of disputed territory. Pope Gregory IX had inserted himself into the controversy and formally relaxed the rules for ownership of property in the order by allowing it to appoint outside regulators who would own its goods and dispense them as needed to the friars. In 1247, Franciscan

Minister General John of Parma sought a return to a more primitive understanding of the poverty of the order and the Franciscan *Rule*. This change caused stress within the order, as some communities supported the papal relaxations, while others found in John (who walked from house to house across Europe) a reflection of the same spirit as Francis.[11] About half a century after Gregory IX intervened, Pope Nicholas III issued a 1279 papal bull entitled *Exiit qui seminat* (*A Sower Went Forth*) that further honed the terminology of poverty, based on Gregory IX's original declaration. It stated that the Franciscans were both individually and corporately considered not to own those things that were being administered by outsiders. After *Exiit qui seminat*, the split into the Conventuals and the Spirituals grew stronger.

But the Spirituals were not merely interested in the issues of ownership and use of property; they were known as the Spirituals because of their belief they were in the spiritual age of Joachim. They overwrote the apocalyptic overtones of Joachim of Fiore's prophecies on their own history and on the conflicts with the church. According to Joachim, the Franciscan order was to be a central figure in the conflict against the ecclesiastical hierarchy. The disputes over the *usus pauper* had a resonating significance in the struggle leading up to the coming of the antichrist: at heart, Olivi was an exegete who probed how scriptural meanings could relate to the problems facing his age. While his disputes about the *usus pauper* would be covered in his Matthew exegesis, his understanding of cosmological history would receive his closest attention in his 1297 commentary on the Revelation.[12] Olivi was writing during a time when, in part thanks to the university settings, there was great progress being made on exegesis of biblical texts and appreciation of the history of exegesis.[13] Olivi himself would write exegeses of Matthew, Isaiah, Job, John, Genesis, and the Apocalypse.

Olivi worked within the mainline Franciscan tradition of apocalyptic work. He used Joachim's idea of the progression of history to emphasize that the time in which they were living was at the boundary of the old Age of the Son and the new Age of the Holy Spirit, giving greater significance to the times and strife between factions in the order. His exegesis of various parts of the Bible—not just Revelation—led him to view sacred history as more than a sum of its parts. Like Joachim, Olivi believed that there was a correspondence between the history of the Old Testament period and of the New Testament period. Steeped deep in a numerology that ascribed a variety of biblical and eschatological meanings to numbers, he composed a schema that interpreted history, using each system to think about it from a slightly different perspective. Thus, he would talk about three ages, corresponding to the three persons of the Trinity. He would also think about seven periods of church history, relating to the seven churches and seals in Revelation. While much of this history was progressive and saw improvements, there were places within this plan that were regressions or times of turmoil in which the church was misled. These schemata were not competing but were ones that he spent time harmonizing.[14] Looking at where one was in the cycle, the mirror from the other period could give guidance concerning what was to happen.

Olivi's Revelation commentary sets forth a Franciscan-centric reading of Revelation as a cypher for the world of his time. He builds on Joachim's three ages of history and sees that the sixth and seventh periods of church history fall within the third age.[15] Humans were about to enter the seventh period and the third age, the Age of the Holy Spirit. He wrote, "The fifth [period] was that of the common life under monks and clergy owning temporal possessions, and was characterized partly by severe zeal, partly by condescension. The sixth was that of renovation of the evangelical life, driving out of the sect of Antichrist . . . a rebuilding of the church on the model of the first period."[16] He names Francis of Assisi as the one who ushered in this sixth period. "The sixth begins in one way with the time of our blessed father Francis, but should begin more fully with the destruction of the great whore Babylon, when the aforesaid angel of Christ, sealed with his sign, will inaugurate the future army of Christ through his followers."[17] The great whore of Babylon is the corrupted church, as Olivi explained: "Around the end of the fifth period practically the whole church from head to foot is corrupted and thrown into disorder and turned, as it were, into a new Babylon."[18] It is during Olivi's time that the corrupted whore of Babylon church thrives. Eventually, a coming of the antichrist would be ushered in. Olivi takes a typical Franciscan idea, that Francis is an *alter Christus*—another Christ—and serves as the role of Christ in this history. It's not as shocking an idea as it seems. In the ordination rite, the words are used to describe the role the priest will assume, as another Christ, when serving the people. Olivi says that the third age church will be one that is led based on charisma, not on ecclesiastical politics and connections. Its spirituality and followers will exemplify apostolic poverty and virtue, and the church of Rome will be replaced by a worthier church. His discussion emphasized that the current era was showing signs of decay and corruption within the church. As can be imagined, this view was not received favorably by the church authorities. Olivi was censured—not just for his position on Franciscan poverty—and in 1283 lost his teaching position.[19] Although he would be rehabilitated and gain another post in 1287, the taint of the original censure never fully left.

Shortly after completing his commentary, Olivi died. He had been well liked by the friars who knew him well in the order and among the laity. Soon other Franciscans and laity began visiting his grave in the choir of the house at Narbonne. March 14, the day of his death, became his feast day. It was perhaps unexpected that a dead friar would provoke such strong reactions from his supporters, but his death elicited a strong response from people who had been repeatedly beaten down in the name of combatting heresy. Olivi had spent much of his time both actively writing for the laity and making sure that his writings had translations in the vernacular.[20] His tomb became a place of pilgrimage for both Franciscans and laity.[21] Olivi's Revelation commentary would later be condemned, first by the order in 1318 and then by the pope in 1326.[22] The attacks on Olivi's writings after his death were more about attacking the people who claimed him as inspiration and less about Olivi himself.

Italian Lay Groups

The Franciscans had significant lay support in both Italy and in southern France. These lay groups ranged from official third-order Franciscan laity who pledged to follow the Franciscan charism to others who imitated the Franciscan charism but never found a place within the order officially. The Franciscan charism would become an inspiration in the High Middle Ages for those who sought the apostolic and evangelical life, including the Arnoldists, Humiliati, Fraticelli, and other penitential groups. Many of these groups had been started in the twelfth century, at the same time as the Franciscans—although some would be incorporated into the church or into specific orders, some, such as the Humiliati, would be condemned as heretics.[23]

Some Spirituals moved from southern France to central Italy and continued to move around to find places that were sympathetic to their beliefs. Angelo of Clareno is credited with being an early leader of Italian Spirituals.

His writings described the movements and beliefs of the Spirituals in Italy as they faced challenges from leadership inside and outside of the order. He wrote a chronicle of the Franciscans that offered a narrative of the lay movements within Italy: it stated that in 1274, a rumor spread in the province of Ancona, saying that the count of Lyon and the pope were about to make the Franciscans accept property. This gossip resulted in a debate about whether the Franciscans should obey. Angelo of Clareno and others answered that they thought the order had strayed from Francis's intent. He thought a division was inevitable, for there was a big, urbanized faction that served universities and churches and a smaller faction that was contemplative and eremitic. Keeping these two groups united would be difficult, he assessed. In 1289, Raymond Geoffroi (who was the only minister general favorable to the Spirituals) was elected to lead the order. In 1290, he arrived in Ancona only to discover Angelo of Clareno and friends in prison and ordered them released. He then sent them to Armenia in response to a request for missionaries, but the other friars were hostile toward them, and they were sent back to Italy a few years later.

Geoffroi next sent them to Pope Celestine V, who removed them from Franciscan obedience and created a new order, the Poor Hermits of Pope Celestine, which was to follow the Franciscan *Rule*. They would no longer be subject to Franciscan politicking but would still follow the charism of apostolic poverty. As was commonplace, their fortunes changed as the leadership of the church did; Boniface VIII came to the papacy next, and fearing the Poor Hermits would not accept his papacy, he put pressure on them. After 1295, a group of Angelo of Clareno's followers would leave for Greece, where Spiritual Franciscans would regroup, seeking a less hostile environment within the Greek church.[24] There they would find support for the idea of both individual and communal poverty in Greek spirituality through the centuries to come.

The Franciscans inspired groups of proximity as well as laity officially associated with the order. One such group of proximity was Gerardo Segarelli's Brothers and Sisters of the Apostles (Apostolici). Gerardo Segarelli had been inspired by the Franciscans and wanted to join the order but had been rejected. After staying near the monastery for a while, he began to imitate them in dress and in a profession of apostolic poverty. In 1260, he had a conversion experience and, like Francis, sold everything he had and distributed the earnings in the marketplace. He would publicly proclaim to people to seek forgiveness. He quickly gained a few dozen followers, including some city leaders. They would file through the streets, singing hymns and begging for food that they would then share with the poor. He looked to the Franciscans as a model for his life of voluntary poverty and even attracted some followers from among their ranks. The people of Parma accepted his group as mendicants, even though they were not an official order.[25] But the papacy was not supportive; at the Second Council of Lyon in 1274, Pope Gregory X promulgated *Religionum diversitatem nimiam* (The Diversity of Religions is Too Great), whose canon 23 restated once again a nontolerance of new religious movements. In 1286, Gerardo was banned from the city of Parma because he was preaching against the church authorities. Pope Honorius IV banned the group with the bull *Olim felicis recordationis* (Once Upon A Happy Memory). Pope Nicholas IV ordered that the group be questioned in 1290. Gerardo and some of his followers broke the ban in 1294, at which point four of his followers (two men, two women) were burned at the stake and Segarelli was imprisoned. He was burned at the stake on July 18, 1300, on the orders of a Dominican inquisitor.

Another group of proximity was that surrounding Guglielma. Her followers looked specifically to the Spiritual Franciscans' apocalyptic ideas for inspiration. She was a noblewoman of Czech and Italian background whose spirituality focused on a female-centered church that she would lead and that anticipated her resurrection. Her death in the early 1280s increased her following, but Guglielma had already attracted a large number. In 1284, just a couple of years after her death, her followers (who called themselves "the Children of the Holy Spirit") were questioned by inquisitors, given light sentences, and reconciled to the church.[26] But the cult would continue. Andrea Saramita, a layman who knew Guglielma would claim that she was the incarnation of the Holy Spirit, similar to Christ being the incarnation of the Son. He would soon join up with Maifreda da Pirovano, a Humiliate sister, who would become a de facto leader of the group. Like Christ, Guglielma would be resurrected and physically ascend to heaven in front of a group of witnessing believers. After the ascension, she would send the Paraclete and would appoint Maifreda to look over the church. With her leadership, women would finally be able to be priests, and Maifreda would be the next pope after Celestine V.[27] Over time, the group gained followers and the stories about Guglielma would grow and be imbued with more biblical overtones. By 1300, the members were once again being questioned. During this questioning, Maifreda donned vestments and began singing the Mass. At the trial, she would be condemned and sentenced to burning. Guglielma would be posthumously condemned, and her bones would be disinterred to be burned as a heretic with her followers. The cult would continue to exist and seems to have geographically expanded for a while after this trial. Apocalypticism would continue to be a feature of lay Italian spirituality of the time, especially among those enamored with the Franciscan ideal of apostolic poverty.[28]

Languedoc
A Conglomeration of Dissent

We now return to where we've already traveled in previous chapters: Languedoc. The south of France would continue to reel in a sort of religious void after Catharism had been attacked. Although the Inquisition had largely suppressed Catharism in the area, it had also left bitterness in the people. The Franciscans had spread across Europe, and when they came to Languedoc, their counterparts in those communities began to rekindle some of the religious fervor that had marked the area for the last century. There the Franciscans, with their focus on evangelism, and a populace hungry for religious fervor would mix with dramatic consequences.

The Béguins of Languedoc were a penitential group who took as their spiritual leader Peter of John Olivi. In the early thirteenth century, the Béguins stood on street corners, announcing the coming apocalypse. The cult continued to grow, especially after Olivi's death in 1298, viewing his gravesite as a martyr's shrine. Olivi worked to spread his ideas to Franciscan circles and to the laity, providing his sermons in both Latin and the local language. The group first came under censure in 1299, when the archbishop of Narbonne, Gilles Aycelin, held a local council at Béziers that condemned them. The claims against them included gathering at night, preaching the end of the world, and engaging in new types of penitential acts. The first Béguins would be handed over to secular justice to be burned as heretics in October 1319 in Narbonne.[29]

With these burnings, the Franciscan dispute was no longer an internal matter. The Spiritual Franciscans of southern France had made a tremendous impact on the local population—after years of heresy and suppression, the Franciscans came in as an order recognized by the church, espousing many of the ideas of simplicity, humility, and poverty that the laity in Languedoc sought. This large group of laity, the Béguins, would follow the ideas of Olivi, although they were more interested in his apocalyptic visions and devotional works than in his work on the *usus pauper*. But they understood and respected that the Spiritual Franciscans took their vow of apostolic poverty seriously.

The Béguins read Olivi's commentary on Revelation in the vernacular and Latin. The movement was to have a spiritual as well as social impact on his followers. They celebrated the anniversary of his death as a saint's day at his tomb in Narbonne. His statements about the unworthiness of the current pope and the moral laxity of the church (especially based on its opulent lifestyle) found resonance among the Béguins as well. Within twenty years, condemnations of Olivi's works would not only affect the Spiritual Franciscans, but their effects would also be meted out on the laity who continued to revere Olivi.

Ubertino de Casale was another Franciscan zealot. In 1287, he met Olivi. He went to Avignon in 1309, under the protection of the cardinal. At issue that year and what Pope Clement wanted answers to were (1) whether the spirituals were infected with the Free Spirit heresy; (2) whether the *Rule* and the *Exiit qui seminat* were being followed; (3) Olivi's orthodoxy; and (4) persecution of the Spiritual Franciscans. Ubertino said that the order was in decline. He saw that the friars' greed caused trouble with the secular clergy and limited the money that went to the poor.[30] Because he said that the majority was unwilling to undertake reform, Ubertino felt that the pope should hand over the order to those willing to reform it. In 1312, the Council of Vienne, which we have already seen in relation to the beguines, decreed *Exivi de paradiso* (*When I Went Forth from Paradise*), the verdict on Franciscan poverty. It agreed that the order needed reform. But it did not agree that the decline of the order was due to papal involvement. It did not think that dividing the order would solve the issues. *Sancta Romana* (Holy Roman) was passed in December 1317, and with it, a new round of attacks on the Béguins would ramp up over the next couple of years.[31] While this bull condemned the Béguins, it did so not for their theology but because they "took the appearance of a legitimate religious order even though they did not have papal approval to do so, and ended by enabling episcopal authorities to act against such individuals."[32] Throughout Languedoc, the persecution of the Béguins increased.

Na Prous Boneta is perhaps one of the best-known names among the southern French Béguins. She was a mystic whose visions often took a decidedly political tone. She was taken into custody to be questioned by inquisitors on August 6, 1325.³³ Shortly after, she was handed over to the local authorities to be burned at the stake as a heretic. At the heart of her confession is a recounting of the times she had mystical visions, many of which began during liturgical moments of importance, such as the elevating of the host after consecration. She claimed that in these visions, she was told how Pope John XXII's treatment of Olivi had offended God so much that "at that time the sacrament of the altar lost its power. This coming Christmas it will have been two years since that occurred."³⁴ She added that "this present pope, John XXII, is like Caiaphas, who crucified Christ."³⁵ A new Age of the Holy Spirit will replace it. And "just as Blessed John prepared the way for the Lord," bringing in the Age of Christ, "so Saint Francis prepared the way for the Holy Spirit" that is the third age, that of the Holy Spirit.³⁶ Her views were further developed through other correspondences: just as two fleshly bodies—those of Mary and Jesus—were the founding of the church, two spirit bodies—namely, Olivi and Prous—will oversee the church in the Age of the Holy Spirit. Christ's body suffered for the church, just as Olivi's did. Prous received a revelation that the Dominicans and Franciscans should stop the Inquisition: "So God ordered the Preachers that they should weep because they have not ruled their order well according to our Lord. And God commands both the Preachers and the Minors that henceforth they should conduct no more inquisitions."³⁷ She compared the condemnation of Olivi's (a Franciscan) writings and the elevation to sainthood of St. Thomas Aquinas (a Dominican) to the biblical story of Cain and Abel, saying that just as Cain killed Abel physically, the Dominicans spiritually killed Olivi by condemning his writings. At the end of her confession, she confirmed that all these claims are pieces of divine revelation given to her, not teachings made by another human. She concluded by affirming that God revealed to her that "just as Eve, the first woman, was beginning and cause of the damnation of all human nature or humankind through Adam's sin, in the same way 'you shall be the beginning and cause of the salvation of all human nature or humankind through those words I make you speak, if they are believed.'"³⁸ She stated her denial of the efficacy of the sacraments was due to a break of the church authorities with apostolic tradition that renders them efficacious. That led to the shortcomings of priests: not their own sinfulness, but illegitimate genealogy. She stated that if one repented, even without confession, it was enough, stating that God had adapted to the sinful state of the church. These ideas certainly were pushing the boundaries of sacramental theology and ecclesiology.

Persecutions of Béguins

Clement allowed the Spirituals some houses in Languedoc. They took over more by force, in Narbonne and Béziers, finding locations where they could not be harassed by Conventuals. He had a twofold understanding of the *usus pauper*. It was the traditional papal vision: they were bound to poverty, chastity, obedience, and to all in the *Rule* that was mentioned specifically, and the rest was left to following the head of house. Thus, it became not an issue of poverty but of obedience.[39] Clement died in 1314, and in 1316, there were two anti-Spiritual moves. First, Michael of Cesena was elected the minister general of the Franciscans. Second, Jacques Duèze of Cahors became Pope John XXII. Both men disliked the Spirituals and wanted to end the Spiritual problem. In 1317, John XXII passed the decretal *Quorundam exigit*. In this decretal, the Spiritual Franciscans were effectively criminalized and were to be subjected to inquisition. While following the writings of Peter of John Olivi would be the source of blame officially bestowed on the Spiritual Franciscans, the source of blame for Béguin mistakes would settle on being ignorant that the writings of Olivi were condemned when it was deemed to be so publicly known.[40]

In the spring of 1317, John acted: he required the Spirituals to appear in Avignon. As a result, sixty or so were held in custody for a year. By March 1318, Paris theologians had been consulted. They agreed that failure to acknowledge the pope's authority to legislate the Franciscans was a heretical position. The pope didn't wait for this ruling; he started persecuting on December 30, 1317. *Sancta Romana* authorized the persecution of the Spirituals and included condemnation of the Fraticelli, the Brothers of Poor Life, the *bizzoche*, and the Béguins. In 1318, the first four Spirituals would be burned in Marseilles after being tried by Michel le Moine. An uprising in Languedoc soon followed. As a result, a more general inquisition followed, centered on Toulouse and Carcassonne. Many were questioned, and a network of safe houses grew as the persecution did.[41] "From 1323 on, it was heresy to deny that Christ and the apostles held property. The doctrine of evangelical poverty that had inspired St. Francis of Assisi was now officially dead."[42] The Béguin strength of resistance was due to two factors: (1) it was only recently declared heretic, and (2) because they were based on the Franciscan third order, there was a backbone of structure and organization.

The inquisitor Bernardo Gui told how the Béguins came to the notice of the church, saying it was because of the attention the Spiritual Franciscans were receiving. But his first description of them focused not on their beliefs but on their geography, showing that he was already associating them with the Cathars and others of the same region a century before. Gui said that they "arose recently in the provinces of Provence and Narbonne and in some parts of the province of Toulouse once belonging to Narbonne."[43] In his description, the Béguins were a short-lived heresy, being condemned only two years after first appearing. They may have been shorter-lived because they were dealt with more severely; over 21 percent of those appearing in Gui's *Liber sententiarum* (*Book of Sentences*) were burned at the stake, over three times as many as the Cathars.[44] In part, the more severe sentences were due to the Béguins refusing to acknowledge papal authority. And in part, the inquisitions had become a machine that was very efficient in producing guilt through the deposition process.

Gui's description focused closely on the Béguins' connection with the Spiritual Franciscans. He called them Poor Brethren, a name meant to evoke the Franciscans, and his description focuses on poverty. He wrote, "Some of these Béguins who live in villages and towns reside together in small dwellings which they commonly call houses of poverty. In these houses they often gather on holy days and Sundays with others who live independently and with friends and companions," a description that sounds neutral, until he continued, "There they read or listen to readings from these tracts and writings from which they suck poison, and yet they also hear readings from the commandments, from the articles of faith, legends of the saints and from the *Summary of Vices and Virtues*, as if in the devil's school this supposed virtue were showing forth the school of Christ."[45] Bernardo Gui's descriptions of the Béguins also depicted them at prayers, claiming that they do not kneel but instead crouch down and pull their hoods so as to cover up their faces.[46]

Gui's was intent to depict the group as a paragon of instability, saying that "it must also be noted that there are some among them who beg openly from house to house because, so they say, they have understood gospel poverty. Others do not beg in public but do manual work and earn enough to lead a poor life."⁴⁷ He ascribed to the laity belief in not possessing material goods, something that there isn't much record to prove. Theologically, he believed that the Béguins were ardent supporters of the Spiritual Franciscans' beliefs about the poverty of Christ and that they extended this principle not merely to the Franciscan friars but also to lay followers. They begged from door to door or were ignorant so as not to understand the errors they committed. Gui described this life as being on the edge of destitution.⁴⁸

The Spiritual Franciscans equated the *Rule* of St. Francis and the gospel. This was hardly surprising, as Francis had thought that his idea of poverty was based on the gospel commandment to not bring a second cloak and to rely on strangers when traveling. But the Béguins took this even further and applied the idea that the papacy could not change the gospel to include that it could not change the example of Francis.⁴⁹ This move effectively put the order's own interpretation of its charism, rules, and governance above the authority of the pope. There were other charges Gui made against the Béguins that do not sound likely to have been issues for the group. He claims that the Béguins objected to the pope allowing Franciscans to transfer to property-owning orders and changing the Franciscan habit.⁵⁰ Some of these allegations sound like they're against the order's Spirituals and not the Béguins. It's hard to believe the laity were truly upset about changes to the length of the habit.

Bernardo Gui described those who were killed in 1318 and how the laity turned them into martyred "saints" of the heretical group. He states, "Many men and women Béguins and their believers have secretly gathered up the ashes and burnt bones of these condemned and burned heretics. They keep them as relics, they venerate and kiss them as relics of saints, just as people kiss the relics of other saints in reverence and devotion."⁵¹ The Béguins also kept martyrologies of their members and refused to take oaths.⁵² Gui clearly thought that the sins of the Spiritual Franciscans should be meted out on their lay followers as well. He insisted that the theological and political matters that the Spirituals took issue with were things that the lay Béguins could and should be asked about. As he explained, the laity "also say that they must not be interrogated by prelates and inquisitors about anything except articles of faith, the commandments and the sacraments. If other questions are asked, they are not bound to reply because they are, so they say, lay persons and simple. But they are astute, cunning and crafty."⁵³ He seemed to believe that the Béguins were secretly more advanced than the ignorant people he'd previously referred to them as.

The apocalypticism of Olivi and his followers made it sound like the new group of Béguins would reestablish an authentic church from the remains of the floundering medieval one. Those who followed Francis's charism were the ones who would comprise the faithful remnant out of which the church would renew itself. "These few will establish the spiritual Church which will be humble and benevolent in the seventh and last age of the Church. This age will begin at the death of Antichrist."[54] This Age of the Antichrist would destroy everything except those true followers of St. Francis, the Spiritual Franciscans.[55] Bernardo Gui claimed that they believed the church consisted of a spiritual church that is the true church, not the carnal church of the Roman hierarchy:

> They teach too that at the end of the sixth age of the Church, which began with St Francis and in which we now live, this carnal Church, the great harlot of Babylon, must be rejected by Christ, just as the synagogue of the Jews was rejected because it crucified Christ. So too the carnal Church crucifies and persecutes the life of Christ in those they call the poor and spiritual brothers of the order of St Francis. By this they mean members of the first as well as of the third order persecuted in the provinces of Provence and of Narbonne as was mentioned above.[56]

Again, this description blends Olivi's apocalypticism with something else—a spiritual church that is primary and valid and an institutional church that is not—probably overlaying the Spiritual position with Cathar dualism. While Olivi did emphasize the corruption in the church, saying it was necessary and signaled the coming of the end, he didn't posit a dualist worldview.

Arrests of the Béguins would start in 1316 in Languedoc and in 1319 around Montpellier. The goal of these arrests was to go after the Béguins who were thought to be aiding the Spiritual Franciscans by giving them money, spreading their doctrines, or hiding them. The inquisitorial tactic took a different approach than in the Albigensian Crusade; here inquisitors were interested in people with leadership positions, thinking that if these roles were removed, the group would lose cohesion and disappear. It encouraged reintegration into the church. The 1310s saw a number of auto-da-fés with burnings of several dozen Béguins at each. The last few years of arrests sought to minimize this result. These arrests would reach their apex in 1325, when the inquisitor claimed to have managed to gather up much of the Béguin community. Among those arrested were several of the most public faces of the group, including Pierre Trencavel (a disciple of Olivi), the visionary Na Prous Boneta, and her sister Alisseta Boneta. Trencavel had been captured twice before and had escaped each time. He had witnessed the 1320 and 1321 burnings of about forty Béguins he had tried to protect.[57] Prous and others who were rounded up were accused of hiding and aiding Spiritual Franciscans. Prous remained defiant, serving as a spiritual leader to the imprisoned Béguins and refusing to change her testimony; she insisted that she was a follower of Olivi and wished to become a martyr. In jail, she encouraged others not to recant their beliefs in the face of death. Trencavel would escape once again within a year and would become a missionary spreading the Béguin message. The Béguin movement was dealt its final blow in 1328, with the martyrdom of a number of leading members of the group. Some would be burned; others would be imprisoned; and still others would be sentenced to undertake pilgrimages.[58] The repression created both martyrs and repentants.

Lasting Impact

One challenge regarding the Spiritual Franciscans and the Béguins of Languedoc is to understand how the targets moved from theological issues regarding the poverty of Christ and papal dispensations for the Franciscan order to a popular heresy. One answer is that Peter Olivi became a martyr and saint of sorts, whose life provided a model and whose burial site became a martyr's shrine. Another is that he sought out this lay attention, knowing the cultural milieu of the time and place. That the laity heard his ideas preached and that he was much loved within the local Franciscan community helped his message to reach both clerical and lay ears. But the strong reaction among the laity to the suppression of the Spiritual Franciscans touches another nerve: Languedoc had been through many suppressions in the last century, and its people reacted strongly to those preachers they'd enjoyed—the ones who lived the poverty they preached—being condemned.

The rhetoric of the Béguins was stronger than that of other groups and apocalyptic. Those who died thought they were doing so in the service of the one true faith. As the persecutions grew, so too did the accusations against the Béguins. There began to be accusations of sexual offenses among the Béguins, an increasingly common tactic against perceived heretics.[59] One of the real challenges is how to describe the social impact of the Béguin movement. Unlike the beguines and beghards of the Low Countries, which were clearly offering new roles to women, the Béguins of Languedoc never tried to organize but were content to simply follow the Franciscans—a group that was recognized within the church. There was no sense of creating new churches; while it existed, its main shrine was in a recognized church in Narbonne.

Ultimately, I want to conclude with a word of caution from the historian David Burr: "Any scholar who writes about Franciscan history between 1279 and the 1330s is likely to devote a great deal of space to the zealots, yet they were a miniscule part of the order. The Tuscan rebels and Languedocian spiritual combined may have added up to around two hundred friars."[60] What I take from these words is that the Spiritual Franciscan and Conventual disagreement might not have had a lasting impact on the Franciscan order, but it does have a lasting impact on the study of heresy, for it shows how close the line between orthodoxy and heterodoxy could be. For example, it could be as simple as a debate about whether a person owns or uses the computer they type on. And it shows how much of a specter the idea of heresy cast over all aspects associated with the suspect groups. At a time when no new orders were permitted and the papacy was trying to consolidate errant movements with extant orders, the Spiritual Franciscans and Béguins did the opposite: they tried to buck the conglomeration of power under the papacy. There were clear reasons for doing so. The papacy had handed down orders about how the Franciscans were to understand the mind of their own founder, something that many Franciscans felt they were better equipped to do. The papacy tried to fit a relatively young order, the Franciscans, into a box that fit its own goals.

This heresy is very short-lived; in the scheme of the heresies seen so far, which have all lasted for a century or much longer, the span of time the papacy was interested in the popular Béguin heresy was only from 1299 to about 1323. It was one where the condemnation machinery wasn't as singularly focused on destruction of the heretics as it might have been and where some associated groups were able to continue to exist. Bernardo Gui's descriptions of the Béguins gave a singular view of them as a community that made them appear as organized as the Spiritual Franciscans, something that was clearly not the case, as the results of their trials showed.

CHAPTER 7

Wycliffe and the Lollards
The Academic and Public Face of Heresy

IT'S UNUSUAL FOR the ideas born within a university to cause widespread popular mayhem or mass resistance, but for John Wycliffe and the Lollards, that's what happened. Wycliffe was an Oxford faculty member and cleric writing and preaching increasingly suspect ideas that crossed over into popular Lollardy, where they were intensified. While the political motivations for the two movements were different—Wycliffe presented his heretical ideas at the service of the crown, and the popular Lollards presented theirs against all forms of authority and power, including the church, the crown, and landlords—they grew from the same seed. As the High Middle Ages gave way to the late Middle Ages, such crossovers between the halls of learning and official theological debates and popular ideas began; a similar crossover between theological debates and popular ideas appears in the next chapter, on Jan Hus. Wycliffe and the Lollards produced ideas deemed heretical because they were both a theological and a politico-social threat. Wycliffe had a uniquely strong impact because he was part of the education system that fed and oversaw the English church's leadership and trained its ministers.

The popular movement took on a new and urgent theological dimension that became increasingly abstracted from Wycliffe's theological ponderings. It borrowed many of the issues that Wycliffe espoused but critiqued aspects of power that expressed economic concerns of the laity as well as the issues of clerical power and its effect on sacramental theology. The effect of Wycliffe and his followers was that they emboldened the people who would become known as the Lollards to seek unmediated religious reading and discussion through vernacular translations of the Bible and an emphasis on the text as the basis for religious doctrine and practice. Adding to the intrigue of the Lollard movement is that England previously had no widespread heresies. Some Templars were jailed during the Europe-wide suppression of the Templar order after

1307, but heresy was not widespread in England before the Lollards. While Wycliffe looks like a proximate source for the flourishing of heresy in the country, there are other exacerbating currents, such as the rise of the mendicant orders in urban areas, that explain the background of this sea change within British religion.

The church in England had held a primary, privileged position both socially and economically in English life and culture throughout the late Middle Ages. During Wycliffe's time and beyond, the church was largely unchallenged, and as such, its response to dissent would be incomplete. There were spontaneous, sporadic attacks on clergy, such as the one on Bury St Edmunds in 1327, which was a response to the great wealth and landholdings of the Benedictine abbey and the way it assessed taxes and rents on an already-squeezed peasantry and artisans. But uprisings like this one were exceedingly rare. The evangelical ideal was in full swing in Britain: the Dominicans and Franciscans both arrived in England during the 1220s, and the Carmelites and Augustinians arrived in the 1240s. Each order brought a reforming zeal as part of their missions to preach to the public, as well as serious interest in intelligent formation of their clergy. By the 1300s, the friars also held dominant positions at both Oxford and Cambridge Universities. Their zeal was matched in the increasing religious fervor of the laity.

Textual discoveries of the last few decades have helped to refine much of what is known concerning the Wycliffite heresy, based on both Latin and vernacular writings, from within the universities and from the parishes. One of the challenges before now has been in understanding how the ideas spread and the nature of the connection between academic Wycliffitism and popular Lollardy. Part of the affinity seems to be based largely on their broad challenges to the seriousness with which church leadership took their charge and to the devotions and practices of the church, which resonated with the laity's economic and political frustrations. Although both heresies had a common root, namely the thought of John Wycliffe, they posed a nuanced threat to the English church because the two prongs of the heresy evolved to attack distinct aspects of the church. The Wycliffites, centered in the universities, offered a theological attack that went to the core of the church teachings and ecclesiastical administration, especially as it related to secular power. The popular attack went after liturgical and core practices within the English church, individual leaders, and the church's understanding of the spiritual basis of leadership. The great combined strength in these two sides (at times even contradicting one another) was in calling into question the church's praxis and commitment to its ideals, raising questions that the Lollards were more prepared to answer than the church was.

Heresy and Inquisition in England before Wycliffe

Because England had only isolated heresy before, it had not developed an inquisitional legal system. Previous heretics tended to be individuals, and incidents were isolated. About 200 years after the continent initiated the Inquisition, England began to institute legal proceedings for heresy. Typically, legislation dealing with heresy fell under two aspects of law: canon law and secular law. Canon law oversaw the processes for deposing those accused of heresy and determining guilt. Secular justice—with the English crown at its apex—was responsible for supporting and protecting the church and, as such, needed to resist heresy. Even before antiheretical legislation in England, secular police were used to arrest accused heretics and compel them to appear in court.[1] On the continent, a heretic found guilty of relapse or one who refused to acknowledge guilt in the face of evidence would be sentenced by the inquisitorial process and then handed over to secular justice for execution.

Once heresy legislation was recognized as necessary, it took a few decades for England to enact it. Parliament passed the Heresy Act of 1382, which required that the chancellor issue commissions to arrest and interrogate suspected heretical preachers; it was repealed by the next parliament that same year, under the claim that the House of Commons did not pass it. In 1401, Parliament and King Henry IV promulgated *De Heretico Comburendo* (*Regarding The Burning of the Heretic*), which was the first legislation to allow the burning of relapsed heretics in England. This law would initiate inquisitorial processes in England, allowing secular justice to mete out the punishments for ecclesiastical charges. Although it alluded to Wycliffe, it did not mention him or his followers by name. The law instructed that any books deemed heretical were to be turned over to the authorities to be disposed of. This part was at the insistence of Archbishop of Canterbury Thomas Arundel, who would come to influence attitudes toward the Lollards.

As the fifteenth century progressed, rooting out heresy would be more clearly etched into English law. The power to inquire into heresy accusations was granted to secular officers in a substantial extension of their powers in 1406.[2] While this ability had been the case on an ad hoc basis previously, it was now enshrined in law. This change was a clear attempt to help mutually strengthen and solidify joint secular and ecclesiastical litigation against heresy. Archbishop Arundel drafted his *Constitutions against Gospellers*, formally published in 1409, which sought to prohibit unlicensed preaching, regulated the orthodoxy of preaching and teaching, prohibited vernacular translations of the Bible, and introduced monthly examinations of the religious belief of those at Oxford. These laws were aimed at addressing problems at Oxford and with the Lollard movement. Finally, in 1414, new statutes would declare that heresy was a crime against common law; these laws would oversee confiscations of property from convicted heretics. The law also sought to clarify who could confiscate this property. Thus, over the span of a few decades, England developed an apparatus for handling suspected heresy that matched similar laws developed in the rest of Western Europe.

Wycliffe's Life

John Wycliffe and his writings were very much a product of the medieval universities and their intellectual climate; he came to Oxford in the early 1350s, where he progressed through his studies and the ranks at the university. He was ordained by 1351 and became a junior fellow at Merton College by 1356, a master at Balliol by 1360, warden at Canterbury Hall by 1365, and a doctor of theology by 1372. By all accounts, he was a rising star—with successful academic careers also came opportunities for work outside of the university, especially in politics. In 1374, he served the king by traveling to Bruges with Bishop Gilbert to negotiate with papal emissaries. In 1376, John of Gaunt, duke of Lancaster, summoned him to London to discuss the topic of disendowment of church properties. Wycliffe also received the living of Lutterworth, which he would hold until his death. His varied career prompted him to develop his theology along lines that intersected with each different direction of his scholarly work and his roles within the church and politics. There were five main areas of his thought that would taint him as a heretic. The first was his thinking on church authority and wealth. The second was his realism, a philosophical stance that would have implications for other areas of his theology. The third was his argument against the wealth of the church and his calls for disendowment. The fourth was his scriptural focus, which led him to question if certain practices of the church—such as pilgrimage, prayers for the dead, and feasts—were necessary; later he would reject them as extrabiblical. The fifth was his denial of transubstantiation as an explanation for the transformation in the Eucharist, which happened during consecration.

Wycliffe's disgust with some aspects of church authority would have its roots in his time at Oxford. In 1365, he encountered his first problem when he was chosen as the warden of Canterbury College, a college founded by the Christ Church Priory at Canterbury and which attracted a mix of secular clergy and monks. Its student body had competing interests, and Wycliffe found himself pulled in opposing directions, satisfying none of them, until the monastics at the college called for his ouster. The Archbishop of Canterbury tried to remove him from office. Wycliffe appealed to the pope, Urban V, but he was removed anyway in 1370. This challenge set him back both financially and politically. The events at the college began to turn him against monasticism and ecclesiastical authority, something that would continue to develop throughout his life.

Based on his university status, the expectation was that Wycliffe would continue to have a career of various administrative appointments in the church. Yet it seems that after a couple more appointments, his career stalled, and despite the others on the Bruges entourage becoming bishops soon after their return, a position he thought he'd been assured never materialized.[3] Upon his return from Bruges, his hostilities bubbled forth more visibly. His job had involved meeting with church representatives to discuss the taxation of clergy; back at Oxford, Wycliffe wrote the treatise *De civili dominio* (*Of the Civil Dominion*), in which he argued that clergy should refrain from property ownership. He had lost his appointment at Canterbury College to a monk, and he now attacked ownership and salaries within the church. This stance got the attention of many, and the Benedictines in England felt threatened by him. One of their monks, Adam Easton, began to investigate aspects of Wycliffe's thought that could be used against him. Wycliffe's manner was brash and caustic; he held grudges; and his philosophical realism (discussed later) meant that he had become embattled in academic debates against a number of his colleagues at Oxford.

In February 1377, Wycliffe was summoned to appear before the bishops at St. Paul's to respond to his several questionable views, including those on property, and to openly preaching these views in London's pulpits.[4] Adam Easton now formally questioned Wycliffe's unorthodox views. The trial unfolded a bit differently than other proceedings we've seen thus far; instead of Wycliffe being questioned alone, as most accused heretics were, John of Gaunt attended to support Wycliffe, as did Henry Percy (the Earl of Northumberland), and representatives from the four orders of friars.[5] Disagreement broke out at the trial between John of Gaunt and Bishop Courtenay of London, and the trial was suspended. In May 1377, Wycliffe received a censure from Pope Gregory XI, who condemned his views, but secular justice did not ensue.

The pope requested that the English authorities ascertain whether Wycliffe held these views or whether, faced with papal condemnation, he recanted them. Pope Gregory XI sent five bulls to various authorities in England.[6] The first bull, *Regnum angliae gloriosum*, requested that the Archbishop of Canterbury and the Bishop of London meet to make themselves fully aware of Wycliffe's teaching and investigate if he were still holding onto the propositions that the pope outlined. In *Nuper per nos*, the pope sent the same request a second time. The third, *Super periculosis*, asked for those clergy addressed to warn the king and secular authorities of the danger Wycliffe and his ideas posed. The pope also wrote directly to King Edward III in the papal bull *Regnum angliae quod altissimus*. He detailed for the king what he had asked the archbishop and the bishop to do to safeguard the church in England against Wycliffe's heretical ideas. The fifth bull, *Mirari cogimur*, was sent to the University of Oxford and to the Diocese of Lincoln to address the problems created by Wycliffe. It stated,

> It has come to our ears that John de Wyclif, rector of the church of Lutterworth, in the diocese of Lincoln, professor of the sacred scriptures (would that he were not also Master of Errors), has fallen into such a detestable madness that he does not hesitate to dogmatize and publicly preach, or rather vomit forth from the recesses of his breast certain propositions and conclusions which are erroneous and false. He has cast himself also into the depravity of preaching heretical dogmas which strive to subvert and weaken the state of the whole Church and even secular polity."[7]

The pope expressed concern that Wycliffe "has polluted certain of the faithful of Christ by besprinkling them with these doctrines, and led them away from the right paths of the aforesaid faith to the brink of perdition."[8] The pope's letter made clear the actions that the masters of Oxford should take, saying, "You are on our authority to arrest the said John, or cause him to be arrested and to send him under a trustworthy guard to our venerable brother, the archbishop of Canterbury, and the bishop of London, or to one of them." Wycliffe was placed under house arrest when the letter arrived at the university, just before Christmas.[9]

During this time, Wycliffe was still working at the court, advising on matters, though not in any capacity where his growing radicalization would be noticed. A group of friends at Oxford, along with friends at court, meant that he was spared any further interference as a result of the papal denouncement of his views, though it was yet another indication that his career had stalled. In 1379, his teachings on the Eucharist changed, and Wycliffe began to support consubstantiation over the accepted church teaching on transubstantiation (described in detail later). When he attacked the doctrine of transubstantiation, saying that it was metaphysically impossible, he found himself losing the powerful friends who had protected him. In May 1382, Archbishop William Courtenay called for the Blackfriars Council to investigate claims about Wycliffe's beliefs. It would come to be known as the Earthquake Council because an earthquake happened in the Strait of Dover while the synod was convened. The earthquake was interpreted as a sign of divine displeasure in Wycliffe. The council found his doctrines heretical; three of his supporters at Oxford—Nicholas Hereford, Philip Repingdon, and John Aston—were also condemned. The tables had officially turned for Wycliffe. Because of this condemnation, he was forcibly retired from Oxford. He went to Lutterworth in Leicestershire, where he continued to write and preach.

In the council, twenty-four propositions culled from his writings were examined.[10] Ten on the Eucharist and church order were found to be heretical; fourteen others were found erroneous and needed correction. Among the propositions were a number that dealt with poverty of clerics—some with the poverty of priests, some with the poverty of the mendicant and monastic orders—and others with the thinking that monastics and mendicants were not to beg but to live only off the work of their hands. One such proposition stated a heretical belief ascribed to Wycliffe: "The pope with all his clergy who have possessions are heretics, because they have possessions, and all in agreement with these, namely all secular masters and other laity."[11] Other propositions dealt with sacramental theology, including the way the substances existed in the consecrated forms, and confession. Yet another condemned statement was that "it is permissible for any deacon or priest to preach the word of God without the authority of the Apostolic See or a Catholic bishop."[12] The council also condemned refusal to believe in the efficacy of indulgences. But Wycliffe's name was nowhere listed as the author of these statements; he would again be summoned to the Oxford Synod six months later. And, again, there would be no decision against him. Some of his previous followers from Oxford, such as Philip Repingdon, were compelled to recant their support of his propositions. Wycliffe, though, was relatively unscathed throughout this process.

At the end of the synod, Wycliffe returned to Lutterworth. Pope Urban VI subsequently summoned him to Rome in 1384, which he refused. As he wrote, "I take it as belief that no man should follow the pope, nor no saint that is now in heaven, but in as much as he follows Christ. For James and John erred when they coveted worldly highness."[13] Wycliffe called Pope Urban VI out of his intellectual league for his "unskilled summoning" when he thought the pope could not understand the philosophical and exegetical foundations of his work. Toward the end of his reply to the pope's summons to Rome, Wycliffe wrote, "If [the pope] summon against reason, by him or by any of his, and pursue this unskilled summoning, he is an open Antichrist."[14] The spring Parliament of 1388 ordered a search for Wycliffite writings, both in Latin and the vernacular. Although he had died in 1384, Wycliffe was condemned a second time for heresy in 1415 at the Council of Constance. In 1428, his corpse was exhumed and burned on a heretic's pyre, and the ashes were scattered in a river to make sure that his mortal body was completely destroyed.

Wycliffe at Oxford

Wycliffe's theological ideas form the basis of the councils' condemnations as well as a substantial part of the popular movement the Lollards. Wycliffe's views would revolve around the following issues. First, the philosophical issue of the problem of universals put Wycliffe at odds with many within Oxford and would come to affect his sacramental theology later in life. Second, he formulated several types of anticlerical attacks on monasticism, church ministers, and the papacy. Third, he espoused clerical poverty, which evolved into a political argument for disendowment of the church in England. Fourth, he expressed reservations about church practices such as pilgrimages and veneration of the saints as he became more focused on the primacy of Scripture;

this point would be a key Lollard complaint. And fifth, Wycliffe's sacramental theology would contest the Catholic understanding of transubstantiation, by which the Eucharist was converted from bread and wine to the body and blood of Christ.

Universals

Wycliffe provoked controversy with his philosophical position on the problem of universals. While this dispute is a specialized philosophical one, it had implications for theology, especially concerning the Eucharist. The problem of universals dealt with differing philosophical systems of understanding the nature of things in the world. Wycliffe had been a nominalist early in his career, drawn to William of Ockham's position that denied the existence of universals. Nominalism was the favored position at Oxford in his time. Wycliffe came to believe that universals emanate from the divine and derivatively manifest in material creation. A philosopher who sees an orange cat and a grey cat is faced with the challenge of how to describe the metaphysical relationship between the two cats: how they share a common nature—how they can both be cats—and how this common nature exists within each of them. A common nature, in this example the idea of "catness," is called a universal because it's something that universally forms all cats. The cat Aelred, the cat Gus, and the cat Freyja must all participate in this nature. But does it exist outside of those cats that currently exist? If the answer is yes, the person is a realist. If not, the person is a nominalist (meaning, it exists in name alone). But if one is a realist, a problem arises. If the universal nature of cat exists in Aelred, how does it simultaneously exist in Freyja or Gus? The philosopher knows that more than one cat exists at any given time. For a realist, a universal can and must be in many things at once, due to being a universal. The next step is to ask about the nature of how this "catness" exists within each cat. Does it exist outside of individual cats or only in live ones, such as Freyja or Aelred? The nominalist position toward the universals denied their existence and posited that only actual things that could be identified by the senses existed. The universals were concepts that were formed based on all the things in any species. But they were concepts only.

Wycliffe's transformation would become the basis for his rethinking of what he said about church authority and the sacraments; he would start to distinguish between an eternal, indivisible church and a visible one that is corrupted. For Wycliffe, following in a Neoplatonic vein rather than in Ockham's Aristotelian one, universals had existence because all created things existed in eternity in the mind of God, even though the accidents in their material existence (such as being a grey cat named Gus) might not. For Wycliffe, the relation between the universals and particulars also affected the relationship between God and humans. Such a difference in philosophical stances likely added to his difficulties and debates around the university as he published *De universalibus* (*On the Universals*), summarizing his position in 1368. What this change in position showed was that Wycliffe had moved away from the standard philosophical positions and was laying the foundation for what would be his heretical positions. It also meant he was making enemies and not playing well with others at the university. While this stance was a topic of intense disagreements among philosophers and theologians, it also had implications for how one understood the nature of the relationship between God and humans and how one understood the sacraments, particular the Eucharist.

Anticlericalism

Wycliffe's anticlericalism developed in stages, beginning with the relationship between secular and ecclesiastical authority, developing into a critique of the wealth of the church and clergy, and culminating with a reconsideration of what the true church was. The Roman view was that the pope was the vicar of Christ and the one who wielded divine power through the position as head of the church on earth. Christian monarchs would support this role and pledge to defend Christendom. They weren't part of the church hierarchy, but they played a significant role in supporting it. In his early 1370s work *Postilla super totam bibliam* (*Commentary on the Entire Bible*), covering the breadth and depth of the Bible as a totality, Wycliffe espoused his hermeneutics of biblical interpretation, but more importantly, he began probing the relationship between secular and religious authority. Soon came *De mandatis divinis* (*On Divine Commandments*) and *De civili dominio*; in these works, he focused his thoughts on religious and secular power, coming to the position that only a human in a state of righteousness could command authority. *Dominum* is lordship granted by God, the type of authority Wycliffe focused on understanding the mandate for. In his view, it could be either secular or ecclesiastical. Authority came not from the office one inhabited but from the moral or spiritual wellness of the occupant of the office. This idea wasn't quite the early church Donatist heresy; rather, Wycliffe focused on the aspect of holding authority rather than on the sacraments at this stage.

In his 1379 tract *De ecclesia* (*On the Church*), Wycliffe further refined his ideas on the nature of the church and its composition. To him, inclusion of the pope and clergy among those in a state of grace was not a foregone conclusion. The difficulty that he identified was that the church was the mystical body of Christ, and yet the institution of the church could not truly be spotless and perfect, being composed of humans who were fallen people. His solution was to say that the true church was the collection of the predestined faithful. Of course, no individual person could know if they or any other person were part of this group. That doesn't sound too radical, but the logic and implications that church members couldn't be assumed to be members of the true church was pretty serious. Wycliffe concluded that if the church leader wasn't a person of righteousness, others did not need to follow that person's orders. That conclusion would have serious implications for church and papal authority. His concern about the fitness of the person in a leadership role resonated with his contemporaries at a time when the church had two rival popes.[15] Wycliffe would later say that the institutional church needed a high level of reform for both the true church and the institutional church to align. The role of the institutional church was to serve as an example of piety, which could happen when its clergy were in a state of righteousness and served in purity and simplicity. Eventually, Wycliffe would decide the only source of Christian authority was Scripture. He was concerned about the pope's supposed temporal authority over secular positions and institutions. He saw it not as being biblically based but a result of the Donation of Constantine, in which the fourth-century emperor transferred secular power over Rome to the pope. Although several leading figures of the church would question its authenticity in the Middle Ages, the document wouldn't be exposed as a forgery until a generation after Wycliffe. To him, papal temporal power came from Caesar, not from Christ.[16]

Clerical Poverty and Disendowment

Another implication of Wycliffe's writings about dominion was his condemnation of the church's wealth and his belief that the church should be stripped of its money and landholdings, a practice known as disendowment. The errors of which Wycliffe was first accused in 1377 were drawn from his work *De civili dominio*, and he wrote a vernacular summary of it, entitled *On the Saviour's Poverty*. His argument was that dominion and power came from God, and that those who received it to dispense must be in a fit state to use it, meaning they must be free from mortal sin; he termed this state "dominion in grace." He further stated that the clergy had been taught by Christ to live simply and in poverty, something that the clergy and bishops were not doing. Like others we have read about, Wycliffe believed that the early church experience gave a deeper model of how clerics should act and live than the contemporary church practiced. Ecclesiastics owning property were in a state of mortal sin and therefore did not have a lawful right to rule over people. His insistence on the standard of poverty meant that the church was not able to fulfill its other roles of leadership, including the interpretation of Scripture, as a result of its inability to live a life of poverty; the result to Wycliffe was that the Roman way of interpreting Scripture made it lose its spiritual and ruling powers.

Wycliffe's example cut across all types of wealth in the church: he called the orders of the church "private religions." His image was of those who hid away and hoarded those things that could help the laity. His position proffered an explicit moral condemnation of the church's acquisition of wealth, a wealth that kept the good that was given to the church from those who could spiritually benefit from it. Disendowment of the church and each order became morally necessary to help the secular authorities and to help save souls from hell.[17] Wycliffe's argument implied that the laity had a right to be involved in theological debate, as they had a stake in it, both spiritually and physically. In fact, in his eyes, the publication of vernacular theological material took on a moral imperative to educate the laity on how to stand up for what the church owed them and was not providing them.

Condemnation of Church Practices

There were many practices of the medieval church that had accrued over the millennia, such as celebrating various saints, offering comfort to believers, and encouraging renewal. With his emphasis on Scripture as the basis for his understanding of church, Wycliffe was alarmed by practices that were not mentioned in the gospel. For instance, he railed against indulgences, a common practice in the church for which he did not find a biblical basis. The Catholic view held that after this life, humans would go to purgatory to atone for the sins they had committed in this lifetime. Under this logic, since the church was the mystical body of Christ, the living could pray to the saints to intercede on behalf of those in purgatory, to erase some of the time and shorten their misery before enjoying the beatific vision. Wycliffe wrote, "I confess that the indulgences of the pope, if they are what they are said to be, are a manifest blasphemy, inasmuch as he claims a power to save men almost without limit, and not only to mitigate the penalties of those who have sinned, by granting them the aid of absolutions and indulgences, that they may never come to purgatory."[18] His concern was that the pope did not have the spiritual authority to guarantee a person would spend less time working off their earthly sins in purgatory or to say where a person would end up after this life.

At the heart of both his views on church wealth and papal indulgences, Wycliffe expressed concern that the contemporary church had set itself up as superior to Christ. But his language showed him growing bolder. He wrote, "It appears that this doctrine is a manifold blasphemy against Christ, inasmuch as the pope is extolled above his humanity and deity, and so above all that is called God—pretensions which, according to the declarations of the apostle, agree with the character of Antichrist; for he possesses Caesarean power above Christ, who had nowhere to lay his head."[19] What may have started as academic disagreements over metaphysics or as a grudge for losing a job because of a monk had hardened into a position that directly attacked the Roman church and the worthiness of the clergy and pope. In *De veritate sacrae scriptura* (*On the Truth of Sacred Scripture*), Wycliffe studied what Scripture said about Christian foundations. This 1378 treatise called for the church to strip away all the nonbiblical practices. Among these, monasticism must go, since monks were not mentioned in the Bible: the practice was not biblically warranted because it caused the separation of monks from the larger church. Wycliffe called it a "private religion." This view in particular would cause clerical objections to be raised against Wycliffe again, particularly from the Benedictines in Oxford.

Sacramental Theology

Although the papal condemnation of 1377 did not list transubstantiation as a problem for Wycliffe, his detractors had already identified a potential issue with his metaphysics from the early 1370s onward;[20] in the wake of the condemnations, Wycliffe began to rethink his position on transubstantiation. In his work *De eucharistia* (*On the Eucharist*, 1379–80), he started to apply his philosophical principles to the doctrine of the Eucharist. He no longer saw the traditional explanation in which the Eucharistic accidents (small, white, round, bread-like) were "hanging" without adhering to a substance to be possible. Accidents without a subject did not make philosophical sense. But at the same point, Christ had said, "This is my body," implying that it was not bread but the body of Christ. One had to either reject Christ's words, call him a liar, and say it is bread, not body (which Wycliffe was not about to do) or say that the traditional explanation of transubstantiation via Aquinas was untenable on metaphysical grounds. Wycliffe did not like being painted into the corner he was, but he jettisoned the idea of transubstantiation in favor of saying that the substance of bread remains in reality but that in signification, power, and effects it was also Christ's body.[21] In other words, the presence of Christ was one of grace rather than of reality.

Additionally, Wycliffe's strong notion of predestination meant that the church was to be a collection of the elect. God would save those who were so chosen and would let those predestined for damnation to be damned. As a result, the actions of God eclipsed the function of the sacraments as a means of his salvation. Although Wycliffe accepted that baptism was scripturally warranted, he acknowledged that the elect would be saved with or without it and that it could not save those predestined to damnation.[22] With this view, he disconnected the sacraments from salvation. After the Eucharist and baptism, other sacraments came under attack by Wycliffe. He questioned both the necessity of confirmation and the episcopal hold over it. He questioned the necessity and scriptural warrant for extreme unction (or last rights). Penance, or individual confession, was another sacrament that he thought there was no need for. Priests to whom people confessed could not tell who was predestined and who was not. Only Christ could truly absolve a person, which meant that priestly penances were blasphemous. Just as he had railed against the episcopal domination of the sacrament of confirmation, Wycliffe railed against the friars' domination of the sacrament of penance. He said that one did not need to confess in private; being contrite was enough, and an exterior confession added no benefit. He also questioned prayers for the dead and the cult of saints.[23] In particular, he noted that if God had foreordained for anyone to end up in heaven or hell, that prayers for the dead would not change the place where God had chosen. Although some of these positions (e.g., those on predestination and baptism) were generally derived from his reading of Scripture, and others (e.g., those on the Eucharistic) were derived from his metaphysics, many derived from his growing anticlericalism. And these last positions were the ones that the Lollards were most interested in, for they would affect preaching and the relationship between clergy and parishioners.

Lollardy

While Wycliffe's positions would be dealt with by trying to condemn him and his university disciples, his ideas would grow harder to respond to as they crossed into the public realm, in part because Lollardy's social practices, beliefs, and strengths adapted among its various locales, from rural to urban and across social strata.[24] While the movement was found in rural counties such as Norfolk and Suffolk, it was also in cities like London. "Early Lollard belief must therefore be seen as highly eclectic rather than as doctrinally homogeneous. The sect's doctrines were systematized only gradually, and this development may have owed less to the activity of its surviving leaders than to the procedures of interrogation employed by the Church authorities."[25] Lollards were hard to spot, even in their own time. They would participate in local church activities, take the yearly communion and confession required, and blend in with other believers. Lollardy would exist in plain sight.[26] It would be recorded in preaching texts, a number of lay pamphlets and spiritual booklets, literature, and the records that condemned the Lollards.

Preaching

The ideas of Wycliffe primarily reached people through the medium of preaching and the Wycliffite Bible; other common texts were placards, pamphlets, and broadsides that were used to put forth ideas as well. A network made up of Oxford graduates, all of whom seem to have known Wycliffe personally, helped Wycliffite ideas spread initially.[27] These men used the preaching benefices to which many of them were appointed as opportunities to spread Wycliffe's ideas among the people; these supporters included Nicholas Hereford, Philip Repingdon, John Aston, and Laurence Bedeman. We know from the condemnation at the Earthquake Council of 1382 that Wycliffe's university followers were required to recant, indicating that Wycliffite preaching was already established. After this condemnation, a sweep to find Wycliffite preachers netted a number near Leicester.[28] But Wycliffite preaching was soon widely sown across England, including the areas of Oxford, London, Bristol, Coventry, Warwickshire, Leicestershire, and East Anglia.[29] The preaching would spread northward in the Midlands as the century wore on, particularly in the western part.

Among the English Wycliffite sermons, 294 were the most frequently copied Wycliffite texts after the Bible itself. These sermon collections date from Oxford during the reign of Richard II and were probably created during the early days of Lollardy. They would have been used to provide the inspiration for more extemporaneous preaching in front of a gathering, or they could have been after-the-fact recordings of what was said.[30] Sermon collections in general were recorded among the clergy of the mendicant orders and the regular and secular clergy, but they were also documented among the Lollards in English, indicating an availability to at least some laity.[31] The sermons affirm the clergy's duty to preach and provide detailed readings of biblical texts, although early ones did not encourage reading the Bible individually, a practice that would grow among Lollards with the publication of the Wycliffite Bible. The sermons also contained occasional attacks on the church, especially on its wealth and on the friars. The sermons discuss the Eucharist, though not frequently, and state that the doctrine of transubstantiation was incorrect. The Wycliffite doctrines that were emphasized in the sermons—an attack on established religion and on the accretion of practices and rituals that the Bible did not institute—would become the focus of Lollard works.

Dissent from Ecclesiastical Authorities

Wycliffitism created an environment that supported dissent from ecclesiastical authority. As was the trend throughout much of Europe, interest in lay piety also arose among people in England. What the average parish saw was the functionally literate priest who was allowed to collect a tithe from parishioners. Anticlericalism was in part a cry for better priests who could inspire and lead the people better, but it was also a cry among other classes against the wealth and landholdings of the church. This demand began in the benefices and pulpits of Oxford students and faculty and spread from there.

Lollardy developed during a time of increasing threats of instability in Britain. There were occasional outbursts against the church, such as an attack on Bury St Edmunds (1327), in which part of the impetus for revolt was the church's taxation of the laity. This uprising lasted the better part of the year, involved armed attacks, and saw several buildings destroyed, a number of monks killed, and the abbey eventually captured. By midcentury, the Black Death (starting in 1348) had caused a substantial shortage of workers, driving up the prices of labor. In response, the Statute of Labourers limited wages to prevent laborers from benefitting from the shortage. Additionally, the poll tax had been imposed to pay for the war with France, and it was levied against every male, regardless of personal income. People also harbored grievances about rents. This situation would come to a head in the 1381 Peasants' Revolt. Alongside the revolt over wages was a religious critique that focused its anticlerical energies on the property of monasteries and the excesses of church spending. Behind the rhetoric of the uprising, the priest John Bull preached a message of divine justice in the reapportionment of money. The uprising culminated in the murder of the archbishop of Canterbury, Simon Sudbury.

The preaching of Wycliffites became associated with this uprising; heresy and sedition were linked in the ecclesiastical mind. The revolt coincided with the ecclesiastical debate over Wycliffe's beliefs on the Eucharist, leading up to his being charged. His *Confessio* (*Confession*), his response to the charges, was dated just weeks before the revolt.[32] Wycliffe commented on the events in his *De blasphemia* (*About Blasphemy*), saying that the peasants should not have been the ones to enact the sentence of beheading the archbishop. "Dominating the whole of the last six chapters of *De blasphemia* is a profound anger, against the clergy, against the king, against the lords, for their collusion in allowing the country to come to a pass such that rebellion of this kind could occur."[33] Wycliffe's disciples would bring his civil dominion ideas to the public, and they would be adapted to fit Lollard concerns. Yet extant treatises from the peasants' uprising do not actually bear any of the traditional Wycliffite points, and this revolt predated Wycliffe's ideas making headway into popular preaching, so the association was anticipatory, not evidenced. Contemporaries such as Nicholas Hereford argued that the preaching of the four orders of friars was actually the proximate cause of the rebellion. During the 1382 Blackfriars Council trial, Wycliffe's followers published vernacular broadsides that were meant to explain their views to the public. Similarly, although the trial was conducted in Latin, John Aston would respond only in English for the benefit of the laity in the gallery, though Archbishop Courtenay kept asking him to respond in Latin.[34] But the Peasants' Revolt in June 1381 meant that those who were investigating Wycliffe linked his ideas to the uprising; although he had been opposed to it, this link was something that with his penchant for rhetoric, he found amusing. What this association reveals is the church had already connected Wycliffe's ideas with Lollardy and social uprisings, even before this relationship had truly been forged.

Ecclesiastic Action

Suppression of the Lollards would focus on identifying people who held Lollard beliefs, owned translations of the Bible into the vernacular or Lollard books, and came into contact with suspected Lollards. In small towns where everyone was in regular contact with one another, this focus would cast a wide net. When a person was suspected of Lollardy, they would be brought before a panel. In the late fourteenth century, inquisitors would develop an internal text, "16 points on which the Bishops Accuse the Lollards."[35] Some of the key elements of Lollardy that the inquisitors would look for included critiques of clerical or church authority (points seven and eight); denial of transubstantiation in the Eucharist (one); rejection of rites of Catholicism, such as prayers to the saints (eleven), pilgrimage (thirteen), reverence of images (fourteen); performance of exorcisms (sixteen); denial that one must tithe, since the church leadership should be bound by poverty (three and nine); belief that all people can preach and teach (seven); and view that the papacy has not been valid since the time of Saint Peter (four). The list identifies the Wycliffite ideas that came to have root in the parishes and how they evolved to focus on the experience and concerns of the faithful.[36]

The 1395 *Twelve Conclusions* provided a strong attack on the church and many of its rites and beliefs. This document summarizing Lollard beliefs was presented to Parliament and nailed to the doors of both Westminster Abbey and St. Paul's Cathedral.[37] Although it contained some statements about sacramental theology, such as talking about how the presence of Christ existed in the consecrated elements, and discussed auricular confession, the document was focused on the lives of the leaders of the church and the church believers. It began with a statement against the fancy rites of the church, stating that they were aggregations of ritual foreign to the scriptural record: "The Roman priesthood is bestowed with signs, rites, and pontifical blessings, of small virtue, nowhere exemplified in holy scripture, because the bishop's ordinal and the New Testament scarcely agree."[38] Concerning typical activities such as pilgrimage, belief in the Trinity, and meditation on the cross, the *Conclusions* noted "that pilgrimages, prayers and offerings made to blind crosses or roods, and to deaf images of wood or stone, are pretty well akin to idolatry and far from alms, and although these be forbidden and imaginary, a book of error to the lay folk, still the customary image of the Trinity is specially abominable."[39] But it was not just the rites of the church that were attacked; even the clergy themselves were viewed as corrupt. The *Conclusions* declared "that the law of continence enjoined on priests, which was first ordained to the prejudice of women, brings sodomy into all the Holy Church."[40] The *Conclusions* called the Eucharist "the pretended miracle" and said that the consecration rites were "the genuine performance of necromancy rather than of sacred theology."[41] Here it argued against the prayers for the dead and railed against the ill-gotten gains of such prayers being offered for sale. The sixth conclusion demanded the separation of church and state, declaring that a person cannot be both a religious authority and a secular leader successfully. It follows that the Lollard focus would take up the clerical reform issues as well as some of the issues of rites and, by proxy, sacramental theology but would avoid some of the issues on predestination, metaphysics, and the operations of grace that Wycliffe had developed. Another text of *37 Conclusions* is mentioned in the *12 Conclusions* and was probably written after Wycliffe's death in 1384 and before the shorter version was publicized in 1395. This version is likely the *Ecclesiae Regimen* (*Government of the Church*) written by John Purvey, a follower and amanuensis of Wycliffe.[42] Similar lists of Lollard beliefs would make their way into the introduction to the Wycliffite Bible and other tracts, helping to mark a growing agreement on the central tenets of the movement and to define it.

The early fifteenth-century Lollards continued to be marked both by rebellion and the threat of rebellion.[43] Leaders and prominent families might be accused and tried for heresy, or they might benefit from friendships, as Sir John Oldcastle benefited from his friendship with King Henry V. He thus managed to escape charges of heresy for several years. He was a Lollard before 1410 and had been accused of heresy; the churches on his properties came under interdict in 1410 for association with Lollardy. He had also written a tract that contained Lollard ideas. In 1413, Oldcastle eventually submitted to the archbishop of Canterbury, having been accused of practicing idolatry and not believing in proper Eucharistic doctrine. He was found guilty of heresy in September 1413, but he escaped and would lead an open rebellion in London and Southampton. In the attack, Oldcastle and his friends had hoped to gather a London crowd to swell their numbers, which never happened because Henry found out about the planned rebellion.

Lollard Literary Culture

The impetus for both creating a lay literate culture so that Lollards could read the Bible and spiritual treatises and wanting more agency in their own religious development was rooted in the same place: desire for people's continued personal religious renewal. And while Lollard beliefs might not have required a literate lay culture, the publication of the Lollard Bible and other texts did encourage literacy among people. Wycliffe believed that a vernacular theology was necessary, and both Lollard and prosecutorial records indicate the existence of numerous Lollard schools.[44] While the exact nature of these schools and their activities is not fully understood, we can make informed guesses about what they included: references in documents indicate that a person would study for at least a year before being considered to understand the Lollard faith. Manuscript copying and dissemination appears connected to these centers as well. In addition, they may have served to either help create literacy or strengthen literacy among adherents.[45] Lollard literary culture would be the foundation of the Lollards' staying power; it was a profoundly written movement despite being centered around preaching. Christ exhorted his followers that the gospel must be "published among all nations," but he also issued a reminder that preaching was important, saying, "When they shall lead you, and deliver you up, take no thought beforehand what ye shall speak, neither do ye premeditate: but whatsoever shall be given you in that hour, that speak ye: for it is not ye that speak, but the Holy Ghost."[46] The most copied Lollard work was the vernacular Bible, or parts thereof. There were also a multitude of sermon collections and other compilations of material that could be used in the composing of sermons.

The area that the Lollards influenced the most was the development of new forms of literature. Broadsides were a popular way of informing the laity of the significance of theological issues and debates; they also became a way of informing the laity of news related to the church and to the Lollard movement. Sermons were written in both Latin and in the vernacular. The Wycliffite sermon cycle was both planned and completed as a whole before it circulated so that the ideas came to fruition by the time they were introduced to the laity.[47] A number of treatises of various sorts arose from avowed Lollard writers, especially shorter tracts. Sir John Clanvowe wrote the prose tract *The Two Ways*, which was a moralizing treatise that took issue with the court life of "eaase and lust." His other work, a Chaucerian dream vision called *The Book of Cupid*, tells of a narrator who witnesses a debate between a cuckoo who despises love and a nightingale who celebrates it. The *Nightingale* is a cypher for the courtly life. The Lollardy here extends beyond the theological to become cultural critique.[48]

The fourteenth century saw a change as English became the more dominant vernacular language of literature and as the audience for literature expanded.[49] Vernacular literature had predominantly been written in French in England, as it was the language of aristocratic audiences. Church preaching was in Latin. But the switch to preaching in English happened when the church took interest in making sure that the laity received instruction in a language they could understand; the Fourth Lateran Council (1215) had promulgated a directive that the laity receive instruction on the substance of their faith, including the six commandments of the church, the seven sacraments, and the Our Father in their own language. This requirement was reinforced in 1281 by decree of Archbishop John Peckham of Canterbury. Preaching in English more often could be construed as an attempt to fulfill this decree to a greater extent.

Even outside Lollard circles, vernacular literature was largely associated with two forms of writing. The first was texts of instruction, largely aimed at priests who used them as a source for educating the laity. These works included sermons, basic instruction manuals on aspects of the faith and sacraments, saints' lives, and texts about miracles. The second was texts about the soul's gradual ascent toward God by orthodox church writers. The latter had begun appearing across Europe in a number of vernacular languages, and Middle English was no exception. Richard Rolle's *Fire of Love* was an exemplar text in this tradition of spiritual growth, as was Julian of Norwich's *Shewings*. These texts took the contemplation of God of the monastic and ascetic life and made it accessible to the laity. The increasing interest in spiritual readings created an opportunity for the writing of Wycliffite texts, partly a result of timing. Alongside these works, another would emerge: the Wycliffite translation of the Bible. The Bible went through two different versions in this period. The first was thought to be the work of Wycliffe and Nicholas Herford. The second translation, overseen by John Purvey, came out between Wycliffe's death and Purvey's condemnation at the Council of Constance. Both versions were officially banned in the 1408 Oxford Convocation, although they continued to circulate. These Bibles gave the laity access to the words of Scripture and encouraged thoughtful reading of biblical stories outside the realm of clerical exegesis.

Lollardy also appears in much of the literature of the time, such as William Langland's *Piers Plowman*. But one of perhaps the best-known authors associated with Lollardy, Margery Kempe, was not a Lollard at all: in her *Book of Margery Kempe*, the rather shrewd and demanding housewife and brewer goes in search of spiritual development, a quest that will take her to a number of pilgrimage spots, such as Jerusalem, as well as to local English shrines and clergy. Throughout her travels in England, clergy repeatedly accuse her of Lollardy because of her knowledge of Scripture and her desire for immediate experience of the divine. *The Book of Margery Kempe* provides a look at what it meant to be accused of Lollardy and how that charge could be levied for power against laity. But there were large gaps between the production of Lollard treatises, the writings of individuals (whether Lollard or not) such as Margery Kempe, and outward rebellions. It also shows just how treacherous things could be for anyone seeking spiritual development or stating their own views on religious matters at that time. And the development of English writings evidenced a movement that the Lollards helped promote but that was also beyond their own circles of influence.

Lasting Impact

Wycliffite ideas were an intellectual heresy that originally affected the university world, where the impact of Wycliffe's thought was somewhat circumscribed. But the connection between the universities and the higher levels of church leadership meant that regardless of the theological impact, there was a practical impact on the church leadership and the laity as the ideas spread within parishes. But more importantly, aside from Wycliffe's thoughts on consubstantiation, very little was truly heretical—rather, Lollardy was a reform movement and would presage the reform movements that would continue to gain momentum. It was perhaps in part because of this steady swell of reforming sentiment that wouldn't be tamped down that the Lollard movement "never died and never joined the mainstream: the mainstream joined it, with the advent of Lutheranism, and hijacked its historiography."[50] Like so many other heresies in this book, the central kernel of the issue is the laity's fervor for having something with significance, taking charge of its spiritual development, and wanting a clergy that met the expectations of the people it served. Lay interest in religion was growing, and in England, it particularly took the forms of affective theology, negative theology, and interest in spiritual development. Wycliffite theology encouraged a number of activities—such as an emphasis on individuals reading the Bible—that overlapped with this interest.

Identifying Wycliffe's beliefs as a heresy actually occurred in multiple stages, first as intellectual beliefs, and then as popular beliefs. Arguably, variations in university thought were more tolerable than were those in the parish. But a number of academics, including St. Thomas Aquinas, Peter Abelard, Meister Eckhart, Siger of Brabant, Wycliffe, and later, Hus, would come under condemnation at one point or another. Most would be rehabilitated; straying thoughts were not unheard of within academic settings. The one counterexample we've seen before Wycliffe is Meister Eckhart, and it was his vernacular works that got him in trouble. It has been noted that for the most part, academics whose ideas were questioned were privileged and not subjected to the full weight of ecclesiastical law like the average person was.[51]

Wycliffe's heretical ideas seem to have started as the unintended consequences of the philosophical stances that he took and progressed to his theological views, especially those concerning grace and the sacraments. What we see in the Lollards is how the popular movement could adapt these ideas to meet their interests and needs. At heart, both heresies shared a frustration with the clergy and their lack of ability to meet the needs of the laity. What this frustration would turn into for the popular movement was a much wider condemnation of ritual and the trappings of empty practices and superstition. In large part, Wycliffe's impact was due to the influence of other forces, such as the mendicant orders and monastics, which in his mind both sowed the seeds of anticlericalism and also charged him with anticlericalism. One of the lasting impacts on Wycliffe's thought will be continued in the next chapter, as it was his influence on Hus that would continue the fomentation outside of England. Wycliffe's legacy in Bohemia would be in its ability to bring together disparate ideas into a new formulation of a system.[52] Another of the lasting impacts of Lollardy is that it was a heresy that didn't get fully suppressed. Because it was so interested in reforming the church, it felt no impetus to remove itself from the organization, and Lollards were able to "pass" as Christians, going to church regularly and participating as needed while studying their Bibles and Lollard tracts in small, discrete groups. These ideas would continue to simmer and would eventually flare up again in the Reformation in England.

CHAPTER 8

The Hussites
The Sociopolitical Nexus of Heresy

As we move from the Wycliffites to Jan Hus, we sweep across the majority of Europe's geography. And in so doing, we move into a world that was socially and politically different from the worlds previously investigated. Like Languedoc and the Waldensian Alps, which had not yet developed the same feudalist history or the same growth of cities as the rest of Europe, Bohemia was behind much of Europe. It was the borderlands, on the edge of Roman Catholicism next to the Slavic lands of Eastern Orthodoxy. As towns developed and a burgher class amassed wealth and started to acquire education and mobility, Italy saw the start of social turmoil as early as the twelfth century, and certainly such tensions were common by the thirteenth century. In Flanders, which had a similarly developed network of trades, guilds, and merchants, tensions would begin in the thirteenth and early fourteenth centuries. France followed suit, especially in the north, and England had contended with uprisings such as the Peasants' Revolt in 1381. Bohemia was slower to urbanize than Western Europe, but it was also incredibly wealthy by the start of the fifteenth century, due to trade routes that passed through Prague. As in parts of Western Europe, hatred would be directed against the church for being the wealthiest landholders. Even as challenges to feudalism were beginning to break up large feudal estates, the church kept accumulating more and more land—it held at least one-quarter and maybe as much as one-third of all the land in Bohemia.[1] As such, any antifeudal revolution was due to have at least some religious aspects to it.

Jan Hus lived at a time when parts of Europe such as Italy were beginning to move from the Middle Ages to the Renaissance, although Bohemia was still developing a bourgeoisie. The legacy of Hus as a thinker and reformer, and even the impact of his being burned at the stake, underscores a complex series of allied movements that were not cohesive; because they were working in social, political, and theological arenas, there were more chances for disagreement among coreligionists. Ultimately, the movement would be partly about theology, partly about ethnicity, and partly about power and authority. The story of Hus's heresy has every bit as much to do with early attempts at nationalism as it does with heterodoxy. Although Jan Hus was condemned as a heretic, there are two ways in which this assessment is unjust: he was the name that would become associated with reform, but it was a reform that began before him and outlasted him, and he was a moderate voice in comparison to many of the voices within the Czech Reformation. In many ways, the story of Jan Hus is a continuation of the Wycliffite story, adapted to the new context of Bohemia, but one that acknowledges the distinction between being reform-minded and wanting to wholesale reject church teachings. That rejection was never Hus's goal.

The Hussite movement began among clergy associated with Charles University in Prague, spread to the laity as well as the clergy, and became steeped with the ideas of Wycliffe from England. Although Hus arguably did not intend to start a movement, he proved to be the one with both the ideas and the timing to bring together a campaign that had been simmering for decades before he became its spokesperson. The movement would continue to be organized by his followers after his arrest in 1414 by King Sigismund and death at the Council of Constance in 1415. Popular disturbances were to follow; these were largely aimed against the clergy, whom the public thought criminally responsible for his death. Just as the Wycliffite heresy affected both politics and especially economic situations, the Hussite revolution was connected to Bohemian cultural identity and the politics of localized lords against German leaders. In fact, Hus was a relatively moderate reforming cleric who never intended to spark the movement that was created in the wake of his death—viewed as a martyrdom by his followers—and during his life he never advocated for the break from the institutional church that many of them later did (although he also did not speak out against reform-minded clergy who advocated extreme positions). Religiously, the Hussite reform movement had a variety of foci, though the most preached-about would come to be the issues of frequent communion and communion under both species.[2]

Bohemian Reform before Hus

Navigating the complex ethnic divisions within Prague, each of these early reformers spoke to a different segment of the capital city's population, and together they formed a strong foundation for the preaching and teaching of Hus and the reform movement to come after him. Czech society consisted of a nobility of German, Moravian, and Bohemian ethnicities, and Bohemia was ruled by a king who, during the time of Charles IV, was also Holy Roman Emperor. This nexus of political alliance and leadership created a multilayered social system within the capital. But there were still significant ethnic divisions within the realm that would bubble to the surface from time to time, especially between German and Bohemian nobility. These reform movements primarily occurred within established parishes in Prague but would also come to be connected to Charles University, which had been established by Charles IV in 1348, near the start of his reign. It was the first university in the Holy Roman Empire and educated both clergy and others, with a number of different ethnic groups represented.

The consolidation of power had been the main focus of the monarchy in the century before Hus. This consolidation of power and strengthening of the monarchy was perhaps most effective in uniting the monarchy with some church institutions. The monarchy had control over church lands, and royal towns as well as estates were held as fiefs of the crown.[3] But the true power was held by the high court, which was staffed by the baronial families in a rotating fashion and met four times a year. This court was the law over all landholders and members of the upper nobility (such as knights and barons). Politically, King Wenceslas IV (1378–1419) was not as effective a leader and did not administer the kingdom as well as his father, Charles, and his relative weakness allowed room for dissent to grow in ways that would have political and religious impacts. Thus, the momentum behind consolidation of power was losing steam.

Conrad Waldhauser (ca. 1326–69) was an Austrian itinerant preacher brought to Prague by King Charles IV in 1363. Charles was interested in fostering stronger ties to the papacy in France and invited the preacher, whom he had heard when in Vienna, back to Prague. From almost the moment Waldhauser set foot in his parish in Litoměřice, his sermons drew crowds large enough that the congregation outgrew the size of his church. Preaching in German, his sermons were primarily attended by the German nobility of Prague. One of his foci was an end to clerical abuses, so he launched a series of attacks on the clergy's excess in lifestyle and misbehavior and on mendicant practices such as simony; these critiques of clergy excess sometimes implicated the lives of his noble listeners as well. His attacks were direct and focused on their lifestyles, such as when he described the mendicants as "loving dances and attractive women, hunting with greyhounds and falcons, thereby arousing pride, sleeping long and delighting in sloth ... sleeping in the forenoon and then till midnight drinking wine and beer, gambling, and keeping impure women."[4] He believed clerical abuses could not be eliminated without cleaning up nobles' vices as well.

Shortly after Waldhauser arrived, the mendicant orders lodged a complaint with the archbishop about his preaching against the lifestyles of the mendicants, which would be resolved in his favor. He continued his preaching on these issues in Prague, although he moved to the Church of the Virgin Mary of Týn, an influential parish that would come to be one center of reform movements in Prague. He had a relatively simple message: the clergy needed to reform itself to return to a sense of apostolic simplicity and purity. His message held up the apostolic and scriptural witness as the standard for how the leaders of the church were to conduct themselves. He was unpopular among the mendicant clergy, who continued attacking him throughout his life, but a growing group of people began paying attention to his messages of clergy reform, and the seed was planted. He also made connections with the university students, who asked him to compile his sermons for them; he did so in the collection *Postilla studentium sanctae Pragensis universitatis* (*Commentary of the Holy Students of Prague University*). Although he preached in German, copies of this collection would soon circulate in Czech as well, expanding the scope of his influence within Prague.[5]

John Milíč of Kroměříž (ca. 1320–74) would carry on the preaching momentum of Waldhauser. He was from Moravia, which lay east of Bohemia, and was an admirer of Waldhauser. Milíč was interested in both clerical reform and the reform of women. He likely studied at the cathedral school (as opposed to a university) and began his clerical career in the court chancery and at St. Vitus Cathedral before moving to Prague to preach. He preached in both Czech and Latin and emphasized the same issues that his mentor, Waldhauser, had. A new emphasis in the thought of Milíč was a focus on the antichrist; he preached to Charles IV that he, the emperor, was the antichrist and was promptly arrested. When in Rome, he likewise stood before church leaders, and later the pope, and preached similarly. Again, he was arrested. He would learn to interpret the notion of the antichrist metaphorically after that. Despite this setback, he preached synodal sermons on at least three occasions at the request of the archbishop, showing he was respected as a preacher among clerics.

Milíč was noted for practicing what he preached; in the record of his life, it was noted that he lived modestly, provided what he could for people—paper and books for students, food for the hungry, alms for the poor—and even paid off debts to madams so prostitutes could leave their brothels.[6] He had a knack for rehabilitating former prostitutes and took ownership of several brothels in the prostitute district of Prague. There, he created apostolic communities for reformed women. Charles IV even granted him one of the largest brothels, named Benátky (Venice). Taking inspiration from the lives of beguines, Milíč created a community unto itself named Jerusalem, with a school, chapel, rooms for the women to live, and work for them to do. They spent their days in simple work and in prayer, and religious brethren came to provide spiritual direction and preaching to the women. In 1373, a group of clergy attacked Milíč, and he had to appear at the papal court to defend himself. They accused the women of Jerusalem of being beguines. His writings mention "the free preaching of the Word of God, the confiscation of the great properties of priests and monks, a requirement for the poverty of priests and monks, and the punishment of public and mortal sins."[7] At Jerusalem, the women were allowed weekly or more frequent reception of the elements at communion, foreshadowing the Utraquist position. Milíč died in jail, and Jerusalem was dismantled. The legacy of Milíč's work was that it foreshadowed the main elements of the *Four Articles of Prague*.

The third and final reformer was a disciple of Milíč named Matěj (Matthew) of Janov (ca. 1340–94). He was both an intellectual and a cathedral canon as well as a student of Milíč for a while and may have also served as a transcriber of his sermons. Sometime in his thirties, Janov enrolled at the University of Paris and first received his license and then a master of liberal arts. He desired a return to the ideals of the primitive church, where worship and daily life would be influenced by what Scripture recorded of the early church and would be stripped of all the added influences and pomp that had accrued over the last millennium and a half. Toward this end, he wrote the prophetic treatise *The Rules of the Old and New Testament*, whose first two books provided four rules from the Old Testament and eight from the New

Testament. Like the others before him, he would say he respected the church but also that it needed to reform. He saw that the last two centuries of the church had secularized it, and he compared the church of his day to the whore of Babylon with the scarlet serpent. His stated purpose in writing this treatise was to rekindle the zeal for living the Christian life among the laity and to help people distinguish between "correct and incorrect (or false) Christianity."[8] In the five surviving books of his treatise, we see the Bible as the central focus of his writing and how he saw it directing the church's leadership and lay activities, all of which were guiding a wide host of church authorities, medieval mystics, and Polish theologians, in addition to thinkers from the University of Prague.[9] The third book provided aids for the reader to discern between true and false spirits among preachers and doctors, and the fourth and fifth books probed the idea of frequent communion.

In 1388, the Prague Synod pronounced that the laity should not receive communion more frequently than once a month. In 1389 and 1392, Janov would be summoned to the archbishop's court and required to recant his views on frequent communion. He was clearly pained by the condition of the church, especially the papal schism and the clergy he saw not fulfilling their duties. He held up Milíč as a model, writing a *Narratio de Milicio (History of Milíč)*, a life of his mentor. Janov wanted frequent communion, seeing it as a potent force to help fight against some of the hypocrisy in the church. He thought one way to combat it was to harness the increased piety of the laity, and frequent communion was often prescribed as a way to help improve the moral quality of the members of the church and to help cure social ills.[10] He would never officially face charges, but in 1388–89, university lawyers and theologians criticized him for his ideas about frequent communion. In 1391, some of those close to Janov built a new chapel that could hold several thousand people and would become the center of the reform movement in Prague, called Bethlehem Chapel. The name was meant to be evocative of two things. First, it suggested the simplicity of the primitive church, the ideal that ran like a thread through Czech reformers. Second, it also alluded to Herod's massacre of the innocents, suggesting the movement saw itself as an innocent victim of political attack.

Wycliffe's Writings in Prague

Wycliffe's writings appeared in Bohemia prior to the 1390s and were known to at least a few in the university by then. Hus would be the first to make full use of Wycliffe's ideas in both teaching and preaching, but the conversations about them had started before Hus made his way to the university. By the early fifteenth century, they were being more widely discussed in the University of Prague. Both Wycliffe's early philosophical work as well as his later political and antiecclesiastical works found eager readers within the university. Students went abroad to study at Oxford, bringing back Wycliffe's ideas and copies of his works. "Master Jan Hus, with his own hand, had copied Wycliffe's philosophical treatises in 1398. This extant autograph—including copies of the treatises *De materia et forma, De tempore, De ideis,* and *De universalibus* (*On Matter and Form, On Time, On Ideas,* and *On Unversals*)—stands symbolically at the start of the Prague dispute about Wycliffe and universals, which soon afterwards erupted at the university."[11] While these philosophical works only somewhat influenced Hus's ideas about the Eucharist, they would more significantly influence others who were part of the Bohemian Reformation.

Hus and His Ideas

Jan Hus was a priest committed to reform within the church and a moderate voice among the variety of voices within the Czech Reformation. He sought not merely a reform of church institutions but also a reform of individuals' lives within the church and their relationship to the church. It would be both his connection to the Bohemian university life and his skills as a popular preacher that allowed his message to have lasting impact after his death—his followers would continue and popularize the revolution. Originally from a small village, Hus was enrolled at Charles University and received his master of arts in 1396; he began teaching that year and was known as a great teacher whose students were devoted to him. In 1400, he decided to enter the priesthood to open further career opportunities. During the formation process, he was required to meditate on the Bible, and this reflective practice had a profound impact on his theological thinking. He would seek to combine his university learning and the Scriptures and to apply these tools to the situations of his congregants.

Hus worked tirelessly as a priest, and in 1402, he would become the personal confessor to Queen Sophie of Bohemia, the wife of King Charles IV, and the primary voice heard at Bethlehem Chapel. His appeal ran deep with a wide swath of people in Prague, from royalty and nobility to students and average workers. Those who heard him preach and administer the sacraments said that he had a strong commitment to the daily life of believers and to serving the people through preaching and administering sacraments.

When Hus began teaching at Charles University, it was the premier university of Eastern Europe and boasted faculty from all over Europe. Within theology, there was a struggle taking shape between the Germans, who favored nominalism, and the Czech faculty, who favored the realism of Wycliffe. The Germans were depicted as being resistant to church reform and holding on to traditions, whereas the Czech faculty were seen as being reform-minded. Wycliffe's works had reached Prague before Hus had entered the university, and Hus read them; he was most impressed with Wycliffe's ideas on clerical poverty and reform. King Charles IV had attempted church reform in response to the church's ownership of so much of the land in the kingdom, so these attitudes coalesced well with the native Prague reform party. Hus would take up the banner of integrating the most promising of Wycliffe's ideas into Czech theology, especially as it related to church reform.

At Bethlehem Chapel, sermons were preached in Czech, and it became known as a center of the church reform movement. Many of Hus's ideas followed from the question of what it meant to follow Christ, in keeping with the contemporary spiritual interest concerning "the imitation of Christ." Hus was particularly interested in what was termed *apostolic faith*. By this term, Hus meant the faith of the early church believers, before the time of Constantine. He saw the first three centuries of the church as an ideal time in which church power had not yet become an institutional power. Rather, the strength of the church's belief and its individual members were what kept the early church strong. In addition to providing examples of the church's history, Hus had an ability to antagonize opponents based on the rhetoric he used against them from the pulpit. At times, he even threatened church institutions when he questioned historical traditions or the idea of papal inerrancy.

Hus defined the church in such a way as to emphasize the tasks that he thought central to the Christian life. He said that all who were baptized from a young age were members of the church, although he separated them into two categories: the sheep, who followed the rule of Christ and were chosen for salvation, and the goats, who were not faithful to the way of Christ and were foreknown by God to be damned. He tempered his double predestination by saying that a person's status could not be known by humans, only by God. This position was similar to Wycliffe's, but Hus said that others could infer the relative status of someone based on the fruits of their actions.[12] Like Wycliffe, Hus emphasized that the worthiness of clergy behavior should be reflected in their ability to do their jobs. He encouraged people to consider only those priests who led holy lives as worthy; by this idea, he meant that they should forbear pomp, luxurious lives, and the accumulation of benefices. "Hus accused the Czech priesthood of frequently living in open fornication, practicing concubinage, and housing women in their rectories openly, all the while lying and hypocritically presenting them as sisters or other close relatives."[13] He would accuse bishops and the pope of similar sexual impropriety as well. Hus stated that people should admonish wayward priests and that if they did not accept correction, the people should consider it unnecessary to follow their leadership.[14]

Hus's spirituality was traditionally Catholic. He emphasized the grace of God as prior to everything in bringing the person to God and in making their efforts to come nearer to God efficaciously. He emphasized the interior working of God to amend the purposes of people and to make them know and ultimately love God. He encouraged the preaching of the word of God to help bring people to faith through their reason. He advocated a social responsibility of almsgiving, suggesting that people give their money to the poor and needy rather than to clergy who were wealthy.[15] Hus challenged some of the traditions of the church that paid reverence to various clergy, from the pope downward, where people would genuflect to them or even kiss their feet. Hus's general concern was that the affluence of many in the church did not reflect its primitive basis and thus showed it straying from its true mission. During the final years of Charles IV's reign, Prague saw a significant increase in urban poverty, increasing tensions among groups in the city and ultimately helping the Hussite reform movement.[16] Wealth bought people opportunities that meant their faith could be tepid. Other aspects of opulence that came under Hus's attack included elaborate singing and the decorative arts that made church services and buildings stand out—vestments, chalices and patens, bells, organs, and statues and paintings. Hus claimed that these elements distracted people from the message of God. Hus's attacks on church decorations, though, were a far cry from Wycliffe's and the Lollards' excoriation of idolatry.

Hus also attempted to separate the basis for sovereign power in the secular and ecclesiastical realms. Archbishops and other high-ranking officials held considerable civic power. The king had combined some of his power and courts with ecclesiastical ones. This move led to the church and monarchial power serving jointly in Bohemia. Hus objected to the pope having temporal power over all within Christianity's realm. He thought the authority of the church should be limited to its spiritual vocation and that it did not have true political or economic authority. Hus was idealistic enough to believe that if he could argue his theological case, churchmen would voluntarily reform themselves. Such did not prove to be the case. Failing that, Hus then suggested that the king and nobles deprive the church of secular powers and dominion. The result would be that the secular leaders would be in charge of the church. At the Council of Constance, this position would put Hus under fire from ecclesiastics. At the heart of Hus's ideas was the inspiration that the laity could follow the example of the apostolic church, regardless of whether the ecclesiastical hierarchy followed that example. Such beliefs had appeared in other places before, from the beguines of the Low Countries to the Petrobrusians and the Franciscan influence on the laity in Italy.

Hus espoused a number of social changes that would impact the way people participated in the church as well. He advocated for Czech and German translations of the Bible, though the institutional church opposed such moves. Hus was not the first to advocate such things for Bohemia. In fact, the lectionary, a selection of passages from the Bible that comprised the readings in church offices, had been translated into Czech for monastic women who did not know Latin. A partial translation of the Bible into German had been commissioned by a wealthy patron in 1381, resulting in an incomplete translation.[17] Similar to other groups, making translations of the Scriptures available so that the laity could read them without needing the priests to mediate them was considered a challenge to church authority. Hus published a copy of the New Testament, Wisdom Literature, and Psalms in 1406.

The Making of a Revolution

Tensions between the Germans and Bohemians would continue to increase, eventually erupting in a series of German attempts to get Czech theologians condemned. Between 1403 and 1408, German academics launched multiple efforts to limit the influence of the Czech masters in the university. A German master presented forty-five articles from Wycliffe at the cathedral chapter in Prague to show the Czech masters were actively dabbling in known heresies; the German faculty pointed out that Wycliffe was condemned by Pope Gregory XI and called his modern-day supporters heretics. In 1408, the accusations increased, and some Czech theologians were accused of specifically teaching Wycliffe's ideas on the Eucharist (consubstantiation instead of the official doctrine of transubstantiation). Two Czech faculty fled to Italy in the wake of this attack, as charges were also filed against them in the court of Gregory XII. The archbishop of Prague asked the Czech masters—all sixty of them—to condemn the propositions in the forty-five articles, but Hus and others refused to, assuming this request was politically motivated. Hus only partly embraced Wycliffe; there were some parts he agreed with, such as the idea that everything should be rooted in reading and understanding Scripture and that Scripture should be accessible to all believers literate enough to read it by being available in the vernacular. But there were other aspects that Hus didn't agree with. He didn't believe in Wycliffe's idea of consubstantiation. He didn't object to the cries that both the bread and wine should be available to the congregation, but he did not offer the Eucharist under both species to his own congregants.

In 1409, the Council of Pisa met with the express goal of ending the Great Schism. The tensions between the German and Bohemian theologians boiled over to this council, along with political lines between the archbishop and the king and exacerbating tensions within the university. The Council of Pisa wasn't a success in that it added a third pope and further increased the fault lines within the church leadership. But after a series of negotiations, the Czech theologians reached a bargain with King Wenceslas that would see him retain control over some local political issues and the voting within the university change so as to favor the Czech faculty.

The change in voting priority gave Bohemia three votes in Charles University's affairs to the German faculty's one vote, leading to a mass exodus of non-Czech masters and students. At stake had been the national character of the university; dominated by German faculty, its governance was out of line with Czech culture. When King Wenceslas gave the Czech faculty more votes, an estimated 5,000–20,000 people left. Overnight, Charles University became a national university rather than one that boasted of scholars from throughout central and eastern Europe. The exodus had two unforeseen consequences. First, the theological variety of the university became much more limited, and Hus's views took central stage. Second, as masters left for other parts of

Europe, Hus's views, and their affinity with Wycliffe, were discussed outside of Prague, often critically. Hus would become university rector later that year. With the position, he had enough visibility to essentially become the de facto figurehead of the reform movement.

Local politics would continue to center around the issue of Wycliffe at the university. Archbishop Zbyněk warned the Pisan pope, Alexander V, about Wycliffite ideas filtering into Charles University. In response, he sent a bull in 1409 condemning the forty-five articles, outlawing preaching in chapels, and supporting the archbishop's attempts to suppress Wycliffe's ideas. After receiving this response, Zbyněk launched a campaign to round up all extant copies of Wycliffe's works. He burned over 200 on a pyre in one day in July 1410. Zbyněk then excommunicated Hus that same year. The pope followed suit in February of the following year. Hus was invited to speak to the pope in Rome but refused, questioning if he would be safe. In response to the pope's communication, large-scale protests erupted across the city, and the archbishop fled, only to die soon after.

The early 1410s were crucial years that saw the faculty of the university becoming a less potent force in the reform movement, as more of the impetus shifted to the work being done in Bethlehem Chapel and other preaching sites around the city. In 1412, the pope placed Prague under interdict because of Hus's continued presence there. This move meant that the residents of the city had been cut off from the saving grace of receiving the sacraments, and those who might die in that time would be prohibited from receiving last rights, putting their souls in jeopardy. Hus was once again excommunicated. To spare the residents of the city from being under interdict, he left to visit various friends who held properties in the surrounding countryside. During this time, he wrote *De ecclesia* (*On the Church*), which rejected the papal claim of divine origins of its office and therefore claimed that the papacy was dispensable. Although strongly influenced by the ideas of Wycliffe, Hus's views were unique to the Bohemian situation and showed marked divergences from Wycliffe. Hus began with the concept of the congregation—a group of people who sought to live under the rule of Christ. His ecclesiology focused on intentional communities rather than structures handed down by a centralized church. This focus would be the first truly heretical belief of his. Then he wrote *On Simony* about the sale of indulgences, which critiqued the sale of offices, sacraments, and properties belonging to the church and argued that a secular management would have been better stewards of the church's and laity's resources.

Hus also called for the participation of women in Bohemian society and church affairs. In his 1412 tract, "Recognizing the True Way to Salvation," which is known by the nickname "The Daughter," he very strikingly made the argument that women, just like men, were created in the image of God. Such a move bolstered support for Hus, particularly among women. This support was to be short-lived, for although women increasingly used Hus's ideas to take more public power, by 1421 these gains had been overturned by men reasserting their masculine privilege.[18] Hus also compared Milíč, Waldhauser, and Janov to Old Testament prophets.[19] He saw them as precursors of himself, and this idea was picked up by other writers during the Bohemian Reformation. In this way, he saw his work as a continuation of the preaching traditions of Bohemia. Another point from previous clerics that Hus discussed was the idea of communion under both species for the laity. This position, called utraquism (from the Latin phrase *sub utraque specie*, "under both forms"), would be formally explicated by Hus's colleague Jacob of Mies in 1414. He upheld the idea that communion should not merely be offered to the laity in the form of bread, as was the standard; rather, the chalice should be offered as well. He stated that it was arbitrary for the church to allow clergy to commune under both the form of bread and wine and to not allow the laity to. The Czech liturgy, in the years after Hus, would allow communion under both forms.

The Condemnation and Death of Hus

Even with Hus living outside of the city, Prague continued to be steeped in controversy. The issue of the lay chalice would continue to dominate theological discussions for years to come. In 1414, Hus was summoned to the Council of Constance. The council was, in truth, preoccupied with the issue of popes and sorting out its own leadership. Hus arrived, thinking he'd have center stage to explain his theology, but that was not to be the case. A group of Paris scholars, including Jean Gerson, sought to have Hus arrested as a Wycliffite.

Among the thirty tenets that Hus was condemned on are a number that speak to predestination and the ability of clergy, bishops, or the pope to do their jobs in accordance with their offices. Hus's works contained statements that predestination trumped how a person chose to live, even saying that "the grace of predestination is a chain by which the body of the Church and any member of it are joined insolubly to Christ the Head."[20] Hus was also condemned for believing that the pope was not the head of the Roman

Catholic Church (tenet 10) and that character traits were all that mattered in church leadership, not whether someone had been appointed according to an apostolic succession (tenet 12). The latter implied that the long-held idea of *imitatio Christi*—trying to act like Christ—was sufficient to receive spiritual power to lead the church, rather than the set rules of ecclesiastical appointments. Hus similarly stated that any priests who were under the stain of sin were inefficacious in their roles as clergy (tenet 8), a reiteration of the early church Donatist heresy. And he was condemned for having stated that "the condemnation of the forty-five articles of John Wyclif made by the doctors is irrational and wicked and badly made; the cause alleged by them has been feigned, namely, for the reason that 'no one of them is a Catholic but anyone of them is either heretical, erroneous, or scandalous.'"[21] To this end, Hus insisted that he and others were the true arbiters of the church's doctrine, not the people who inhabited its ecclesiastical offices.

After seven months' imprisonment and interrogation, Hus still did not concur that his ideas were heretical and refused to submit to correction. For his part, when investigated by the council, he insisted that he did not currently, nor had he in the past, held any of the condemned Wycliffite positions.[22] What the council sought was textual linkage to prove that Hus's texts contained Wycliffe's ideas. Some went so far as to declare that his work was nothing more than extractions from Wycliffe. Scholars have now determined that Hus's *De ecclesia* contained 1,602 borrowed lines from Wycliffe's *De ecclesia*—which amounted to 23 percent of the text.[23] Hus was presented with thirty articles that he should answer to. His contemporary, Peter of Mladoňovice, left an account of the examination:

> The above-named Master Jon Hus in the month of June of the year of the Lord 1410, as well as before and after, preaching to the people congregated in a certain chapel of Bethlehem and in various other places of the city of Prague, at various times contrived, taught, and disputed about many errors and heresies both from the books of the late John Wyclif and from his own impudence and craftiness, defending them as far as he was able. [A]bove all, he held the error hereafter stated, that after the consecration the host on the altar remains material bread. To that charge they produced as witnesses doctors, prelates, pastors, etc. as it is stated in the said testimony.[24]

What becomes obvious from the records of the examination is that the examiners had brought many people to testify to the accuracy of the charges and to present evidence against Hus. His responses were defiant. He told the investigators that he would be judged by God. Other times, he claimed he was unable to answer for fear of his safety.[25] This statement may have been true; Hus had been living in protective exile. Sometimes Hus was brought face-to-face with articles from Wycliffe and interpreted them in accordance with church fathers. He also denied the teaching of Wycliffe that wealth of the clergy was against Christ's teaching. In the end, the council found Hus guilty of being "a disciple, not of Christ, but of the arch heretic, John Wyclif."[26]

The ending of Peter's text is very telling about the worries that the authorities had regarding the execution of John Hus. It began by narrating the way in which Hus died:

> When the executioners at once lit [the fire], the Master immediately began to sing in a loud voice, at first "Christ, Thou son of the living God, have mercy upon us," and secondly, "Christ, Thou son of the living God, have mercy upon me," and in the third place, "Thou Who are born of Mary the Virgin." And when he began to sing the third time, the wind blew the flame into his face. And thus praying within himself and moving his lips and the head, he expired in the Lord.[27]

In Peter's text, Hus's death looks like that of a typical martyr's: going to the Lord singing hymns and uttering prayers. What Peter records next suggests that Hus was in the right and that the executioners were brutes:

> When the wood of those bundles and ropes were consumed, but the remains of the body still stood in those chains, hanging by the neck, the executioners pulled the charred body, along with the stake, down to the ground and burned them further by adding wood from the third wagon to the fire. And walking, they broke the bones with clubs so that they would be incinerated more quickly. And finding the head, they broke it into pieces with the clubs again and again and threw it into the fire. and when they found his heart among the intestines, they sharpened a club like a spit, and, impaling it on its end, they took particular [care] to roast and consume it, piercing it

with spears until finally the whole mass was turned to ashes. And . . .
the executioners threw the clothing into the fire along with the shoes,
saying, "So that the Czechs would not regard it as relics; we will pay
you money for it." Which they did.[28]

Hus's ashes were then dumped in the river (as were Wycliffe's after exhumation and burning). Clearly, this annihilation was overkill, but it signified a concern at the council that Hus had too many followers, ones that would be willing to turn him into a martyred saint, and any physical remains could be venerated as the physical remains of their leader. Peter's record makes Hus out to be quite Christlike; his death is also meant to recall the crucifixion scene. Like the two thieves who died next to Christ, Hus had his legs broken with truncheons. His side was pierced (though his executioners then became cannibalistic). And whereas the Romans cast dice for Christ's clothes, they bought Hus's clothes so that they could be consigned to the fire. Nothing remains of the body, as was the case after Christ's ascension. Compared to many of the descriptions of heretical deaths, Hus's attitude toward death is serene, like that of so many Christian martyrs.

In Prague, the situation would not be serene. On the one hand, the movement was searching for its next leaders. Hus had been a mild voice compared to many of the reformers, but he was also a voice of unity. The movement also needed to decide how the work in the parishes, the work within the university, and the political arm of the movement would all coordinate. And the issue of the lay chalice would come to dominate the movement after Hus. A Hussite league would be formed to protect Hus's followers; 452 local nobles would sign a letter protesting the Council of Constance's decisions; and the university theologians and lawyers would help defend these nobles. Hus had become a martyr and a rallying point for the reform movement.

The Revolution after Hus

In the wake of his condemnation and death, Hus was upheld as a martyr by his followers, whose ideas would grow more radical than his own. He was memorialized by "popular songs, hymns, hagiographic 'lives', and graphic images."[29] The Hussite heresy would take on multiple shapes. There were the actual ideas and preaching of Jan Hus and the transformation of them by his followers, who gave them greater political and theological shape in the generation after his execution.

Even though after his death, Hus's place was among those most revered by the Czech people, he still had some detractors during and after his life. They were both homebred from within Bohemia and from other places in Europe that sent preaching missions to help correct and redirect the Bohemian church. The Hussite heresy was chronicled by Aeneas Sylvius, a humanist papal diplomat. As he catalogued the errors of the Hussites, he blamed the theologians, saying that errors only come through them.[30] His would be the standard account of the Hussite heresy, composed in 1458:[31] Sylvius claimed that it was founded on the Wycliffite movement. The heresy entered Bohemia through the teaching of a student named Nicholas, and other heresies filtered in through Germany. John Hus and Jerome of Prague, who was martyred a year after Hus, preached this new teaching until they were condemned. Jan Žižka, who would be associated with the Taborites (part of the Hussite reform in the generations after Hus), was portrayed by Sylvius as a man of violence. Sylvius reported that Žižka attacked churches, expelled monks from their homes, and was involved in the destruction of religious artifacts and other iconoclastic activities. The worst of these claims was that Žižka herded Catholics into churches and burned the buildings and people. The portrait that Sylvius developed was one in which Žižka was relentless and merciless, an archvillain. At his death, his followers were nicknamed "the Orphans" by Sylvius in his chronicle. The Hussite heresy was also linked to nationalism, Sylvius noted. At a time when national sentiment was increasing, he said that nationalism fanned the flames of heresy and led people astray. He also noted other causes of the rise of heresy, including the growing number of heretics among the university masters and an increasing isolation of the kingdom.[32]

In the span of a few years, the Hussites would have to reorganize and rededicate itself to a new and clearer mission as it passed on its leadership to new people. The nobility would come to unite themselves; Hus's condemnation in 1415 was the spark that began to bring them together. The Hussite nobility created a group of lords who pledged to uphold Hus's ideals, including free preaching of the gospel and obedience only to those bishops who lived in accordance with the Bible. The social landscape of Bohemia not only split along lines of town and country, but the city of Prague also stood out as distinct from other cities and towns. From the time the nobles signed the 1415 protest letter, it was clear there was support from the nobility as well as the populace. Heresy was occasionally about money, as in the case of the Templars, but it was more often about the papacy exerting control rather than about those with money trying to counteract ecclesiastical power. When Wenceslas IV died, in 1419, the power issues came to a head in the temporal realm as well. Hussite Bohemia opposed the legal heir, King Sigismund of Luxembourg.

Yet following Hus's death, the movement would fracture into several groups. The lasting effects would be a series of Hussite wars, which crested and receded in waves for the next half century. Following Hus's martyrdom, his followers drew up the *Four Articles of Prague*, which established their main demands. These commands included reception of the Eucharist under both forms by the laity, the freedom of preaching, the curtailment of clerical wealth, and the punishment of sin. The Hussites would split into groups of varying extremism. The Utraquists, or Calixtines, so-called because they wanted communion to be offered under both forms for the laity, were the moderate group. The Taborites, who were more closely aligned with Wycliffite beliefs, demanded the abolition of all church property and accepted Wycliffe's views on the Eucharist, something Hus had not done. Eventually, the Utraquists would be reconciled to Rome with the *Compactata (Compacts) of Basel* signed in 1436 and ratified in 1437, which granted one of the four demands of the *Four Articles*; namely, declaring that communion under both species was not heretical.

Still a matter open for discussion is the nature of the Hussite revolution and its fraternity with Wycliffite beliefs. One of the big distinctions between Wycliffe and Hus can be seen here—all that Wycliffe wrote, he did in service of the English crown, as an attempt to show how the church did not have power over the interests of the crown, especially financial interests. In the case of Hus, he was sometimes writing at odds with the crown, which had allied itself with the church and was seeking to bolster its own authority from such a close connection.

It is unique among the heresies in this book that one became a political movement that in part was also an ethnic or nationalist movement. The Cathars certainly had a social element among them, and the Waldensians had a familial element, though the latter might have been largely due to geographical isolation. But the condemnation of Hus was a significant event in making him a social revolutionary. His importance moved beyond the ecclesiastic. Granted,

Wycliffe's ideas spread to popular uprisings as well, but they didn't have the lasting identity that Hus's did. Somehow, Hus's words became emblematic of Czech nationalism and the power of the populace.

Another reason why this revolution differed from the Wycliffites and Lollards is that Hus unambiguously sought to have popular influence. Working in the same vein as Waldhauser, Milič, and Janov, he used a popular pulpit in town to bring new theological ideas from the university to the people.[33] Additionally, he became a voice of the people through the consequences of his thoughts on the laity's role. Hus believed that the church's authority was related to the spiritual realm only. Peter had the keys to the kingdom, but it was the kingdom of heaven, not the temporal kingdom of earthly rulers. As such, Hus said that clergy served as leaders only inasmuch as they were role models for good holy behavior. He empowered the laity to read and interpret the Bible in their own languages. This idea meant that the Bible was translated into Czech, and the people could encounter the word of God in their own idiom. A Prague burgher had helped to fund a translation of the Bible into German in 1381. By 1392, there was a Czech translation. Hus published a Czech translation in 1406, with other versions appearing in the years that followed. All these views meant that the average person was being encouraged to think for themselves and to stand up against clergy who were not serving them.

Lasting Impact

Hus's legacy was, as a martyr to the cause of church reform and the fight against the abuses of the clergy, more than a legacy of ideas. The ideas of the Hussite movement would move far beyond the ideas that Hus personally espoused. He helped bring those ideas to his university, took them seriously, and espoused some of them, but he did not adopt as many as his followers in the university and in the church did. Hus is often viewed as a precursor to the Protestant Reformation, in part due to his reforming zeal. The movement has been called a premature Reformation in the sense that it encapsulated rethinking of the theological issues of the day. It was premature in the sense that it occurred before the Lutheran Reformation in Germany and before a groundswell of public opinion would make for successful reformation. But even this name oversells the motives and goals of the person of Jan Hus. There are a number of heresies that we've seen—the Waldensians, the Wycliffites, and now the Hussites—that the scholarly literature makes this claim about. These statements are all an attempt, later in history, to see the movements as foreshadowing the Lutheran Reformation. If they were such, they'd offer a sense of the advancement of such groups and areas, suggesting that they had their finger on the pulse of where intellectual and ecclesiastical trajectories were headed. If these groups are proto-Protestants, then it looks like the church, in suppressing them, is reactionary. But being a proto-Protestant also suggests that there would be a continuity of thought between what a proto-Protestant group believes and what the Reformers, when they came along, believed. The desire for reform alone doesn't make one proto-Protestant. The church did attempt—sometimes too slowly—to reform itself, and there were many orders in the church that were founded on goals to reform various aspects of the church.

The Middle Ages were focused on internal reforms; where the clashes occurred was on how to implement or allow reform. It is not a case of reform against people who refuse to change. Ultimately, such discussions of whether a group is proto-Protestant are red herrings. They point out the useful fact that such groups encouraged lay participation and did so through direct access to the Scriptures in vernacular languages. But while this shift in literacy and reading patterns does correspond with the Reformation, it wasn't a descriptive factor in determining allegiance to it. From the time of the High Middle Ages, there had been a growing desire among people—among nobles at first, then the burgeoning bourgeoisie—for spiritual treatises, books of prayers, and so forth. They'd have encountered biblical quotations and paraphrases, often in languages other than Latin, through these writings. The idea of the Bible in the vernacular, while not encouraged by the Papacy, isn't a surety of being a Protestant, even at this time. Rather, the economy of power explains the church's willingness to reform or not in various places and times. To lose clerical wealth was to lose clerical social and political status. And it could also perhaps harm the church's own ability to lead its flock.

Another thing to note is that we really need even more scholarship focused on Hus. What's been created is good, but much of the work is in Czech and remains inaccessible either by limitations on the availability of materials or by language. Hus's relationship with Wycliffe is to this day a source of scholarly discussion. The thesis can be seen in its extreme in the work of Johann Loserth, which compares the two men's work as a literal borrowing that established the utter dependence of Hus on Wycliffe. Loserth carried this view to a radical conclusion, asserting that it was emblematic of the utter lack of creativity that characterized Czech intellectualism.[34] Recent scholarship has found influences of other continental universities in the work of Hus's followers, especially the influence of the University of Paris, where the followers Vojtěch Raňkův of Ježov, Matěj of Janov, and Jeroným Pražský all studied.[35] At the start of Hus's career, Charles University was a cosmopolitan place, and it was likely that the theologian would encounter the ideas of many different thinkers. Learning more about the intellectual realm in which Hus and other Czech reformers worked could shed even more light on understanding their appeal to the laity and the disjunct between the inquisitors' questions and Hus's answers. It can also help us to better understand the nature of the innovation of their ideas in the milieu in which they taught and preached.

The significance of the Hussites was something much more important than being mere foreshadowers of the next century's Reformation. Rather, the Hussites stepped into a situation in late feudalism in the eastern edge of Western Europe and used the reform of the church as a way to reform society and as a countermeasure to the attempts at consolidation of monarchical power and baronial power. That this circumstance became a revolution of the lower landowners and the people, and that it was coupled with new ideas in the church, shows that it had reminiscences of the Free Spirit heresy, which was similarly located at a time when there was a shift in the social structure following urbanization. And it also has parallels with some of the Languedoc movements, such as Catharism, which sought a spirituality that fit their regional identity.

CHAPTER 9

Late Medieval Witchcraft
The Movement Back Toward Individual Heresy

IT'S APPROPRIATE TO end a look at medieval heresy with a group that signals, in many ways, the transition from the medieval to the early modern church. Late medieval witchcraft was a phenomenon that shared a number of elements with other movements already covered in this book: those identified as witches were primarily women; they were individuals who did not have the backing and authority of an influential group supporting them; and these women were accused of having visions or claimed to have access to supernatural or divine forces.[1] One way to interpret the late medieval preoccupation with witchcraft—and the attempts to test whether women were witches—is as a continuation of the medieval concern about women's spirituality.[2] When a mystic was found to be operating in the church, it was necessary to test the spirits and determine whether the inspiration was divine. These tests have their foundations in Scripture, and throughout the Middle Ages, women's mystical visions were tested by men in charge (be they spiritual directors, ecclesiastical authorities, or university scholars). Savvy, connected women such as Hildegarde of Bingen sought out ecclesiastical support from both the monastic men of power, such as Bernard of Clairvaux, and popes. Read in this way, the witchcraft trials of the late Middle Ages and early modern period emerge from the same vein that erected boundaries around the literary work and spiritual expressions of earlier women such as the beguines. Witchcraft merely focused on those whose inspirational spirits were discerned to be demonic, not divine.

We enter at the time following the black death. Europe was buffeted by a disease whose waves had killed up to one-third of the population in some places and brought economic crisis and warfare, causing flare-ups of accusations and suppression. In reality, witchcraft was a crime that had been punished by the church throughout the Middle Ages, and it was not a new uprising. Accusations against witches would slowly become formulaic, showing few aspects of innovation. The *Nuremburg Handbook* began with a definition of witchcraft that would place it firmly within the context of heresy when it said, "This depravity of sorceresses consists of two elements: the heresy and apostasy from the Faith and the temporal loss that she inflicts."[3] The witch was seen to be someone who had joined another sect, one centered around the devil. Witchcraft became identified through the High Middle Ages and into the late Middle Ages with previously examined heretical groups, but it really took on its own life; this disjunct will highlight just how society had changed considerably since the creation of a medieval heresy machinery and how the machinery had not adapted.[4] In many ways, the prosecution of late medieval witchcraft represents the end of an effective machinery dealing with heresy and an end to the manufacture of definitions of heresy for social control. Heresy once again became individual in its attacks. This heresy didn't have the widespread effect of leading others into error as much as causing individual physical effects, such as blighted crops and sickly cattle. Witchcraft pointed to a change in the theology, one that saw a struggle between God and the devil, with the orthodox on God's side and witches on the other.

Some of the challenges involved when talking about late medieval witchcraft in the context of a book on medieval heresy are the ways in which witches were talked about, the identification of the forces they harnessed in their magic, and the crimes purported to be committed by witches; all these overlap somewhat with accusations against heretics. As witchcraft accusations often found women to be their targets, there are correlations between women's power and accusations in late medieval witchcraft, just as there were for the Free Spirit heresy.

The Emergence of Witchcraft

Witchcraft is a phenomenon that is attested to in the Bible and in the ancient texts of Greece and Rome (such as Medea being described as the Colchian witch). By the time of its being defined in the early medieval *Canon Episcopi*, witchcraft was already associated with women. It was less about a set of theological beliefs than it was about a set of folk practices, setting it apart from the heresies discussed thus far. Europe had largely been converted to Christianity by the second millennium, but part of that conversion process included a syncretistic adaptation of local traditions and beliefs to fit alongside

Christianity. These types of local superstitions and practices—such as the use of special herbs for healing, prayers to local spirits, charms, and magical sayings for good luck or the belief that geographical features are imbued with supernatural benefits—indicate that magic was commonplace. Some of these practices would make their way into medical texts, hagiographic materials, and Christian practices.[5]

For the most part, the type of witchcraft that the church would become concerned with was that with a negative impact, known as *maleficium*. As early as the seventh century, Isidore of Seville wrote in the *Etymologies* that "consequently, this foolery of the magic arts held sway over the entire world for many centuries through the instruction of the evil angels. By a certain knowledge of things to come and of things below, and by invoking them, divinations (*aruspicium*) were invented, and auguries (*auguratio*), and those things that are called oracles (*oraculum*) and necromancy (*necromantium*)."[6] He discussed *sortileges* (interpreters of lots), *horoscopus* (drawers of horoscopes), *hydromatius* (hydromancers, who draw up the shapes of demons by gazing into water), *divinus* (diviners), and *incantator* (enchanter); magic had many subspecialties. Isidore then singled out one particular type of magic, saying, "There are magicians who are commonly called 'evildoers' (*maleficus*) by the crowd because of the magnitude of their crimes. They agitate the elements, disturb the minds of people, and slay without any drinking of poison, using the violence of spells alone."[7] Isidore equated the beliefs of Simon Magus and the magician Menander with heresy, and his treatment of all the subspecialties of magic show a clear condemnation for the practice of *maleficus*. He demonstrated that the terminology for those practicing such actions would vary considerably, often based on the precise suspected nature of their actions. Another type of magic that received scholarly attention was the practice of necromancy (*necromantia*). It had its roots in the types of magic listed here but was a more developed form meant to conjure demons and other spirits. The study of it involved both understanding the material objects needed in its rituals, as well as the rituals themselves, and determining what demons can be conjured to accomplish various results. The books from which this knowledge came were secretive and tied to the scriptoria of the universities and monasteries. It was infrequently practiced and was protected by the learned, so only a few ever studied it. Necromancy works were attested to by several inquisitors and other writers of the times.

Magia was a catchall term for magic that would often be intertwined with beliefs in other deities or with heresy. The church defined *superstitio* (superstition) as a type of illogical false belief. *Superstitio* appears in medieval sermons through the early and High Middle Ages as an occasional theme of attitudes to be corrected, not for its connection to magic as such but rather due to its being something ascribed to the unlettered, ignorant rural populations as an incorrect worldview. If a learned priest believed that his learning explained the reason for something occurring (such as a harvest failing or a calf dying), then the local farmer who believed it was due to elemental or supernatural forces would be seen as superstitious, having an infantile understanding of the world and God's power in it. What would begin to happen in the High and late Middle Ages, though, was that the power behind the words uttered and the power behind the forces summoned would be taken more seriously and taken to be real. That was what suddenly made magic a force that needed to be controlled and eliminated. Witchcraft began being persecuted slowly in the years 1300–1500; toward the end of this period, the persecutions would become more common.[8] The mechanisms for dealing with witchcraft had their foundations in those used to control heretics and wayward religious orders.

Accusations of Witchcraft

Just as we've seen with heretics, there were stock accusations against witches. Witches were primarily individuals, not groups, although some stock accusations assumed that the individuals were part of a witches' network. They could be from any social class, although women of the middle and gentry classes were more likely to be accused. Although society was postfeudal during part of this time frame, witchcraft accusations mainly occurred in rural agrarian areas; in these closely connected communities where most were related by marriage or by blood, accusations of witchcraft meant accusing neighbors and relatives within a highly interdependent society. Witchcraft served as a theory of causation for ill health, crop failures, weather problems, and animal death or blight.[9] The behaviors that witches were accused of became part of the standard list of behaviors. A *maleficus* (male) or *malefica* (female) might commit "crimes such as theft or murder by magical means, causing pestilence or disease, withering crops or afflicting livestock, and conjuring lightning and hail."[10] Witchcraft accusations included flying, celebrating the Sabbat with the devil, consorting with familiars, and making pacts with the devil. The 1437 *Errores Gazariorum*, although titled *The Errors of the Cathars*, actually spoke about witchcraft and included details that should seem familiar, saying that the devil appears "in the appearance of another animal, but most commonly in the shape of a black cat."[11] There were similarities to be found between the descriptions of witches' Sabbats, especially in Gregory IX's papal bull *Vox in Rama* (*A Voice in Ramah*) from 1233 and John of Winterthür's descriptions of the Austrian Waldensians' secret meetings in the mid-fourteenth century.[12] These descriptions became a pattern that would include a devil's Sabbat, often on Friday nights, in which the women would attend some type of meeting. They were able to travel there by will and were often described as flying to the meetings, often on the backs of animals. The Sabbat saw the gathering of witches with the devil in meetings at night in varying places. It was seen as a supernatural parody of true religious meetings: the devil presided while the women danced, and it ended with a sexual orgy. Witches would confess the evil things they had done since the last meeting, but in a reversal, the penance would come if their deeds were insufficient. As the 1437 *Errores Gazariorum* described, "The poor seduced person adores the presiding devil and pays homage to him; and as a sign of homage kisses the devil, whether the devil appears as a human or some kind of animal, on the anus or the ass."[13] This demonological text, written by an inquisitor, developed a theory of how the witches acquired and used demoniac powers for their rites and attempted to explain why these witchcraft practices were a threat to the entire church.

Witches were identifiable by the fact that they practiced *maleficium*, or harmful magic, that included acts that would sicken humans and cattle or destroy crops by means of poisonous fogs.[14] This ability caused witches to inspire fear in their neighbors. Harming cattle or crops could lead to starvation or financial ruin among subsistence farmers. "Storms and bad weather have been commanded by many devils together on the top of a mountain to break up ice . . . using their staffs to destroy the crops of their enemies or of certain neighbors."[15] Pacts concluded at midnight were another common claim. The devil appeared in either the form of a Black man or in the form of a black goat. The devil would preside over the Sabbat and would have sex with the witches present. Their relations would produce monsters, and at the banquet, newborn babies would be devoured. Other charges leveled against the witches included having ecstatic experiences and walking with or visiting with the dead. Visiting the afterlife had given rise to a number of literary works, including Dante's *Divine Comedy*, and among the Waldensians, there was literature that claimed their elders needed to visit heaven regularly to have their powers to loose and bind renewed.[16]

Witches' attacks on neighbors could take an even more malevolent turn, causing the deaths of newborns and young children. It was noted that, "when they want to strangle children while their father and mother are sleeping, in the dark of night with the silent help of the devil they enter the houses of the parents and grasp the child by the throat or the sides and strangle him until he is dead." One can imagine how, in a time before medicine, the sudden death of a child—not an uncommon experience—could lead to suspecting one's neighbor of being a witch. But the witch wasn't content merely to cause death:

> In the morning, when he is taken for burial the man or woman or group who have killed the child appear at the burial and lament the death with the mourning parents and friends. But the next night they open the grave and take the body, sometimes leaving the head, and they never take hands and feet unless they need to make some magic with the hand. When they have taken the corpse of the child and filled the grave again, they carry it to the synagogue, where it is cooked and eaten.[17]

The child becomes part of a religious sacrifice for the witch. This passage combines a list of fears and taboos—the removal of a corpse from consecrated ground, the destruction of a corpse, and cannibalism—to overwhelming effect.

Witchcraft and Heresy

Witchcraft had already begun to appear around the margins of some heresy trials. The Waldensians were sometimes accused of witchcraft. In the Cathar inquisitional proceedings, examples of witchcraft existed, such as a story of a person named Arnoldo Mondo bringing a young girl to neighbors who would help her look into a mirror and find who had stolen his items. While the person telling the story said Mondo did not want to watch the art performed, he was appreciative of sorcery being able to help him recover his goods.[18] The word *Cathar* came to be a synonym for witch, as the title of the book *Errores Gazariorum* shows; the word *Vaudois*, used to mean Waldensians, also came to refer to witches. Templars similarly were connected to sorcery and said to venerate a demonic head of Baphomet. Witchcraft was traditionally condemned on legal grounds (especially relating to bad magic, or *maleficium*, where there would be potentially criminal actions such as harming a cow or killing a person) or on the basis of it being antisocial or immoral (such as a love potion that forced a person, against their free will, to love another person). Witchcraft also was associated with pagan rites. For social and moral cases, the focus would be on reconciliation and rehabilitation.

In early and high medieval law, accusations of witchcraft were dealt with on an accusatory model. Under this procedure, the person making the accusation had the burden to prove the *maleficium*. Witchcraft was by nature secret, involving travel at night and clandestine meetings, and thus it was hard to prove. If the accuser was unable to prove the claims, they faced punishment. This practice effectively limited accusations of witchcraft. Over the course of the twelfth through fourteenth centuries, the Inquisition forced a move from the accusatory model to the inquisitorial model for witchcraft, as it had for heresy. Under this new model, once a person accused another of witchcraft, the burden then fell on the officials of the court to prove the charges. Charges could be brought against a person either by another individual or by the court, even without a formal accusation by another person. The proof would come largely from a series of interrogations. The inquisitor would have a list of questions associated with a particular heresy and would use them to get proof of guilt or, better, a confession. As a result, the courts began using torture to obtain evidence for a conviction. Although there were limits on torture, they were regularly set aside.

It would take a reinvestigation of heresy for witchcraft to become associated with it, but afterward, new methods could be employed in the attempt to rout out witches, and witches would seem more capable of greater harm than ever before. The association would also clarify whom inquisitors would seek to charge with witchcraft, expanding the net by considering most or all types of witchcraft to be types of sorcery. "Clearly, all three elements of full-blown witchcraft—divine permission, diabolic power, and especially the pact—existed in the early Middle Ages. The distinctive contribution of the fourteenth century was not so much a fall from healthy skepticism into the sewers of superstition as it was an attempt to combine secular and ecclesiastic thought."[19] Inquisitors would come to believe that all witchcraft was *maleficium*, causing harm to humans and things associated with them, like their property and farm animals. They would assume *diabolism*, which referred to magic that included elements where the devil or demons were invoked or whose powers were needed to perform a ceremony, was an element of all witchcraft. The categories of witches and sorcerers would collapse into one. In the early Middle Ages, a sorcerer was an intentional practitioner with harmful intent, whereas a witch need not be a regular practitioner and might not have evil intent. Originally, only sorcerers would be investigated. By the time of the late Middle Ages, they both were seen as being in a pact with the devil and therefore harmful to the mystical body of the church.

Developing a Framework for Trials

During the fourteenth century, the concerns over the cultic nature of sorcery and witchcraft increased, and attempts to codify how to investigate, judge, and punish such offenses grew. In his 1324 *Practica inquisitionis heretice pravitatis* (*Inquisitor's Manual*), Bernardo Gui barely mentioned sorcery; it was a form of heresy as far as he was concerned, but it did not merit the attention that the more organized heretics such as the Béguins of Languedoc, the Cathars, or the Waldensians warranted. Compared to these groups, witches seemed minor and not a large, organized sect. The short section on witchcraft in his *Manual* focused on the method of examination, as Gui did not yet see it worthy of much concern. He wrote of sorcerers, "The error and pestilence of sorcery, fortune-telling and the summoning of demons occur in many forms in many countries and regions, depending on the various inventions and false and worthless assertions of superstitious persons who pay heed to the spirits of error and to demoniac doctrines."[20] In short, practitioners of witchcraft were merely people in error, not heretics. Fifty years later, in 1376, the inquisitor Nicholas Eymeric would offer a view in his *Directorium* that sorcery involved the invocation of the devil and thus constituted an opposite pole to Christian worship.

Witch trials and the attendant structure of the Inquisition developed through four distinct phases between 1300 and 1500. In the first period, between 1300 and 1330, witchcraft trials were few and far between.[21] They began in the French- and German-speaking regions of the western Alps and in northern Italy, areas associated with the Waldensians. Key to the development of witch hunts at this time were stereotypes of witches and their harmful effects on local society. In the earliest stages, those who were accused of witchcraft often were prominent figures, and the accusations were seen as retribution. These accusations were often tied to increasing political instability and the loss of the Capetian dynasty in France.[22] These trials were infrequent, averaging about one per year across Europe. Prior to the development of a more robust idea of witchcraft, singular witchcraft trials were the norm; with the association of witches and diabolical communities, a single trial could result in multiple trials of people associated with the first accused. The development of seeing the witch both as a heretic and as someone working within a community meant that sorcery was taken more seriously, and it would be dealt with in the same way that heretics were, with no mercy to be given. Thus, the number of trials increased, and they spurred further trials for people associated with the original accused.

Early witchcraft trials started with a simple accusation of *maleficium* brought against people by neighbors or people in their local craft, trade, or community. Once the trials were taken over by the courts, and run by people with experience investigating heresy, the accusations took on the added hues of practicing demonic worship and heresy and of acting as part of a diabolical community. Location influenced the spread of witchcraft accusations and trials, just as it had for the construction of the Free Spirit heresy; in towns and cities, it was likely that a person would be labeled a heretic, but in the outlying countryside, the accusations and investigations were more likely to be about witchcraft. The assumption here was that the villagers and country dwellers were more likely to be illiterate and given to superstition and hysteria, while those who lived in the towns were more able to use reason to combat prejudice and baseless fears.

The first period of widespread witch hunts began in southeastern France and northwestern Italy (in Savoy and Dauphiné) and in Swiss territories, including Bern, Fribourg, Lucerne, Lausanne, and Sion (Vaud and Valais). One can also see the influence of the Templar trials in the paranoia of political leadership and loss of power in these first witchcraft trials.[23] The Templars were accused of "sodomy, blasphemy, and other species of immorality, they are supposed to have venerated the Devil in the guise of an animal named Baphomet."[24] The similarity with the Templars underscored the political aspect of these accusations in a time of widely changing French fortunes in secular power, as we can infer from the political aspects of the Templar trials. Scholars point to connections between the growth of sorcery accusations against the Templars and the growth of witch hunts in the next century. Sorcery became a way of swaying general popular fear against the Templars. What these accusations note is that both accused witches and the Templars were relatively well-off defendants, highlighting that accusations of witchcraft were wielded in the early fourteenth century against political or economic targets.

Yet despite the connections to politics, these charges were usually mild in their accusations at this stage. Charges of sorcery and diabolism had been leveled against heretics such as the Cathars and Waldensians through the centuries before, but they were not the primary focus of the accusations against either group; both were found to be heretics based on deviations from church doctrine and practice. And the witches at this time were not given theological examinations or propositions to assent to like the heretics were. In looking through the literature, it is clear that some modern authors see the Waldensians as having been accused of witchcraft in the court of public opinion; rumors of Waldensian pacts with the devil seem to appear in the later Middle Ages.[25] Witchcraft was beginning to be associated with heresy to an increasing extent.

The second period stretched from 1330 to 1375. During this time, the character of prosecution changed, and the accusations were not primarily against political targets. In fact, political trials abruptly stopped as a semblance of stability come to England and France. Rather, the trials focused on sorcery and invocations. The third period lasted between 1375 and 1435, and it was in this period that the number of trials saw a great increase in numbers. Part of the reason for believing there was a rise in number is due to an increase in the number of extant records of trials, but there was also a corresponding increase in the number of secular courts that began to oversee witchcraft trials, signaling that such proceedings were becoming not only an ecclesiastical issue but also an issue that temporal authorities felt needed to be addressed.

The nature of accusations and investigations also changed during this time. Whereas there were few accusations of diabolism (direct worship of the devil) prior to this period, it took an increasingly central role in accusations.

Witchcraft became a clearly defined cultus.[26] The *Malleus Maleficarum* (*Hammer of Witches*) would identify six characteristics of witchcraft that this time, that inquisitors looked for during investigations:

1. Entering into a pact with the devil, which necessarily caused the person to be in a state of apostasy
2. Having sexual relations with the devil
3. Flying, especially to meet up with others
4. Attending meetings that were overseen by the devil (It was often at these meetings that sexual improprieties would take place, such as having sex with the devil or engaging in forbidden sexual acts such as incest.)
5. Practicing maleficent magic (magic meant to harm)
6. Committing infanticide[27]

As with other heresies, the list became the basis for the questioning that inquisitors put to suspected heretics.

There have also been claims that during this third period, the increase in witchcraft proceedings could be attributed to the fact that prosecutors turned to witches when the Cathars and Waldensians had been sufficiently routed. But it should be acknowledged that witchcraft trials increased widely, not only in the areas where the Cathars and Waldensians were most prevalent. As was the case in previous periods, outbreaks were recorded in France and Germany. But part of the acceleration has been traced to Switzerland, an area that overlapped but was larger than some Waldensian locations.[28] In fact, prior to 1383, there exists no evidence of investigation in most of the area at all, though by the beginning of the fifteenth century, investigators were dealing with an outbreak in Simmenthal, which the Dominican John Nider would help investigate.

Further outbreaks were reported in Italy. And it would be in this country where the strongest evidence of accusations of diabolism would come from during this period. Nicholas Consigli was accused of witchcraft and endured several trials. After being found guilty, he escaped from prison before his death sentence could be carried out. In his case, the authorities did not seem all that interested in attempting to recapture him. In Italy, people were regularly accused of a mix of folk belief and religion that was often misconstrued by church authorities who were not local. It was also a time that saw an increase in preaching about the dangers of witchcraft, which may have helped fuel accusations. The reformer Franciscan friar Bernardino of Siena instituted reforms that regularly muddied the lines between sodomy, witchcraft, and heresy. His sermons, which tended toward the sensationalist, lingered on the frequent tales of sexual immorality among the witches. His work triggered many witchcraft trials, and he was involved in prosecuting a group of women in Rome in 1424. He reported that a witch, "confessed, without being put to torture, that she had killed thirty children by sucking their blood; she also said that she had let sixty go free. She said that every time she let one of them go free, she had to sacrifice a limb to the devil, and she used to offer the limb of an animal. She had done this for a long time." The woman's confession further revealed that one of the children she sacrificed was her own son, whom she ground up into powder to feed to others. Other abominations he described included witches anointing themselves with foul-smelling diabolical ointments and killing adults.[29]

Another notable case was that of Gilles de Rais (1404–40), a nobleman from southern France. He was a chief commander in the army that Joan of Arc led, and he had a distinguished military career. He was the one she called on after her unsuccessful attack on Paris in September 1429. While she was facing heresy charges, he fell afoul of court politics. By 1433, his patron, Georges de Tremoille, had fallen from power and this defeat effectively ended Gilles's career. In 1440, in response to legislation that King Charles VII put forward regarding a national army that meant to put an end to the free soldiers like Gilles, he took the brother of the local duke of Normandy hostage while serving Mass. This act led to an outrage in the ecclesiastical courts and to Gilles being charged with a number of backdated crimes—including necromancy and the murders of countless children. After undergoing torture, he went into court admitting alchemy, devil worship, infanticide, sodomy, and other faults. His death, especially alongside that of Joan of Arc, showed that although the investigation of witchcraft had moved on from its first stages, charges of witchcraft could still serve as a political expedient to bring down political enemies.

The fourth period of witchcraft trials extends from 1435 to roughly 1500. This period saw trials occur in waves, particularly cresting around 1455–60 and 1480–85.[30] It was the period with the most trials, and it was also the one in which the machinery of accusation brought together many of the disparate elements and types of allegations into a more formulaic set. When people think of late medieval witchcraft trials, these are the ones they tend to think of. The brunt of accusations occurred in France, Germany, and Switzerland; England and Italy's witchcraft accusations had decreased significantly. One such example is the witchcraft trials of 1459–61 in the Burgundian town of Arras that didn't end until 1491: the trials lasted from 1459–60, but the appeals process took a full thirty years. They began when a hermit, under suspicion of heresy, reported that two neighbors were witches. After one was caught and tortured, she provided other names. Consequently, several witches were accused by neighbors and during the torture process were asked to provide names of those who consorted with them. They did so, and another eight people were arrested after being told that if they confessed, they would go free. Eventually, a series of trials of all charged would begin; when the witches were found guilty, they appealed. All told, fifteen from the area were burned as witches; many were set free; and the legal proceedings helped to bolster the approach of prosecuting witchcraft within canon law.

The Legal and Inquisitorial Machinery

One challenge of magic and witchcraft being turned into a type of heresy was that it varied in both its execution and intent. When the Italian Benedictine monk Gratian compiled his code of canon law (church law), he spent time organizing different cases into types and considering the penalties that had been enacted. His law code contained more than 4,000 texts about various issues related to church law, creating categories to classify and organize the materials; in this compendium, known as the *Concordia discordantium canonum* (*Concordance of Conflicting Canons*) (otherwise known as the *Decretum*), magic was one such category he created, one that to him was simply silliness or ignorance on the part of a practitioner who didn't know it was inefficacious or a trick. During his time, magic was not taken as a serious threat to belief; it was just something the unlearned and simple people occasionally engaged in without any malice.

There were some attempts to slow down the wave of witchcraft trials. In 1258, Pope Alexander IV ordered all inquisitors to refrain from involving themselves in sorcery trials unless the sorcery was a direct result of heresy.

He was particularly concerned with what the proper scope of inquisitorial jurisdiction was when he wrote, "The inquisitors of pestilential heresy ought not to intervene in cases of divination or sorcery unless these *clearly* savour of manifest heresy."[31] He continued by glossing this statement with the examples of "praying at the altars of idols, to offer sacrifices, to consult demons, to elicit responses from them."[32] For a while, witchcraft trials were investigated only by secular justice, which meant that there was sporadic, localized investigation only. In 1320, Pope John XXII reversed this practice, ordering all inquisitors to investigate all aspects of sorcery that involved invocation or worship of demons. His Cardinal William would write to the inquisitors of Carcassonne and Toulouse that the pope "fervently desires that the witches, the infectors of God's flock, flee from the midst of the House of God." He instructs the inquisitors, saying,

> He ordains and commits to you that, by his authority against them who make sacrifice to demons or adore them, or do homage unto them by giving them as a sign a written pact or other token; or who make certain binding pacts with them, or who make or have made for them certain images or other things which bind them to demons, or by invoking the demons plan to perpetrate whatever sorceries they wish; or who, abusing the sacrament of baptism, themselves baptize or causer to be baptized an image or wax or some other material; and who themselves make these things or have made them in order to invoke demons; or if knowingly they have baptism, orders, or confirmation repeated; then, concerning sorcerers and witches, who abuse the sacrament of the eucharist or the consecrated host and other sacraments of the Church by using them or things like them in their witchcraft or sorcery, you can investigate and otherwise proceed against them by whatever means available, which are canonically assigned to you concerning the proceeding against heretics."[33]

In the beginning of the instruction letter, Cardinal William's focus is on the supernatural forces by which the magic or sorcery finds its power. It was a type of idolatry, and witchcraft was viewed as antisacerdotal. As the letter continues, the connections to heresy taint the description of what witches do, making it akin to a separate church with its own sacraments. Cardinal William compares the rites of witches to being a reissuance of sacraments of initiation: baptism, confirmation, or the rite of a vowed religious taking orders and joining a religious community. Here, the emphasis is on becoming something other than Christian. The passage then discusses the abuse of the sacrament of the Eucharist, which perhaps makes the most sense in this paragraph; it was a known folk practice in some places to plant a consecrated host in the ground during sowing season as a way to find divine favor for the coming season's yield. While not the purpose the consecrated host was to be meant for, it seems a far cry from the passage's suggestion that the person was practicing heresy or worshipping idols or other gods. If anything, the practice reinforced belief in the power of the Christian God, even if not along the lines of official sacramental theology.

In 1326, in the decretal *Super illius specula* (*Upon His Watchtower*), John XXII formally excommunicated all who were found guilty of practicing sorcery or invoking demons. In the span of seventy years, witchcraft came to be a forefront concern of the church's inquisitorial apparatus.

On December 5, 1484, Innocent VIII issued the papal bull *Summis desiderantes affectibus* (*Desiring with Supreme Ardor*); while not stating a new policy or change of action, this bull was frequently reprinted and thus attained its lasting significance. It stated that the pope had heard of cases in southern Germany in which people were allied with evil spirits and were having an effect on crops and animals, encouraging people to masturbate, and preventing people from being able to procreate.[34] One of the effects, the pope saw, of this *maleficium*, was that the spiritual crime led to physical acts and crimes. His bull suggested that local clergy were ignoring the problem, and he called for the Bishop of Strasbourg to investigate these allegations. The bull focused on *maleficium* as coming from the devil rather than ritual incantations and charms. In the wake of this document, the German Dominican inquisitors Heinrich Institoris (Heinrich Kramer) and Jacob Sprenger, who worked at the behest of Pope Innocent VIII, stepped up the persecutions and within two years had executed forty-eight witches in Constance. They also completed the *Malleus Maleficarum* at this time (1486); it contained information on determining who was a witch and delineated methods to bring them to trial and sentence them. By this time, witch-hunting had become a full-time preoccupation and would continue to be bolstered by the development of manuals on how to interrogate witches.

The Intellectual Machinery

The legal and inquisitorial framework demonstrated the necessity of and provided a structure for the intellectual exploration of witchcraft and its effects on scholarship. This period of late medieval witch-hunting was not a time of doctrinal innovation. There was much written about witches, and how to conduct investigations and trials, but little of it represented new ways of seeing things. Instead, it was a retrenched, reactionary attempt to limit expression. Witches were to be tried as others had been. As Pope Eugene IV wrote in 1434 to the inquisitor Pontus Fougeyron, "Among many heretics there are also found many Christian and Jewish magicians, diviners, invokers of demons, enchanters, conjurers, superstitious people, augurs, those who use nefarious and forbidden arts, through whose efforts the Christian people, or at least a numerous and simple-minded part of them, are stained and perverted."[35] The manuals produced, such as the *Formicarius* (*The Anthill*) and the *Malleus Maleficarum*, provided the user with a set of rubrics that required little understanding of theology or witchcraft. Concerns for harmful sorcery existed in the time of the early church. It was only as witchcraft became associated with a diabolical community that appeared organized and met regularly that it became an issue that needed to be theologically addressed. In the early medieval period and before, harmful magic, or *maleficium*, was dealt with in both the code of canon law and in secular law.

The scholastic tradition also spent time attempting to determine the place of witches within the orderly scholastic worlds. Interest in identifying women not as wayward mystics but as a malignant force was evident in a variety of theories both among the church tradition and among the men at university. This interest led to new practical work on identifying malevolent women by their late medieval clergy. Scholasticism developed elaborate demonologies, describing the exact abilities of both the angels and the fallen angels in extraordinary detail. Furthermore, a whole theology developed around questions about the powers of the devil and the Christian God. While the theology granted complete power to the Christian God, it allowed that he had given powers over to the devil.[36] Because the devil was a fallen angel, he had the creaturely powers ascribed to the angels. He could move people's souls, or their souls and bodies together, since he was an entirely incorporeal creature. At the same time, he had acquired the power of prescience, or foreknowledge. But the devil could not do miraculous things, such as raising the dead. Witches' pacts with the devil were discussed by a number of theologians, separate from examples of witchcraft in their time, and became part of the established demonology of writers such as Albertus Magnus, Aquinas, and William of Paris.[37] The pact with the devil was the essential crime of witchcraft.[38] It was thought that with the help of a witch, the devil could accomplish more destruction; for the Scholastics, understanding the powers of the devil helped them to understand what witches could be capable of when they called on him.

But accompanying this pact were other elements that made up witches' actions. Foremost were the heretical conventicles and the Sabbat, in which witches met with the devil. Everyone knew witchcraft was not a new phenomenon in the high and late medieval church. And many of the actions associated with it were similar through the centuries, although attitudes about them changed. In the ninth century, the canon *Episcopi eorumque* expressed its condemnation of the belief that women accompanied the goddess Diana riding in the night on animals. The canon explained the apparently popular belief of women riding around at night as its own form of the delusion caused by the devil. The error that these women fell into was to believe that the devil was capable of divine powers, which, since he was a mere creature, was not the case.[39] Transvection, or nocturnal flying, would be a common belief by the fifteenth century, when witches flying on brooms or animals was firmly established as part of the folklore of witches.[40] In the late Middle Ages, those investigating witchcraft once again attempted to understand how the phenomenon helped the devil and what role of assent the women played in these pacts.

Nicholas Eymeric (ca. 1320–99) was a Dominican inquisitor who served in Aragon and authored the handbook *Directorium Inquisitorum* (*Directory of the Inquisition*) in 1376. His book contained the most comprehensive discussion of sorcery among the late medieval wave of reinterest in witchcraft. The book was rooted both in his work as an inquisitor and in his theological studies. Although a number of people had written about the diabolical nature of sorcery by this point, it had once again become a matter of increasing ecclesiastical concern. Sorcery complaints had appeared in the trials of the Templars, as well as in a number of other trials that had both a political and ecclesiastical taint to them, but there had been no real theological framework with which to handle such complaints. As a result, sorcery complaints were sometimes ignored in heresy trials as mere "further evidence" in favor of theological and doctrinal issues that were more easily investigated. Eymeric first treatise on the subject was written around 1359 and later incorporated into the *Directorium*. He discussed in detail the rituals that the demons required their servants to perform, and he related them to heresy. His work built on the demonology of Augustine and Aquinas, as well as Scripture, Innocent V, and the *Canon Episcopi*. He considered sorcery and heresy to be a form of idolatry and apostasy, having turned away from true belief and put a new worship in its place.

Eymeric would directly address the question about the relationship between witchcraft and heresy, beginning with how witches and sorcerers were subject to the judgments of inquisitors. Next, he considered whether they were to be considered heretics. In Scholastic fashion, he further distinguished two types of diviners and magicians. "Some are to be considered magicians and diviners just as are those who act purely according to the technique of chiromancy, who divine things from the lineaments of the hand and judge the natural effects and the condition of men from this."[41] Another type of witch or sorcerer, however, doesn't gain their insights in this way but instead "[is] contracted to heretics, as are those who show the honor of *latria* [idolatry] or *dulia* [veneration] to the demons, who rebaptize children and do other similar things."[42] In this instance, Eymeric viewed this form of witchcraft in terms of devotion to a god other than God, involving rituals akin to the Catholic sacraments but performed for that other god. As he continued to gloss the different types of veneration or worship some witches and sorcerers give their gods, he wrote, "In this manner the Saracens invoke Mohammed as well as God and the saints and certain beghards invoke Petrus Johannis [Peter of John Olivi] and others condemned by the church."[43] Here, Eymeric connected the prayer and worship of Muslims—people outside of Christianity—with the Béguins; Peter of John Olivi, by comparison, is seen as worshipped not as a saint but as a foreign god. Eymeric concluded that witches and sorcerers worship in this way as well.

Eymeric continues, attacking superstition, which previously was considered benign although foolish. He says, "Superstition is a vice opposed to the Christian religion or Christian worship. Therefore, it is a heresy in a Christian, and as a consequence those who sacrifice to demons are to be considered heretics."[44] His argument is that if a person does something superstitions, it shows that they are honoring the thing that they think holds the power in that situation. So if a person creates a charm for an easy birth, they are honoring the power they think can bring that about over and above God. Most people assumed that these charms, amulets, and potions tapped into either God's or local saints' powers, not into a power outside of God, so this reading of the situation is contrary to popular understanding. Eymeric, writing from the security of the university, attempted to hold up a very rational view with no folk practices within it.

Just as Bernardo Gui's handbook described the errors of five heretical groups (including lightly touching on witches), other, fifteenth-century handbooks both catalogued the beliefs and instructed inquisitors on how to deal with witches. The 1458 *Flagellum haereticorum fascinariorum* (*The Scourge of Heretical Witches*) by the Dominican inquisitor Nicholas Jacquier argued that modern witches were a different sect with new powers and abilities, including flying. *Flagellum* means a scourge, and the scourge that Jacquier used was that of Scripture and the teachings of the saints. His book began with a discussion of demonic illusions and their nature. It focused on skeptics who doubted the existence of witchcraft in the late Middle Ages and was based on his own experience. Although Pope Alexander V had said in 1409 that the *Canon Episcopi* did not fully describe the activities of witches because new witches were of a new sect, Jacquier dealt with the disjunction between the canon's lack of discussion of transvection and the apparent contemporary belief that witches flew on broomsticks and animals. Chapter 7 of his book described the sect of witches, showing how he had proof of their nocturnal flights through their exhausted frames. He also identified the witches with the Waldensians. The *Flagellum* was often printed alongside or as a supplement to the *Malleus Maleficarum*, which became the most-used guide for the detection of witches. Jacquier's lasting role was to investigate the contemporary witchcraft trials as both a continuation of heresy and a new and unique phenomenon.

The tradition regularly spoke of the Cathars and Waldensians as witches and of the inquisition of witches as a continuation of the work of stopping heresy. One such text that makes this connection, in its title at least, is the 1430–40 *Errores Gazariorum*. It originated somewhere in Val d'Aost, northwest Italy. This text dedicated energy to elaborating the connection of witchcraft with heresy and focused on the witches' Sabbat and transvection. The text is found in a long version and a short (six-page) version that circulated widely. It addressed Sabbat and flights, the oath and reverence for the devil required of witches, the ritual meal that was cannibalistic, sexual orgies, and the profanation of the consecrated host. It described how the witch is seduced by the devil and forced to swear allegiance:

> When the devil has heard and accepted the oath of fidelity from the seduced person, this is what is said first: he swears that he will be faithful to the master who presides over the whole society; second, that he will assemble with the society; third, that he will not reveal the secrets of the said sect, not even until death. Fourth, that he will kill all of those children he is able to injure or kill and will take them to the synagogue, and by this is to be understood children under three years old. Fifth, that he will hurry to the synagogue whenever he is called upon to do so. Sixth, that he will impede sexual intercourse in every marriage that he is able to, using *sortilegium* and *maleficium*. Seventh, that he will avenge all injuries to the sect or any act that may impede or divide it.[45]

These oaths of course sound rather similar to the six characteristics listed at the start of this chapter, which were pulled from the *Malleus*. But the *Errores* offered additional grisly details of the actions of witches. It said that they make an unguent "of the said fat of children" that they then combine "with the most poisonous of animals such as serpents, toads, lizards, and spiders, which are all mixed mysteriously" and the result of a person having this unguent applied is "an evil death, sometimes for a time in a persisting illness, sometimes dying quickly."[46] This document further explored the reasons for why one might become involved with a sect of witches, and the text emphasized the fact that witchcraft is communal: it must involve groups of people rather than individuals.

It becomes readily apparent that these descriptions of witches appeal to sensationalism. This tendency would expand to providing stories for the pulpit and preaching in the work of Johannes Nider (1380–1438), a Dominican theologian and reformer contemporaneous to the *Errores Gazariorum*. Nider was part of the Vienna School, a fifteenth-century reform movement within the Dominican order that stressed the pastoral aspect of theological reflection and training. He was particularly interested in sorcery, superstition, and the diabolical.[47] His accounts of witchcraft in the early fifteenth century would become very influential. His *Formicarius* was written around 1437 and would prove to be a key source for the *Malleus Maleficarum*. He also wrote two other works that touched on the topic of witchcraft, the *De lepra morali* (*On Moral Leprosy*) and *Praeceptorium divine legis* (*Preceptor of Divine Law*). Nider also attended some of the sessions at the Council of Constance (1414–18) and was a leading member of the Council of Basel (1431–49). *The Formicarius* took the form of a dialogue between a theologian and a lazy student. Much of the dialogue was constructed around providing edifying stories that could be repeated in sermons. The form meant that Nider not only presented a discussion of witchcraft theologically, but he also provided detailed examples. And he anticipated a derivative lay audience for the ideas, not just an academic audience. His histories and stories seem to have been collected mostly from the western Alps, particularly the areas around Lausanne and Bern. His source was the secular judge Peter of Bern, supplemented with stories from the Dominican inquisitor of Autun, personal discussions and observations from his time in Vienna with a former necromancer who had become a Benedictine monk, and the accounts of delegates to the Council of Basel regarding the burning of Joan of Arc and others whom Nider considered witches. Johannes Nider's accounts of witchcraft, superstition, and magic discuss these subjects alongside moral questions, heresies, and statutes of faith.[48] His writings traverse a considerable span, for he also talked about the beguines and the Hussites (both of whom were topics of discussion at the Council of Basel). In his writings about heretics, although he opposed heresy, he did not have the same level of vituperative attack or the fearmongering that his writings about witches entailed. And he supported the beguine movement, appreciating the laity's approach to the religious life as laudable, believing that religious reform could be done by laity as well as others. Nider's focus was on reform, and he believed that demons used witches as a proxy to stifle it. Reforming witches, Nider thought, was part of the necessary foundation to strengthen and improve the church.

Nider would largely be responsible for the picture of witchcraft that emerged, and his descriptions contained most of the elements that would go into the definition of witchcraft: practitioners were simple people, usually rural, who performed bad magic that was harmful. Often the effects would be infertility, animal death, human sickness or death (including children), or destroyed or stolen crops. Witches had these abilities through their associations with demons and their power over the demons by renouncing the Catholic faith. The women would gather for secret meetings at night, where they would engage in sexual orgies and in cannibalistic feasts. The only element of the picture that Nider did not attribute to the witches was night flight, which he dismissed as a delusion. His account was also underscored by strong misogyny, where he explained that women were more susceptible to the devil because of the weakness of their sex. Because of the great variety of sources that he used, Nider also was able to include some sections on people outside of the main; for instance, he includes the story of the man Staedelin, who was a "great witch" who worked alone, a story he heard from Peter of Bern.

The culmination of the intellectual discussion of witches would be the *Malleus Maleficarum*, which without question became the most widely circulated treatise on witchcraft and how to investigate it. Its authors, Joseph Sprenger and Henricus Institoris, produced their work in three parts, each one intended to serve a different purpose for a unique audience. The book began with an apology that served as an introduction. In this part, it defined sorcery as "a particular element in Satan's final assault on God during the end times."[49] The *Malleus* explained that the main danger of witchcraft was in the physical danger to the faithful, and the authors used many examples to prove this point. In so doing, they emphasized the part of the devil in making *maleficium* so dangerous. The introduction also contained the papal bull from Pope Innocent VIII in 1484, which charged the authors with countering witchcraft. The first part intended to counter skepticism about the existence of witchcraft. It looked in depth at the sorceress, at the demon that encourages witchcraft, and at God's permission. Much of this first part was based on the ideas of Aquinas, and the book followed the Scholastic tradition of presenting questions with objections and replies. The second part focused on the types of behavior that witches undertook. Then it discussed appropriate ways to counteract witchcraft. The sources of this part were numerous and include Aquinas and Nider's *Formicarius*, as well as other works. Part three dealt with the interrogation of suspected witches and was based in large part on Eymeric's *Directorium Inquisitorum*. Whereas Eymeric wrote for inquisitors, this section was meant to guide the civil lawyers and judges. It's also worth noting that the vast majority of the sources were Dominican, continuing a trend that Dominicans were the ones at the forefront of theorizing witchcraft and also writing about how to question it and combat it.

Of course, the writing of manuals was only part of the process that led to the condemnation of witches. These manuals often gave the outline for how to question suspected witches and what sorts of witchlike behaviors to investigate. The other element that would be involved was the development of both a canonical and secular legal framework for actually trying the cases of those convicted of witchcraft. In 1437, Pope Eugene IV issued a general decree about devil worship: magic by touch, signs, or words. It would be followed in 1440 by the papal bull *Ad perpetua rei memoriam* (*In Perpetual Memory of the Matter*), which was directed against Amadeus VIII of Savoy, whom the Council of Basel had elected the antipope Felix V (1439–49). The bull declared that the heresies, devil worship, and sorcery of his diocese were due to the false pontificate.[50]

Lasting Impact

We've ended this chapter, unlike the others, without a clear condemnation. In the development of witchcraft, there would be a number of condemnations along the way and a gradual shift of inquisitorial efforts from heresy to witchcraft. While there were clear shifts in how witchcraft was defined, described, and understood, they were not codified in anathemas the same way as the heresies before. The big European and American witchcraft trials of the early modern era would still be on the horizon. What this chapter has shown is the impetus building and the mechanism and theory of developing witchcraft as a category that will allow the early modern witchcraft trials to explode on the scene later. In attempting to discuss the beginnings of witchcraft trials in Europe, I hope to show that they bear an affinity with the trials of heretical groups, particularly the Cathars, Waldensians and Templars, which we have already discussed in this book.

In its early years, accusations of witchcraft were somewhat different from other types of "heresy" in that they involve a level of social judgment, fear, and response, a social aspect that wasn't present in the other heretical groups we've seen. Cathars may have made good neighbors—or they may not have—but what got them into trouble wasn't what their neighbors thought; it was what officials of the church thought. Part of this difference is a natural extension that began halfway through this book, as heretics began being handed over to secular justice for punishment, as with the beguines, and secular justice decided to use heresy as an excuse to suppress, as was the case with the Templars. The yoking of secular and religious justice paved the way for accusations of witchcraft, which moved in their earliest days from being political ploys to social ones, perhaps the best example being the Salem witch trials in America, where family lines were a large part of who was accused, an accuser, or a defender.[51]

One of the issues is what causes a switch from popular heresy to a more localized form of trials for individual accounts of witchcraft. While each of the heresies had individuals, what we've seen has been a slow progression from individual wandering preachers to larger movements, whether real or imagined. To move back to individuals is unexpected, but the way in which the individual is treated is substantially different at this later time. The witchcraft trials in the late medieval period certainly continued many of the themes we've already seen, such as the persecution of women, which we saw with the beguines. And just as the first couple of heresies saw the development of the inquisitorial method, these trials brought forth a new industry in witchcraft manuals. It also points to the continued efforts that the Dominicans made to keep to their order's charism, fighting heresy at every turn, if not by preaching then by inquisition.

Looking back on the sweep of the history of these chapters, these witches represent, in many ways, the dangers of the individual even in the late Middle Ages. We began with a wandering preacher whose fervor was questioned; the beguines and beghards were investigated as rogue mystics spreading a heresy of being too free in spirit with God. The witches also bucked the social conventions expected by family and local society. Individuality was dangerous and met with suspicion. Yet in this final turn of heresy, the witches are never fully alone—they're always seen as part of a Sabbat, diabolical gatherings, and witchy networks, hearkening back to the idea that all heresies spring forth from the same impulse.

CHAPTER 10

Conclusions

THE FOURTH LATERAN Council declared that whilst heretics had different faces, their tails were twined together; each heresy is merely a different version of the same old mistaken beliefs.[1] By this, the church exerted that heresy sprang from one source, later identified as diabolical. But from what we have seen, it is obvious that from the twelfth to fifteenth century, heresy was far from a singular phenomenon. What each so-called heresy had in common was that it offered a new expression of the same reforming fervor shared with church-approved movements. While there may have been a single origin, it was shared with accepted movements, and it was not unique to those deemed heretical. The church's view of heresy developed as a category that was applied inconsistently but one that was used largely for the development of church authority based on the exclusion of once insiders. The past nine chapters have tried to understand how such movements formed and how they viewed themselves, over and against how the central, institutionalized church viewed alleged heretics and dealt with them.

Conclusions about the nature of such movements would notice that centrally they share a reforming zeal with not only themselves but also with many orthodox movements within the church. Each was seeking out a new way in which to enact reform, and sometimes new ideas were met with skepticism or contempt. The Templars, a recognized order within the church with substantial financial and military resources, looks quite different from the Petrobrusians, a loosely organized set of people following of a charismatic wandering preacher. The Hussites, with their necessary entanglement in the Bohemian political scene, bear little relationship to mystical writers such as Marguerite Porete, condemned as a Free Spirit heretic with no ties to other heretics or power. We see heresies develop in small towns, in the countryside, in the city centers, and even in Crusading lands. We see heresies develop among individuals and large orders. We see them among both men and women. What is clear is that until the development of the intellectual or academic heresies in the late Middle Ages, the heretics only rarely had a concept of themselves as opposing the church in a way that would sow schism. They saw themselves as enacting an extension of the evangelical role of the church through a new charism.

Structure

One of the questions that always bubbles just below the surface is why these individuals and groups. What made one particular individual or group be pursued as heretics, while another was embraced in the bosom of the church? Some of the heresies were more focused on the individual: the Petrobrusians, while focused on individual wandering preachers, began to advocate separate preaching and worship, never fully left the church, and continually tried to renew Christians. Heresy like this one relied more on the influence of wandering preachers who were accepted in some areas by church leadership, often in the absence of a strong church structure. The beguines of the Low Countries and Rhineland worked within the urban orders, setting up communities of pseudoreligious that clearly worked from the same impetus as the established orders and probably with the assumption that they too would receive official approval eventually—something that happened in some locations before the Council of Vienne put an end to it. But this similarity could also serve to spotlight heresies' difference from traditional orders. Sometimes the structure of these groups could enhance the likelihood of being considered heretics. When the Cathars and Waldensians set up parallel ecclesiastical structures that looked like the church, it could suggest they were trying to supplant the institutional church. While orders within the church could have their own structure, lay groups could not. The Templar order, whose organization was somewhat shrouded in mystery and with a complexity more pronounced than in other orders, was clearly still an order—a structure governed by a *regula* (rule) that delineated power and responsibility and made clear a member's role based on their place in the structure.

The Records

Through this book, we've relied on a variety of texts, and the fragmentary record of this time must be viewed with caution. The orderly destruction of many texts—whether they in fact were all destroyed—demonstrates that there was a tradition of trying to prevent ideas from being passed along. Marguerite Porete's *Mirror of Simple Souls* was one such text consigned to the fires. The accidents of history have also meant that few texts survive from various locations or orders—for instance, the Templars' archive, which was lost in Cyprus. More importantly, as some groups tried to remain below the radar, few records of their exact strength, organization, and beliefs exist for us. We may know of one or two people burned as heretics and may want to assume that behind them, there are many more. And then there's just fate, the luck of what survives, what was found collectable by people through the centuries, what didn't get recycled into material to bind the next book.

There's also the variety of records and their uses. While inquisitorial records tell us something, they use tropes and strict categories to talk about the accused and are not meant as an objective description of them. Hence, when Bernardo Gui writes about several heretical groups, the Cathars are viewed as contemporary Manichaeans, whereas the Waldensians' errors arise from the sin of pride, and the Béguins of Languedoc are in the middle of a Franciscan disagreement, one that the Dominican Gui is happy to pronounce on. But these accounts are still far from complete pictures of heresy, and the pictures vary considerably whether we look at the sources of inquisitors or the sources of the groups and individuals themselves, so even with the advances in textual research at the end of last century and the beginning of this century, we still need to exercise caution in understanding exactly how these groups viewed themselves. Inquisitors had no motivation to make their subjects look good. Their purpose in questioning the accused was to elicit a confession that reinforced how the heresy had been defined and showed its seriousness. Subjects had every reason to try to look orthodox to investigators.

Geography

Another aspect that distinguished heretical groups was the vagaries of geography. Repeatedly, we returned to the area of Languedoc, for the Petrobrusians, the Cathars, and the Béguins. By the end, we had moved much further east: Bohemia and Germany became late hotbeds of heresy, areas where the Reformation would arise in the following century. Heresy was more easily routed from areas where there was a strong central authority and where it could work with other authorities such as the bishops and papacy. In areas such as the German city-states and Languedoc, where central authority was lacking, heresy smoldered, and for longer than other areas before being addressed. It is not surprising that it also flourished in the rural areas of Britain in the form of Lollardy. It is important to remember that in a time when areas were more often distinguished by ethnicity and language and boundaries were still fluid, the concentration of power was something that not only the papacy was interested in. Having a population easily controlled was important to local bishops, local leaders, and monarchs as well. Religion was one vehicle through which the population both expressed its independence or fit within the structures of power. This consolidation of power, even within areas easily geographically defined—such as mainland Britain—could easily change over space and time.

Spirituality

Perhaps the defining aspect at the heart of medieval heresy is the desire for the apostolic life. This desire would lead the founders of new orders such as the Cistercians in 1098, the Victorines in 1108, the Franciscans in 1209, and the Premonstratensians in 1120, and it would also lead a number of groups that did not receive official support to still try to establish their own communities, often falling foul of the church hierarchy. Additionally, the church made this result more likely as it restricted the formation of new orders at the Fourth Lateran Council in 1215. Talking of the rise of Catharism, and the missionaries who set out to spread its ideas and demonstrate their asceticism, the historian of heresy Malcom Lambert noted that "the greatest strength of the movement lay in its ethical appeal to populations who had been sufficiently affected by the religious sentiment of the age to value poverty and self-sacrifice, yet lacked orthodox instruction."[2] The people yearning for something more and following these new movements saw a guiding ideal of spiritual growth. The other side of this coin, viewed from the perspective of church authorities, was obedience. Those who failed to remain obedient to the local church (however deficient it may be) and who were too carried away with their zeal, were the ones who found themselves in trouble. That they called for changes to the church was not alarming in itself. Just as the orders such as the Cistercians sought to extend the reform ideal espoused by the Gregorian reform by reforming the institution of monasticism, many of these heretical groups sought to extend the reform to the laity. But the Gregorian reform also added to the problem of lay piety; it oversaw an increasing clericalization and institutional hierarchy of the church, which no longer had the confidence or flexibility to allow lay piety to lead movements. Hence, lay-organized movements came under suspicion as disobedient and were repressed whenever possible.[3]

Genealogies of Heresy

To return to the issue we started the conclusions with, of heretics springing from the same source: Is there a benefit to trying to discern genealogies of the heretical beliefs? At stake is the issue of which groups are related and how. While there are some clear lines of connection, there are even more lines of speculation, and for the most part, other than obvious sources of connection or where the state of scholarship has demanded that I touch on tit, I have left speculation aside. For the most part, the scholarship of these genealogies roots itself in the works of inquisitors, whose reflections created genealogies such as the Cathars coming from the contemporary Manichaeans as a way to embellish the seriousness of new sects. The inquisitors deny self-determination and self-identification and try to define new movements into monstrosity, sometimes before the movement was a true movement. Historians have tried to understand the reasons for the precipitous rise in heresy in the Middle Ages and for its appeal, as well as which layers of society each heresy appealed to. In part, both are determined by an increase in modern churches talking about heresy and charging dissenters with heresy, even in nondoctrinal issues. In the modern case, part of the issue seems to be the inability to find ways to disagree respectfully or to assume that any divergence is a major divergence. In that respect, a study of medieval heresy can be effectual for reminding people that heresy was more often a method of social control than a method of doctrinal control. That's not to say that there were not serious doctrinal differences. There were. But what these chapters should show is that doctrinal deviance, while a part of the equation for medieval heresy, was often only one part.

Lasting Impact of Heretical Suppression

Given these many dissimilarities between heretical movements, the question we must answer is what main goal the attacks on heresy served the church. A simplistic way to think about the development of heresy is to see it as the development of the intellectual framework, on the part of the church, that distinguished correct and incorrect belief. Once these categories were established, individuals and movements could be tested, and even preemptive measures (as in the case of the beguines) could be set up. In this sense, the development of heresy was a development of the vocabulary of both inclusion and separation. Judaism and Islam were expanding in areas where Christians lived in the early Middle Ages, and Christians had recently separated themselves from the eastern half of Christendom; the question of what constituted Christianity in the face of outsiders and against other insiders was a significant one. In the wake of increasingly violent encounters with Jews and Muslims in the Crusades and in the expulsion of the Jews from Western European countries, Christianity was identifying not only those of other religions as outsiders but also some of those who claimed to be Christian. Inclusion could be determined by permission, professions of faith, rites and rituals of inclusion or exclusion, sacramental participation, submission to authority, or formal recognition of a distinct charism. Internal and external confrontations like these also led to heresy's identification resulting in the development of a new institutional structure to investigate the church and its adherents and to convict them legally and hand them off to secular justice. It was the development of a series of organizational structures working in common—papal, religious orders, and local bishops—that was the real defining element of the Inquisition. And the various aspects of the Inquisition we've seen in the preceding discussions show just how institutionalized the response to heresy became. Part of the church's institutionalized vocation was to test its adherents. It was this new definition of the church that was much more groundbreaking than that of any heretical sect. Throughout this book, we've seen how the prosecution of heresy developed over time, from being sporadic efforts on the local level to being accomplished in lockstep with local authorities, to finally being centrally promulgated and ordered to be followed by bishops in their local areas.

But the development of heresy was not merely the development of categories of correct and incorrect belief. What we've also seen is that there were a number of structures of power that were challenged continually by the church and by the accused heretics. We also see those various types of power, such as the decentralized power of the beguinages, called into question because they did not easily dovetail into the centralized hierarchy of the Roman church and dependent orders. Power challenges from different geographic areas—such as Cyprus's eastern concentration of wealth and power with the Templars, or Languedoc, where feudalism was not yet entrenched—were also problematic for the Papacy. Increasing papal centralization of power brought with it, ironically, a decrease in flexibility and ability to adapt to social movements, leading to reactions against its own members. Whereas before, a local bishop could investigate, amend, and guide the local population, by the thirteenth century their ability to do so was denied. Such changes meant that a religious community living a quiet life that served the needs of their neighbors—such as the beguines—found that the church had no official room for it in the categories of religious life. The apparatus of power had become totally separated from the apparatus of religious sentiment, apostolic life, and renewal in the spirit. That was the real tragedy.

NOTES

PREFACE

1. Sharon Crowley, *Toward a Civil Discourse: Rhetoric and Fundamentalism* (Namur: University of Pittsburgh Press, 2006), 3–4. ProQuest Ebook Central.

INTRODUCTION

1. Michael Goodich, *Other Middle Ages: Witnesses at the Margins of Medieval Society* (Philadelphia: University of Pennsylvania Press, 1998), 189. ProQuest Ebook Central.
2. Andrew P. Roach and James R. Simpson, *Heresy and the Making of European Culture: Medieval and Modern Perspectives* (New York: Taylor & Francis Group, 2013), 27.
3. Gordon Leff, *Heresy in the Later Middle Ages: The Relation of Heterodoxy to Dissent, c. 1250–1450* (Manchester, UK: Sandpiper Books, 1999), 1.
4. Leff, *Heresy in the Later Middle Ages*, 2.
5. Malcolm D. Lambert, *Medieval Heresy: Popular Movements from Bogomil to Hus* (London: E. Arnold, 1977), 3–4.
6. J. A. F. Thomson, "Orthodox Religion and the Origins of Lollardy," *History* 74, no. 240 (1989): 52.
7. Jacques LeGoff, *The Birth of Purgatory* (Chicago: University of Chicago Press, 1984). Also see J. H. Van Engen's critique in "The Christian Middle Ages as an Historiographical Problem," *American Historical Review* 91 (1986): 519–62.
8. See Norman Cohn, *Europe's Inner Demons: An Inquiry Inspired by the Great Witch Hunt* (London: Chatto, 1975); Robert Ian Moore, *The Formation of a Persecuting Society. Authority and Deviance in Western Europe, 950–1250* (Oxford: Blackwell, 2007).
9. Peter Biller, "Goodbye to Waldensianism?" *Past and Present* 192 (August 2006): 5.
10. Biller, "Goodbye," 7.
11. Biller, "Goodbye," 8.
12. Lutz Kaelber, "Weavers into Heretics? The Social Organization of Early-Thirteenth-Century Catharism in Comparative Perspective," *Social Science History* 21, no. 1 (Spring 1997): 111–13.

13. Leff, *Heresy in the Later Middle Ages*, vii.
14. Jeffrey Burton Russell, *Dissent and Reform in the Early Middle Ages* (Berkeley: University of California Press, 1965).
15. Michael Frassetto, *Heretic Lives: Medieval Heresy from Bogomil and the Cathars to Wyclif and Hus* (London: Profile, 2007), chapter 1; Lambert, *Medieval Heresy*, chapter 1.
16. Caterina Bruschi and Peter Biller, *Texts and the Repression of Medieval Heresy* (Woodbridge, UK: York Medieval Press, 2003), 148.

CHAPTER 1

1. Michael Frassetto, *Heresy and the Persecuting Society in the Middle Ages: Essays on the Work of R.I. Moore* (Leiden: Brill, 2006), 27–37.
2. Lambert, *Medieval Heresy*, 41.
3. Heinrich Fichtenau, *Heretics and Scholars in the High Middle Ages, 1000–1200*, trans. Denise A. Kaiser (University Park, PA: Pennsylvania State University Press, 1998), 57; James Fearns, "Peter von Bruis und die religiöse Bewegung des 12. Jahrhunderts," *Archiv für Kulturgeschichte* 48 (1966): 313–15.
4. Fearns, "Peter von Bruis," 317.
5. Bernard Hamilton, "The Albigensian Crusade and Heresy," in *The New Cambridge Medieval History*, ed. David Abulafia (Cambridge: Cambridge University Press, 1999), 165.
6. Fearns, "Peter von Bruis," 318.
7. Fearns, "Peter von Bruis," 318.
8. Fichtenau, *Heretics and Scholars*, 57.
9. Fearns, "Peter von Bruis," 318.
10. Adolphe Dieudonné, *Hildebert de Lavardin, évêque du Mans, archevêque de Tours (1056–1133) Sa vie.—Ses lettres* (France: A. Picard et fils, 1898), 23.
11. Walter Leggett Wakefield and Austin Patterson Evans, eds., *Heresies of the High Middle Ages* (New York: Columbia University Press, 1991), 108–9; narrative of Henry's actions at Le Mans.
12. Fichtenau, *Heretics and Scholars*, 60.
13. Dieudonné, *Hildebert of Lavardin*, 74 (translations are mine when texts are not in English).
14. Dieudonné, *Hildebert of Lavardin*, 75.
15. Dieudonné, *Hildebert of Lavardin*, 75.
16. Dieudonné, *Hildebert of Lavardin*, 75.
17. The Gregorian reforms could and did lead to attacks on clergy because they focused on correcting clerical luxury and depravity. Those that took these ideals to extremes found themselves espousing antisacerdotal and anticlerical notions (Fearns, "Peter von Bruis," 328).
18. Dieudonné, *Hildebert of Lavardin*, 23, 74.

19. Lambert, *Medieval Heresy*, 51; Dieudonné, *Hildebert of Lavardin*, 75. Dieudonné mentions that in Bernard's letter (241) to Hildefonse, the count of Toulouse, that Henry was probably not at all the same as he was 30 years before, when preaching in Le Mans. Henry's condemnations of infant baptism and prayers for the dead and his denial of transubstantiation in the Eucharist seem to have dated after Henry met Peter.
20. To trace the genealogy of these views, see Marcia L. Colish, "Peter of Bruys, Henry of Lausanne, and the Façade of St-Gilles," *Traditio* 28 (1972): 456.
21. It is from Peter the Venerable's treatise that we glean the most details about the beliefs and practices of Peter of Bruys and his followers. In fact, this letter serves as the only historical record of the person of Peter of Bruys.
22. Dominique Iogna-Prat, *Order and Exclusion: Cluny and Christendom Face Heresy, Judaism, and Islam, 1000–1150*, trans. Graham Edwards (Ithaca, NY: Cornell University Press, 2002), 109.
23. Fearns, "Peter von Bruis," 319.
24. Fearns, "Peter von Bruis," 319.
25. Fichtenau, *Hildebert de Lavardin*, 57.
26. Lambert, *Medieval Heresy*, 53. Fearns notes that the discussion of infant baptism had preoccupied reforming groups within the church for a couple of centuries at this point; their discussions usually focused on Mt 28:19; Peter of Bruys's focus on Mk 16:16 is a shift in the focus of this discussion. The rejection of infant baptism was something that would be found around this general time in a number of different groups in Bucy-Le-Long, Toulouse, Trier, Liège, Cologne, and Brittany, among other places. See Fearns, "Peter von Bruis," 321.
27. Fearns, "Peter von Bruis," 318.
28. Iogna-Prat, *Order and Exclusion*, 116.
29. Fearns, "Peter von Bruis," 321.
30. Fearns "Peter von Bruis," 323.
31. Fichtenau, *Heretics and Scholars*, 124. See also Raoul Manselli, "Il Monaco Enrico e la sua eresia," *Bolletino dell'Instituto Storico Italiano per il medioevo e Archivo Muratoriano* 65(1953): 46.
32. Fearns, "Peter von Bruis," 327.
33. Fearns, "Peter von Bruis," 327.
34. The fourth Council of Toulouse, in 1229, put forth 45 canons that aimed to extinguish heresy in the region. It was clearly a threat that did not diminish over the next century.
35. Giovan Domenico Mansi, *Sacrorum conciliorum nova et amplissima collectio: in qua praeter ea quae Phil. Labbeus et Gabr. Cossartius . . . et novissime Nicolaus Coleti in lucem edidere ea omnia insuper suis in locis optime disposita exhibentur*, t.52 (France: H. Welter, 1901–27, 1927): c. 3, 21:226f.
36. Fearns, "Peter von Bruis," 316.
37. Peter the Venerable, dedicatory letter. C 10.5.

38. Fichtenau, *Scholars and Heretics*, 61.
39. Iogna-Prat, *Order and Exclusion*, 113–14.
40. Wakefield and Evans, *Heresies*, 119.
41. Colish, "Peter of Bruys," 455.
42. This point has long been a matter of contention among scholars, although English-language scholarship is finally acknowledging that if there was an influence, it was constructed in the minds of the contemporary detractors and not based on Peter and Henry themselves.
43. Lambert, *Medieval Heresy*, 53.
44. He uses words such as *peregrinus* ("foreign") to describe Peter and his ideas; see Fearns, "Peter von Bruis," 328.
45. Lambert, *Medieval Heresy*, 51.
46. Beverly Mayne Kienzle, *Cistercians, Heresy and Crusade in Occitania, 1145–1229: Preaching in the Lord's Vineyard* (Woodbridge, NY: York Medieval Press/Boydell Press, 2001), 91.
47. Jonathan Sumption, *The Albigensian Crusade* (London: Faber & Faber, 1978), 45.
48. Sumption, *Albigensian Crusade*, 45.
49. Constant Mews, "Accusations of Heresy and Error in the Twelfth-Century Schools: The Witness of Gerhoh of Reichersberg and Otto of Friesing," in *Heresy in Transition: Transforming Ideas of Heresy in Medieval and Early Modern Europe*, ed. Ian Hunter, John Christian Laursen, and Cary J. Nederman (Aldershot, UK: Ashgate, 2005), 43–57.
50. Bernard of Clairvaux, "Letter 317," in Bernard of Clairvaux, *Letters*, trans. Bruno Scott James (Kalamazoo: Cistercian Publications, 1998), 389.
51. Bernard, *Letters*, 389.
52. Bernard of Clairvaux, "Sermon 66," in Bernard of Clairvaux, *Sermons on the Song of Songs*, vol. 3, trans. Kilian Walsh, OCSO, and Irene M. Edmonds (Kalamazoo: Cistercian Publications, 1996); see also *Rule of Benedict*, chapter 1, 202–6.
53. Bernard, *Letters*, 387–91.
54. Bernard, "Sermon 66.1, 9, 11," *Sermons*, 190–203.
55. Lambert, *Medieval Heresy*, 43–44, states that this situation is due to a dualism; others (Zerner and Moore) will say it's not a dualism in Peter and Henry as much as a dualism imposed by their detractors. What seems certain is that the ideas are on a spectrum, and those of Peter and Henry are considered just out of range. See Zerner, Monique, ed. *Inventer l'hérésie? Discours polémique et pouvoir avant l'inquisition*. Nice: Centre d'Études Médiévales de Nice, 1998. and Moore, Robert Ian. *The Formation of a Persecuting Society. Authority and Deviance in Western Europe, 950–1250*. Oxford: Blackwell, 2007.
56. Lambert, *Medieval Heresy*, 49.

57. Stamatia Noutsou, "'We are not to believe that he hesitated to give correction, for his ministry is applauded': Politicizing the Fight against Heresy in the Writings of Geoffrey of Auxerre," *Cistercian Studies Quarterly* 57, no. 1 (2022): 79.

CHAPTER 2

1. Lambert, *Medieval Heresy*, xiii.
2. As an aside, brulology, the study of burn-wound care, has its modern origins in the time of the attacks against Cathars, where heretic burnings were commonplace. See Michel Costagliola, "Fires in History: The Cathar Heresy, the Inquisition and Brulology," *Annals of Burns and Fire Disasters* 28, no. 3 (2015): 230–34.
3. While the verity of the declaration is debated by scholars, the vehemence of the rhetoric ascribed to the crusaders shows the fervor of the crusading spirit against their own countrymen. Jacques Berlioz, *'Touz-les tous, Dieu reconnaîtra les siens': La croisade contre les Albigeois vue par Césaire de Heisterbach* (Loubatières: Portet-sur-Garonne, 1994).
4. Jonathan Sumption, *Albigensian Crusade*, 79.
5. Robert Ian Moore, *The War on Heresy: Faith and Power in Medieval Europe* (London: Profile, 2012).
6. Antonio Sennis, *Cathars in Question: Heresy and Inquisition in the Middle Ages* (Woodbridge, UK: York Medieval Press, 2012), 2.
7. Lutz Kaelber, "Weavers into Heretics?":113.
8. Sumption, *Albigensian Crusade*, 18–19.
9. For an overview of how some scholars are continuing to insist on an unbroken line of dualist thought threatening Christianity from the fifth century Manichaeans onward and a map of updated methodology regarding Cathars in historical records, see Mark Gregory Pegg, "On Cathars, Albigenses, and Good Men of Languedoc," *Journal of Medieval History* 27, no. 2 (2001): 181–95.
10. The necessity of a good genealogy for administration of *consolamentum* was most markedly noted when Pope Nicetas/Ninquita required that the Cathar bishop re-receive *consolamentum* from him, as Mark had been associated with a different Bogomil group, not Nicetas.
11. Pegg, "On Cathars," 185.
12. Sandra Pott, "Radical Heretics, Martyrs, or Witnesses of Truth?: The Albigenses in Ecclesiastical History and Literature (1550–1850)," in *Heresy in Transition: Transforming Ideas of Heresy in Medieval and Early Modern Europe*, eds. Ian Hunter, John Christian Laursen, and Cary J. Nederman (Aldershot, UK: Ashgate, 2005), 181–94. On the other side, people such as Biller and Lambert find similarities between the Cathars and some heretics, such as the Bogomils, in an attempt to catalogue them.

13. This view, instead of the church being founded in the West or by Bogomils in the East and carried West, is seen in Bernard Hamilton, "Wisdom from the East: The Reception by the Cathars of Eastern Dualist Texts," in *Heresy and Literacy, 1000–1530*, eds. Peter Biller and Anne Hudson (Cambridge: Cambridge University Press, 1994), 44–45.
14. This definition was largely false, for the Bogomils of the East consisted of several distinct churches.
15. Janet Hamilton, Sarah Hamilton, and Bernard Hamilton, *Hugh Ereriano: Contra Patarenos* (Leiden: Brill, 2004), 37.
16. Bernard Hamilton, "The Cathars and the Seven Churches of Asia," reprinted in *Crusaders, Cathars and the Holy Places*, ed. Bernard Hamilton (Aldershot, UK: Ashgate, 1999), XII: 282.
17. Hamilton, *Hugh Ereriano*, 47.
18. Eckbertus Abbas Schonaugensis, in J. P. Migne, *Patrologia Latina*, vol. CXCV, 1855, col. 16–17, 24.
19. Thus, the contemporaries of this idea were not viewing it as a repeat of an old classic. See S. R. Maitland, *Facts and Documents Illustrative of the History, Doctrine, and Rites of the Ancient Albigenses and Waldensians* (Gloucester: Edward Power, 1832), 392–94.
20. Peter Biller, "Christians and Heretics," in *The Cambridge History of Christianity: Christianity in Western Europe c. 1150–c. 1500*, eds. Miri Ruben and Walter Simons (Cambridge: Cambridge University Press, 2010), 179–80. The word *mission* is used by scholars; it implies a network of communication and shared purpose.
21. Malcolm Barber, "Moving Cathars: The Italian Connection in the Thirteenth Century," *Journal of Mediterranean Studies* 10, no. 1 (2001): 5–19.
22. It would also reinforce trade and financial transactions between the areas that Cathars traveled.
23. Biller, "Christians and Heretics," 181.
24. Pott, "Radical Heretics," 182 n. 3. Amended by Kienzle, Beverly Mayne, "Cathars." In *Encyclopedia of Genocide and Crimes against Humanity*, edited by Dinah L. Shelton (Detroit: Macmillan Reference USA, 2005): I.151–55.
25. Kienzle, "Cathars," 152.
26. Kaelber, "Weavers," 113–14.
27. Deborah Schulevitz, "Following the Money: Cathars, Apostolic Poverty, and the Economy in Medieval Languedoc, 1237–1259," *Journal of Medieval Religious Cultures* 44, no. 1 (2018): 24–59.
28. Kaelber, "Weavers," 118.
29. Kienzle, *Cistercians, Heresy and Crusade*, 48.
30. Kaelber, "Weavers," 117.
31. See Guillaume Besse, *Histoire des ducs, marquis et comtes de Narbonne, autrement appellez princes des Goths, ducs de Septimanie et marquis de Gothie* [...] *par le sieur Besse* (Paris : A. de Sommaville, 1660).

32. Seen by the request that each take *consolamentum* a second time from Nicetas.
33. These would have been northern France, Albi, Lombardy/Italy, Toulouse, Carcassonne, and Agen, according to the records of the Council of Saint-Félix-de-Caraman in 1167.
34. Sumption, *Albigensian Crusade*, 47.
35. Beverly Mayne Kienzle, "Religious Poverty and the Search for Perfection," in *The Cambridge History of Christianity: Christianity in Western Europe c. 1150–c. 1500*, eds. Miri Ruben and Walter Simons (Cambridge: Cambridge University Press, 2010), 49.
36. Kaelber, "Weavers," 120.
37. Schulevitz, "Following the Money," 26.
38. Bernardus Guidonis, *The Inquisitor's Guide: A Medieval Manual on Heretics*, ed. and trans. Janet Shirley (Welwyn Garden City, UK: Ravenhall Books, 2006), 41.
39. See Bernard Hamilton, "The Cathars and Christian Perfection," in *The Medieval Church: Universities, Heresy and the Religious Life. Essays in Honour of Gordon Leff*, eds. by Peter Biller and Barrie Dobson (Woodbridge, UK: Boydell Press, 1999): 5–23.
40. Wakefield and Evans, *Heresies*, 556.
41. Antoine Dondaine, *Le Liber "De Duobus Principiis": Un Traité Néo-Manichéen Du Xiiie Siècle; Suivi D'un Fragment De Rituel Cathare* (Rome: Instituto Storico Domenicano S. Sabina, 1939), section 13; Wakefield and Evans, *Heresies*, 523.
42. Although one challenge to this rigid morality was that there was nothing in place to deal with major lapses or with lapses of the ascetic regime.
43. Bernardus Guidonis, *The Inquisitor's Guide*, 37.
44. Bernardus Guidonis, *The Inquisitor's Guide*, 42. Gui is at pains here to portray the Cathars as hard-hearted and hard-minded, thus making their view appear to be one of obstinacy.
45. Lambert, *Medieval Heresy*, 109.
46. For minor offenses, the rite of *apparellamentum* was a communal confession of minor faults.
47. For copies of these rites, see Catherine Léglu, Rebecca Rist, and Claire Taylor, *The Cathars and the Albigensian Crusade: A Sourcebook* (London: Routledge, 2014); Dondaine, *Le Liber "De Duobus Principiis."* For sources of the rituals, see René Nelli and Anne Brenon, *Écritures Cathares* (Monaco: Editions du Rocher, 1995).
48. Wakefield and Evans, *Heresies*, 480.
49. Lambert blames the majority of its downfall on the Cathars, not on the external forces amassed against them. What he saw was the internal divisions sown as doctrinal squabbles among the Italian Cathar churches; Lambert, *Medieval Heresy*, 143.
50. As Andrew Roach notes in his article on the development of the Inquisition, there's still much to be explored on how the inquisitorial machinery warmed up

in the years between 1215, when it was outlined in Fourth Lateran, and 1242, when the first inquisitorial manual came into being. Andrew P. Roach, "Penance and the Making of the Inquisition in Languedoc," *Journal of Ecclesiastical History* 52, no. 3 (July 2001): 410.
51. Sumption, *Albigensian Crusade*, 43.
52. Sumption, *Albigensian Crusade*, 46.
53. Sumption, *Albigensian Crusade*, 46–47.
54. Roach, "Penance," 411. Among other penances Roach discusses are being required to wear a cross and being required to join a crusade, along with financial penalties for heretics.
55. Roach, "Penance," 415.
56. Sumption, *Albigensian Crusade*, 54.
57. Noutsou, "Geoffrey of Auxerre, 90, 92.
58. Indeed, the previous series of pronouncements and judgments had focused on the necessity of the knights no longer protecting the heretics, as noted in Cicely d'Autremont Angleton, *Two Cistercian Preaching Missions to the Languedoc in the Twelfth Century, 1145 and 1178* (Washington, DC: Catholic University, 1984), 182.
59. Ian Forrest, *The Detection of Heresy in Late Medieval England* (Oxford: Clarendon Press, 2005), 32.
60. Hamilton, "Albigensian Crusade," 166.
61. Lambert, *Medieval Heresy*, 144.
62. Leff, *Heresy*, 42. See Paul Fredericq, *Corpus Documentorum Inquisitionis Haereticae Pravitatis Neerlandicae: Verzameling Van Stukken Pauselijke En Bisschoppelijke Inquisitie In De Nederlanden* (Gent: Vuylsteke, etc., 1889–1903), 77–78.
63. The two inquisitors murdered were William Arnold and Stephen of St. Thibéry, who were among eleven men in their entourage murdered by Cathars.
64. This change would be formalized by *Ad extirpanda* in 1252, which has the religious orders take over as inquisitors; at first, the two mendicant orders—the Dominicans and Franciscans—would hold these posts.
65. Kaelber, "Weavers," 117–18.
66. Bernardus Guidonis, *The Inquisitor's Guide*, 41–42.
67. Sumption, *Albigensian Crusade*, 40.
68. James Given, "The Inquisitors of Languedoc and the Medieval Technology of Power," *The American Historical Review* 94, no. 2 (1989): 338.
69. Given, "The Inquisitors of Languedoc," 339.
70. One of her sermons against heresy comes down to us as a letter; see *Epistolarum* i. XVr, pp. 34–44 and for additional passages, see the appendices.

CHAPTER 3

1. Lambert, *Medieval Heresy*, 70.
2. Wakefield and Evans, *Heresies*, 209.

3. Euan Cameron, *Waldenses: Rejections of the Holy Church in Medieval Europe* (Oxford: Blackwell, 2000) devotes chapters to each of these regions. See also Lutz Kaelber, "Other- and Inner-Worldly Asceticism in Medieval Waldensianism: A Weberian Analysis," *Sociology of Religion* 56, no. 2 (Summer 1995): 93.
4. Cameron says that sources cannot show a continuity between Valdesius and the Southwestern Alps Waldenses, who were not discovered until the mid-fourteenth century.
5. Eugene Smelyansky, "Heretical Refugees and Persecution of German Waldensians, 1393–1400," *Journal of Medieval History* 48, no. 3 (2022): 400.
6. Smelyansky, "Heretical Refugees," 416.
7. See Cameron, *Waldenses*. The book is organized into these three stages.
8. For someone looking for a much more in-depth look at the Waldensians, see Cameron's *Waldenses* and Gabriel Audisio, *The Waldensian Dissent: Persecution and Survival, c. 1170–1570*, trans. Claire Davison (Cambridge: Cambridge University Press, 1999).
9. A scholarly project focused on a trove of over 200 Waldensian sermons is currently underway. Some selected studies of parts of this collection have begun to appear as the project works on a critical edition of the sermons. See Andrea Giraudo, "The Critical Edition of the Medieval Waldensian Sermons," *Medieval Sermon Studies* 59, no. 1 (2005): 74–77.
10. Luciana Borghi Cedrini and Andrea Giraudo, "Chapter 20: Ancient Waldensian Literature," in *A Companion to the Waldenses in the Middle Ages*, eds. Marina Benedetti and Euan Cameron (Leiden: Brill, 2022), 460. See also Cameron, *Waldenses*, 4–5.
11. For more on this topic, see Euan Cameron, *The Reformation of the Heretics: The Waldenses of the Alps, 1480–1580* (Oxford: Clarendon Press, 1984), especially the first few chapters, which lay out the social context of later Waldensianism.
12. Biller, "Goodbye to Waldensianism?" 20.
13. Biller thinks the Gui and Zwicker inquisitorial records are good, truthful sources, thinking of them as akin to protomodern historiographic approaches, an interpretation I disagree with.
14. Kienzle, "Religious Poverty", 49. In fact, this emphasis on the ability of the laity to preach and interpret Scripture is perhaps the aspect scholars most agree on.
15. Biller, "Christians and Heretics," 177.
16. Cameron, *Waldenses*, 11.
17. Noutsou, "Geoffrey of Auxerre," 64–65.
18. Sumption, *The Albigensian Crusade*, 39.
19. The origins of the Waldensians being linked to Valdesius are attested to in the *Universal Chronicle* of Laon and the *Life of Pope Alexander III* by Richard of Poitiers. *Universal Chronicle* in Robert Ian Moore, *The Birth of Popular Heresy* (Toronto: Medieval Academy Reprints for Teaching, 1995), 200–203.
20. It is one of the oldest poems in French. For the text and commentary, see Alison Goddard Elliott, *The Vie de Saint Alexis in the Twelfth and Thirteenth Centuries:*

An Edition and Commentary (Chapel Hill: UNC Dept. of Romance Languages, 1983). For more on the significance of the poem across academic fields of study, see the study by Karl D. Uitti, "The Old French 'Vie de Saint Alexis': Paradigm, Legend, Meaning," *Romance Philology* 20, no. 3 (1967): 263–95.
21. Matt 19:21.
22. Wakefield and Evans, *Heresy*, 209; see also Edward Peters, ed., *Heresy and Authority in Medieval Europe* (Philadelphia: University of Pennsylvania Press, 1980), 144.
23. An Anonymous Chronicle circa 1228, translated in J. H. Robinson, *Readings in European History* (Boston: Ginn, 1905), 381.
24. Cameron, *Waldenses*, 14. Wakefield and Evans, *Heresy*, 202.
25. Cameron, *Waldenses*, 16, for the issues surrounding what might have been early prohibitions on Valdesius preaching.
26. Kienzle, *Cistercians, Heresy and Crusade*, 129.
27. Noutsou, "Geoffrey of Auxerre," 80.
28. Noutsou, "Geoffrey of Auxerre," 91.
29. Peters, *Heresy and Authority*, 148.
30. Cameron, *Waldenses*, 18.
31. Peters, *Heresy and Authority*, 148.
32. Noutsou, "Geoffrey of Auxerre," 65.
33. Peters, *Heresy and Authority*, 149.
34. Adam L. Hoose, "Durán of Huesca (c. 1160–1230): A Waldensian Seeking a Remedy to Heresy," *Journal of Religious History* 38, no. 2 (2014): 173–74.
35. Kaelber, "Other- and Inner-Worldly Asceticism," 91–119.
36. Giovanni Gonnet, "The Influence of the Sermon on the Mount upon the Ethics of the Waldensians of the Middle Ages," *Brethren Life and Thought* 35, no. 1 (Winter 1990): 35.
37. Gordon Leff, "The Making of the Myth of a True Church in the Later Middle Ages," *Journal of Medieval and Renaissance Studies* 1, no. 1 (1971): 13.
38. Biller, "Christians and Heretics," 178.
39. Kaelber, "Weavers," 123.
40. Robert Lerner, "A Case of Religious Counter-Culture: The German Waldensians," *American Scholar* 55 (Spring 1986): 241.
41. Lerner, "Religious Counter-Culture," 242.
42. Bernardus Guidonis, *The Inquisitor's Guide*, 58.
43. The approach stood in some contrast with the views of the Petrobrusians and the Cathars, whose evangelical focus caused them to shift from favoring the whole Bible to rejecting the Old Testament. The Waldensians managed to keep both sets of books as favored. Fearns, "Peter von Bruis," 326.
44. B. Marthaler, "Forerunners of the Franciscans: The Waldenses," *Franciscan Studies* n.s. xviii.2 (June 1958): 376.
45. Marthaler, "Forerunners," 376.
46. Kienzle, "Religious Poverty," 50; Lambert, *Medieval Heresy*, 80.

47. Lambert, *Medieval Heresy*, 77.
48. Lerner, "Religious Counter-Culture," 243.
49. Lerner, "Religious Counter-Culture," 243.
50. Herbert Grundmann, *Religious Movements in the Middle Ages: The Historical Links between Heresy, the Mendicant Orders, and the Women's Religious Movement in the Twelfth Century, with the Historical Foundations of German Mysticism*, trans. Steve Rowan (Notre Dame and London: University of Notre Dame Press, 1995), 41–42.
51. Leff, "The Making of the Myth," 14.
52. Leff, "The Making of the Myth," 13.
53. Lerner, "Religious Counter-Culture," 244.
54. Leff, "The Making of the Myth," 13.
55. Leff, "The Making of the Myth," 14.
56. Bernardus Guidonis, *The Inquisitor's Guide*, 59.
57. Bernardus Guidonis, *The Inquisitor's Guide*, 59.
58. Alan C. Kors and Edward Peters, *Witchcraft in Europe 1100–1700: A Documentary History* (London: J. M. Dent & Sons: 1972), 158.
59. Bernardus Guidonis, *The Inquisitor's Guide*, 53.
60. Lerner, "Religious Counter-Culture," 241.
61. Sources for the history of the Waldensians come from the *Chronicon universal anonymi Louunensis*, which was a document ca. 1220 from a Premonstratensian monk of Laon, and the *Tractatus de septem donis spiritus*, which was the work of the Dominican inquisitor Stephen of Bourbon.
62. Noutsou, "Geoffrey of Auxerre," 88.
63. This decree was a reaffirmation of Lucius III's 1181 decree in which he stated: "We decree to put under a perpetual anathema the Cathari and Patarini and those who falsely call themselves Humiliati or Poor of Lyon, the Passagini, Josephini, Arnaldistae." See Henry C. Vedder, "Origin and Early Teachings of the Waldenses, according to Roman Catholic Writers of the Thirteenth Century," *The American Journal of Theology* 4, no. 3 (1900): 467.
64. Lambert, *Medieval Heresy*, 73.
65. Grundmann, *Religious Movements*, 42.
66. Grundmann, *Religious Movements*, 43–44.
67. Gonnet, "Influence," 35.
68. Leff, *Heresy*, 40.
69. Hoose, "Durán of Huesca," 178.
70. Grundmann, *Religious Movements*, 48.
71. Grundmann, *Religious Movements*, 44.
72. Grundmann, *Religious Movements*, 46.
73. Antonio García y García, editor, *Constitutiones Concilii quarti Lateranensis una cum Commentariis glossatorum* (Vatican City: Biblioteca Apostolica Vaticano, 1981), 50–51.
74. Hoose, "Durán of Huesca," 175.

75. Hoose, "Durán of Huesca," 178.
76. Marthaler, "Forerunners," 133.
77. Later, Innocent would in fact insist that Francis be ordained as a deacon in order to continue preaching.
78. Biller, "Christians and Heretics," 175.
79. Jean-François Gilmont, "Les Vaudois: Sources et Méthodes," *Revue de L'Histoire Des Religions* 217, no. 1 (2000): 19, notes that this discovery has both its advantages and disadvantages. Scholars from other fields often find them in nontheological document caches but often don't know how to approach theological issues.
80. Calvin and his cousin Olivetan completed this work in 1535.
81. Grundmann, *Religious Movements*, 50.
82. Grundmann, *Religious Movements*, 50.

CHAPTER 4

1. Robert E. Lerner, *The Heresy of the Free Spirit in the Later Middle Ages* (Notre Dame and London: University of Notre Dame Press, 1972), 5–6.
2. As the heresy scholar Robert Lerner declared, "heretics of the Free Spirit were condemned before very many of them can be proved to have existed." Lerner, *Heresy of the Free Spirit*, 61. Strictly speaking, it was defined after one person was condemned to death and their book burned, but there certainly was no grounds for the thousands of inquisitional investigations that followed.
3. Lerner, *Free Spirit*, 37–38.
4. Lerner, *Free Spirit*, 38.
5. The earliest references to Lollards were in 1309 and were in reference to wandering beghards.
6. Leff, *Heresy*, 20.
7. Lerner, *Heresy of the Free Spirit*, 45.
8. *Canons of the Council of Vienne*, 28.
9. *Ad nostrum*, Canon 28.1.
10. *Ad nostrum*, Canon 28.8.
11. The last official beguine died in 2013, in Sint-Amandsberg, Belgium. Gloria Satto, "The Last Beguine," *L'Osservatore Romano*, September 26, 2020. https://www.osservatoreromano.va/en/news/2020-09/the-last-beguine.html.
12. Penelope Galloway, "'Life, learning and wisdom': The Forms and Functions of Beguine Education," in *Medieval Monastic Education*, eds. George Ferzoco and Carolyn Muessig (London: Leicester University Press, 2000), 153.
13. Grundmann, *Religious Movements*, 76–80.
14. Backtracked is in part a misnomer, for women had been only semi-accepted into the order in a couple of geographical locations.
15. Grundmann, *Religious Movements*, 93.

16. Kienzle, "Religious Poverty,", 42 n. 13; *Sancti Bernardi Opera* (SBO) 2. sermon 55.2; SBO 7. Ep. 64.158. James, Letters 67, 91.
17. L. J. M. Phillipen, *De begijnhoven: oorsprong, geschiedenis, inrichting* (Antwerp: Veritas, 1918), 40–57. Cited by Ernest W. McDonnell, *The Beguines and Beghards in Medieval Culture* (New Brunswick, NJ: Rutgers University Press, 1954), 5. Hans Geybels, *Vulgariter Beghinae: Eight Centuries of Beguine History in the Low Countries* (Turnhout: Brepols, 2004), 39–54, has a good, detailed development of this group in English.
18. Walter Simons, *Cities of Ladies: Beguine Communities in the Medieval Low Countries, 1200–1565* (Philadelphia, University of Pennsylvania Press, 2001), 7–8.
19. Grundmann, *Religious Movements*, 83.
20. These lives are all collected in Thomas de Cantimpré, *Thomas of Cantimpré: The Collected Saints' Lives*, ed. Barbara Newman, trans. Margot H. King and Barbara Newman (Turnhout: Brepols, 2008).
21. When he talks of Marie d'Oignies, he talks of a woman who was married and who forsook relations with her husband in favor of a life serving God. He also does not use the word *beguine* to refer to these women, seeing it as a word made up by their detractors; see Robert Bartlett, "Jacques de Vitry (d. 1240) and the Religious Life of His Time," *History (London)* 108, no. 379–380 (2023): 3–19.
22. Simons, *Cities of Ladies*, 114.
23. Simons, *Cities of Ladies*, 115.
24. Leff, *Heresy*, 21.
25. Lerner, *Free Spirit*, 62.
26. Thomas de Cantimpré, *The Life of Christina the Astonishing*, ed. and trans. Margot H. King and David Wiljer (Toronto: Peregrina Publishing., 1999), 63.
27. Thomas de Cantimpré, *The Life of Christina the Astonishing*, 67.
28. Thomas de Cantimpré, *The Life of Christina the Astonishing*, 13.
29. Thomas de Cantimpré, *The Life of Christina the Astonishing*, 79.
30. Thomas de Cantimpré, *The Life of Christina the Astonishing*, 85.
31. Kathleen Garay and Madeleine Jeay, *The Life of Saint Douceline, a Beguine of Provence* (Rochester, NY: D. S. Brewer, 2001), 10. The role of Franciscan poverty in the development of heresies near her convent is discussed in the chapter on Spiritual Franciscans.
32. Marguerite Porete, *The Mirror of Simple Souls*, trans. and intro. Ellen L. Babinsky (New York: Paulist Press, 1993), chapter 61, 138–39.
33. Marguerite Porete, *Mirror*, chapter 68, 143.
34. Marguerite Porete, *Mirror*, chapter 12, 92.
35. Marguerite Porete, *Mirror*, chapter 12, 93.
36. Lerner, *Free Spirit*, 76.
37. 2 Cor 3:17.
38. Lerner, *Free Spirit*, 82.
39. Lerner, *Free Spirit*, 83.

40. Lerner, *Free Spirit*, 48.
41. Geybels, *Vulgariter Beghinae*, 54.
42. Geybels, *Vulgariter Beghinae*, 55.
43. Lerner, *Free Spirit*, 66.
44. Leff, *Heresy*, 32.
45. Meister Eckhart, *The Essential Sermons, Commentaries, Treatises, and Defense*, trans. and intro. Edmond College and Bernard McGinn (New York: Paulist Press, 1981), sermon 6, 187.
46. Meister Eckhart, *The Essential Sermons*, sermon 48, 197.
47. J. M. Clark, *The Great German Mystics* (Oxford: Basil Blackwell, 1949), 12.
48. Robin Vose, "Heresy Inquisitions in the Later Middle Ages," in *Origin, Development and Refinement of Medieval Religious Mendicancies*, ed. by Donald Prudlo (Leiden: Brill, 2011), 157.
49. Meister Eckhart, *Teacher and Preacher*, trans. Bernard McGinn, Frank Tobin, and Elvira Borgstädt (New York: Paulist Press, 1986), 350.
50. Meister Eckhart, *Teacher and Preacher*, 351.
51. Meister Eckhart, *Teacher and Preacher*, 363.
52. Meister Eckhart, *Teacher and Preacher*, 358.
53. Meister Eckhart, *Teacher and Preacher*, 383.
54. Leff, *Heresy*, 18–19.
55. Grundmann, *Religious Movements*, 75.
56. Leff, *Heresy*, 19.
57. Grundmann, *Religious Movements*, 140–41. Lincoln had a thriving cloth trade in the High Middle Ages, linking the city to Flanders, and thus it would make sense that religious ideas from the Low Countries would make their way back to Lincoln.
58. Grundmann, *Religious Movements*, 141.
59. Leff, *Heresy*, 14.
60. Simons, *Cities of Ladies*, 119.
61. Meister Eckhart, *The Complete Mystical Works of Meister Eckhart*, trans. Maurice O'C. Walsh (New York: Herder & Herder, 2009), 48.

CHAPTER 5

1. Lambert, *Medieval Heresy*, 172–73.
2. A. J. Forey, "The Emergence of the Military Order in the Twelfth Century," *Journal of Ecclesiastical History* 36, no. 2 (April 1985): 176.
3. Peter W. Edbury, "The Old French William of Tyre and the Origins of the Templars," in *Knighthoods of Christ: Essays on the History of the Crusades and the Knights Templar Presented to Malcolm Barber*, ed. Norman Housley (Aldershot, UK: Ashgate, 2007), 151–64. William's text is in chapter XII.7.

4. Malcolm Barber, *The New Knighthood: A History of the Order of the Temple* (Cambridge: Cambridge University Press, 1994), 44.
5. Bernard of Clairvaux, "Letter 32," in *Letters*, trans. Bruno Scott James, intro. Beverly Mayne Kienzle (Kalamazoo: Cistercian Publications, 1998), 65.
6. Helen Nicholson, *The Knights Templar: A Brief History of the Warrior Order* (London: Robinson, 2010), 2.
7. Barber, *New Knighthood*, 13.
8. Forey, "The Emergence," 176.
9. Barber, *New Knighthood*, 27.
10. Nicholson, *Knights Templar*, 13.
11. Nicholson, *Knights Templar*, 24.
12. Bernard of Clairvaux, *In Praise of the New Knighthood*, trans. Conrad Greenia (Kalamazoo: Cistercian Publications, 2000), chapter 11.
13. Bernard, *In Praise*, 5.10.
14. Bernard, *In Praise*, 4.1.
15. Jean Leclercq, "Un document sur les Débuts des Templiers," *Revue d'Histoire Ecclésiastique* 52 (1957) : 91.
16. Bernard, *In Praise*, 4.8.
17. Bernard, *In Praise*, 4, end.
18. J. M. Upton-Ward, *Rule of the Templars: The French Text of the Rule of the Order of the Knights Templar* (Woodbridge, UK: Boydell, 1992), 32.
19. Upton-Ward, *Rule of the Templars*, 12.
20. Upton-Ward, *Rule of the Templars*, 12.
21. Upton-Ward, *Rule of the Templars*, 14.
22. Forey, "The Emergence," 186.
23. Upton-Ward, *Rule of the Templars*, 33.
24. Saint Thomas Aquinas, *Summa Theologica*, Question II-II.188.6 ad 2.
25. Forey, "The Emergence," 187.
26. Barber, *New Knighthood*, 1.
27. Sophia Menache, "Contemporary Attitudes Concerning the Templars' Affair: Propaganda's Fiasco?" *Journal of Medieval History* 8 (1982): 136. In studying propaganda used by the French royalty during the Templar trials, the scholar Sophia Menache notes, "The French propaganda campaign during the Templars' trial reveals, from its initial stages, an acute awareness of favorable public opinion."
28. Malcolm Barber, "Introduction," in *The Debate on the Trial of the Templars (1307–1314)*, eds. Helen Nicholson, Paul F. Crawford, and Jochen Burgtorf (Farnham: Taylor & Francis Group, 2010), 26.
29. Nicholson, *The Knights Templar*, 69.
30. Malcolm Barber and A. K. Bate, *The Templars: Selected Sources* (Manchester: Manchester University Press, 2002), 245.

31. Barber, "Introduction," 23.
32. Barber and Bate, *Selected Sources*, 245.
33. Barber and Bate, *Selected Sources*, 257 (Esquin); 251 (Geoffrey of Charney).
34. Barber and Bate, *Selected Sources*, 273.
35. Barber and Bate, *Selected Sources*, 277.
36. Nicholson, *The Knights Templar*, 70.
37. Malcolm Barber, "James of Molay, the Last Grand Master of the Order of the Temple," *Studia Monastica* 14 (1972): 108.
38. Nicholson, *The Knights Templar*, 73.
39. Probably the primary reason why Jacques would confess: a heretic who confessed was treated more leniently that a recalcitrant one too obstinate to give up their ways. He probably saw that no one would believe his innocence, so confessing would at least lead to life imprisonment rather than excommunication and death by burning.
40. Barbara Frale, "The Chinon Chart: Papal Absolution to the Last Templar, Master Jacques de Molay," *Journal of Medieval History* 30, no. 2 (2004): 109–34.
41. Lambert, *Medieval Heresy*, 173; Menache, "Propaganda,"136.
42. Evelyn Lord, *The Knights Templar in Britain* (London: Longman, 2002), 250.
43. Lord, *Knights Templar in Britain*, 255.
44. Elizabeth A. R. Brown and Alan Forey, "*Vox in Excelso* and the Suppression of the Knights Templar: The Bull, Its History, and a New Edition," *Mediaeval Studies* 80 (2018): 3, 6.
45. Brown and Forey, "*Vox in Excelso*," 4.
46. Barber, "James of Molay," 118.
47. Roach, "Penance," 428. Citing Upton-Ward, *Rule*, 74, 79.

CHAPTER 6

1. James M. Matenaer, "Franciscan Poverty as Virtual Perfection: The Description of the Apostolic Life in Peter of John Olivi's Matthew Commentary," *Cithara* 62, no. 1 (November 2022): 18–32.
2. Jennifer Kolpacoff Deane, *A History of Medieval Heresy and Inquisition* (Lanham, MD: Rowman & Littlefield Publishers, 2011), 77.
3. Decima L. Douie, *The Nature of the Effect of the Heresy on the Fraticelli* (New York: AMS Press, 1978), 2.
4. David Burr, "Effects of the Spiritual Franciscan Controversy on the Mendicant Ideal," in *Origin, Development and Refinement of Medieval Religious Mendicancies*, ed. Donald Prudlo (Leiden: Brill, 2011), 278.
5. Lerner, *Free Spirit*, 35 n.1; Louisa Burnham, *So Great a Light, So Great a Smoke: The Beguin Heretics of Languedoc* (Ithaca, NY, and London: Cornell University Press, 2008), 30ff.
6. Matenaer "Franciscan Poverty," 19.

7. Leff, "The Making of the Myth," 4–5.
8. Brett Whalen, "Joachim of Fiore, Apocalyptic Conversion, and the 'Persecuting Society,'" *History Compass* 8/7 (2010): 684.
9. For more on how Bonaventure's theology of history relied upon the ideas of Joachim of Fiore, see Joseph Ratzinger, *The Theology of History in St. Bonaventure*, trans. Zachary Hayes (Chicago: Franciscan Herald Press, 1971).
10. Matenaer "Franciscan Poverty," 21.
11. As Flood points out, part of what was at stake was also a concerted effort of the papacy to shape the order from one that showed solidarity with the field workers to one of book learning. See David Flood, "Peter Olivi and Franciscan Poverty," *Franciscan Studies* 74 (2016): 177–84.
12. A critical introduction and critical edition of this text can be found in Warren Lewis, "Peter John Olivi, Prophet of the Year 2000: Ecclesiology and Eschatology in the *Lectura super Apocalypsim*; Introduction to a Critical Edition of the Text" (PhD diss., Universität Tübingen, 1976). Reprinted excerpts in Paul Halsall, "Petrus Iohannis Olivi: Selections from the Apocalypse Commentary," *Internet Medieval Sourcebook*, https://sourcebooks.fordham.edu/source/olivi.asp.
13. David Burr, "Early Olivi and the Parables," *Franciscan Studies* 78 (2020): 110.
14. David Burr, "Olivi, Christ's Three Advents, and the Double Antichrist," *Franciscan Studies* 74 (2016): 16.
15. David Burr, "Olivi, Maifreda, Na Prous, and the Shape of Joachism, ca. 1300," *Franciscan Studies* 73 (2015): 279.
16. Halsall, "Petrus Iohannis Olivi."
17. Halsall, "Petrus Iohannis Olivi."
18. Halsall, "Petrus Iohannis Olivi."
19. Burr, "Effects," 281.
20. Burr, "Olivi, Maifreda, Na Prous," 276.
21. Burnham, *So Great a Light*, 138–39.
22. Burr, "Olivi, Maifreda, Na Prous," 277.
23. Vose, "Heresy Inquisitions," 155.
24. Nickiphoros I. Tsougarakis, "Heretical Networks between East and West: The Case of the Fraticelli," *Journal of Medieval History* 44, no. 5 (2018): 529–42.
25. Brian R. Carniello, "Gerardo Segarelli as the Anti-Francis: Mendicant Rivalry and Heresy in Medieval Italy, 1260–1300," *Journal of Ecclesiastical History* 57, no. 2 (2006): 230.
26. Burr, "Olivi, Maifreda, Na Prous," 283.
27. Burr, "Olivi, Maifreda, Na Prous," 283.
28. Burr, "Olivi, Maifreda, Na Prous," 293, acknowledges that a clear line of geneaology of thought from Olivi or Joachim to Maifreda cannot be established, but like him, I believe it's obvious that the apocalyptic ideas of ages and being on the cusp of a new age were alive and well within her sect.

29. Delfi I. Nieto-Isabel, "Beliefs in Progress: The Beguins of Languedoc and the Construction of a New Heretical Identity," *Summa* 15 (Spring 2020): 95, 97.
30. Burr, "Effects," 287.
31. Nieto-Isabel, "Beliefs in Progress," 101–2.
32. Nieto-Isabel, "Beliefs in Progress," 102.
33. Text of her confession in Latin can be found in William Harold May, "The Confession of Prous Boneta Heretic and Heresiarch," in *Essays in Medieval Thought: Presented in Honor of Austin Patterson Evans*, eds. John H. Mundy, Richard W. Emery, and Benjamin N. Nelson (New York: Columbia University Press, 1955), 3–30. An English translation can be found in Paul Halsall, "Na Prous Bonnet," *Internet Medieval Sourcebook*, https://sourcebooks.fordham.edu/source/naprous.asp.
34. Quotation from Halsall, "Na Prous Bonnet." For more on her equating recent events with apocalyptic history, see Burr, "Olivi, Maifreda, Na Prous," 289.
35. Halsall, "Na Prous Bonnet."
36. Halsall, "Na Prous Bonnet."
37. Halsall, "Na Prous Bonnet."
38. Halsall, "Na Prous Bonnet."
39. Burr, "Effects," 294.
40. Nieto-Isabel, "Beliefs in Progress," 107, 105.
41. Burnham, *So Great a Light*, 51.
42. John Monfasani, "The Fraticelli and Clerical Wealth in Quattrocento Rome," in *Renaissance Society and Culture: Essays in Honor of Eugene F. Rice, Jr.*, ed. John Monfassani and Ronald Gusto (New York: Ithaca Press, 1991), 181.
43. Bernardus Guidonis, *The Inquisitor's Guide*, 91–92.
44. James Given, "The Béguins in Bernard Gui's *Liber Sententiarum*," in *Texts and the Repression of Medieval Heresy*, eds. Caterina Bruschi and Peter Biller (Woodbridge, UK: York Medieval Press, 2003), 155.
45. Bernardus Guidonis, *The Inquisitor's Guide*, 94–5.
46. Bernardus Guidonis, *The Inquisitor's Guide*, 96.
47. Bernardus Guidonis, *The Inquisitor's Guide*, 95.
48. Bernardus Guidonis, *The Inquisitor's Guide*, 97.
49. Bernardus Guidonis, *The Inquisitor's Guide*, 97.
50. Bernardus Guidonis, *The Inquisitor's Guide*, 102.
51. Bernardus Guidonis, *The Inquisitor's Guide*, 105.
52. Bernardus Guidonis, *The Inquisitor's Guide*, 106.
53. Bernardus Guidonis, *The Inquisitor's Guide*, 106.
54. Bernardus Guidonis, *The Inquisitor's Guide*, 111–12.
55. Bernardus Guidonis, *The Inquisitor's Guide*, 112.
56. Bernardus Guidonis, *The Inquisitor's Guide*, 111.
57. Bernardus Guidonis, *The Inquisitor's Guide*, 168.
58. David Burr, *The Spiritual Franciscans: From Protest to Persecution in the Century after Saint Francis* (University Park: Penn State University Press, 2001), 246.

59. Lambert, *Medieval Heresy*, 164–66.
60. Burr, "Effects," 301.

CHAPTER 7

1. Forrest, *The Detection of Heresy*, 35.
2. Forrest, *The Detection of Heresy*, 41.
3. Some sources state that this job was the vacant see of Worcester; Rex says it wasn't Worcester but was Prebend of Caistor in Lincoln Cathedral; Richard Rex, *The Lollards* (Basingstoke: Palgrave, 2002), 26.
4. Rex, *The Lollards*, 29.
5. Henry Ansgar Kelly, "Trial Proceedings against Wyclif and Wycliffites in England and at the Council of Constance," *Huntington Library Quarterly* 61 no. 1 (1998): 4.
6. These bulls are contained in E. M. Thompson, *Chronicon Angliae* (London: Longman and Company, 1874), 173–83.
7. Peters, *Heresy and Authority*, 271.
8. Peters, *Heresy and Authority*, 272.
9. Kelly, "Trial Proceedings," 8.
10. Vilém Herold, "Wyclif's Ecclesiology and Its Prague Context," in *The Bohemian Reformation and Religious Practice: Papers from the IV. International Symposium on The Bohemian Reformation and Religious Practice under the auspices of the Philosophical Institute of the Academy of Sciences of the Czech Republic held at Vila Lanna, Prague 26–28 June 2000*, eds. Zdeněk V. David and David R. Holeton, 5 vols. (Prague: Academy of Sciences of the Czech Republic Main Library, 2002), 15.
11. Among those dealing with poverty were 10, 21, 24, 32, and the quoted 36.
12. Peters, *Heresy and Authority*, 275. Based on the Council of Constance, 1415.
13. Peters, *Heresy and Authority*, 273.
14. Peters, *Heresy and Authority*, 274.
15. The schism began the year prior, in 1378, and would last until 1417; during part of the time, there would be a third rival pope, further undermining a sense of authority.
16. Howard Kaminsky, "Wyclifism as Ideology of Revolution," *Church History* 32, no. 1 (1963): 60.
17. Steven Justice, "Lollardy," in *Cambridge History of Medieval English Literature*, ed. David Wallace (Cambridge: Cambridge University Press, 1999): 662.
18. On indulgences, see Peters, *Heresy and Authority*, 268.
19. Peters, *Heresy and Authority*, 269.
20. Rex, *The Lollards*, 43.
21. Rex, *The Lollards*, 45.
22. Wycliffe, *De ecclesia*, 467–68.
23. Wycliffe, *De ecclesia*, 524–48; 44–45 for cult of saints.

24. Maureen Jurkowski, "Lollardy and Social Status in East Anglia," *Speculum* 82 (2007): 121.
25. Thomson, "Orthodox Religion," 50.
26. Peter Marshall, "Identifying Heresy in Sixteenth-Century England," *Saint Anselm Journal* 14, no. 2 (Spring 2019): 61.
27. Rex, *The Lollards*, 57.
28. Rex, *The Lollards*, 56.
29. Rex, *The Lollards*, 64.
30. Alan J. Fletcher and Anne Hudson, "Compilations for Preaching and Lollard Literature," in *The Cambridge History of the Book in Britain*, eds. Nigel J. Morgan, and Rodney M. Thomson, vol. 2, *1100–1400* (Cambridge: Cambridge University Press, 2008): 318–19.
31. Fletcher and Hudson, "Compilations," 327.
32. Anne Hudson, *"Poor Preachers, Poor Men*: Views of Poverty in Wyclif and His Followers," in *Studies in the Transmission of Wyclif's Writings*, ed. Anne Hudson (Burlington: Ashgate, 2008), 43.
33. Hudson, *"Poor Preachers,"* 46.
34. Steven Justice, "Lollardy," 667.
35. Anne Hudson, *Selections from English Wycliffite Writings* (London: Cambridge University Press, 1978), 19–24.
36. The format of these sixteen listed items both gives the list of the problematic propositions and then gives an answer restating correct belief on each point.
37. Hudson, *Selections*, 24.
38. Peters, *Heresy and Authority*, 277.
39. Peters, *Heresy and Authority*, 279.
40. Peters, *Heresy and Authority*, 278.
41. Peters, *Heresy and Authority*, 278. Notice here that the Lollards accuse the church of necromancy; usually, the tables are reversed.
42. For a text of the XXXVII Conclusions, see Reginald L. Poole, "The Thirty-Seven Conclusions of the Lollards," *The English Historical Review* XXVI (1911): 738–49.
43. Justice, "Lollardy," 674.
44. Anne Hudson, *The Premature Reformation: Wycliffite Texts and Lollard History* (Oxford: Oxford University Press, 1988), 174–227.
45. Margaret Aston, "Lollardy and Literacy," *History* 62, no. 206 (1977): 352–53.
46. Mark: 13:10–11.
47. Thomson, "Orthodox Religion," 41, citing Anne Hudson, *English Wycliffite Sermons, I* (Oxford, 1983): 46–7, 193.
48. Justice, "Lollardy," 671.
49. Rex, *The Lollards*, 11.
50. Justice, "Lollardy," 662.
51. William J. Courtenay, "Inquiry and Inquisition: Academic Freedom in Medieval Universities," *Church History* 58, no. 2 (June 1989): 170. He points out that

there were at least fifty judicial procedures against university officials regarding heresy in the century before Wycliffe and also notes that as of yet, there's no book-length study of academic heresy as a category.
52. Kaminsky, "Wyclifism as Ideology," 58–59.

CHAPTER 8

1. Josef Macek, *The Hussite Movement in Bohemia* (Prague: Orbis, 1958), 15, says one-third; John Martin Klassen, *The Nobility and The Making of the Hussite Revolution* (New York: Columbia University Press, 1978), 369, says 28 percent.
2. David R. Holeton, "The Bohemian Eucharistic Movement in its European Context," in *The Bohemian Reformation and Religious Practice*, ed. David R. Holeton, vol. 1, *Papers from the XVIIIth World Congress of the Checoslovak Society of Arts and Sciences, Prague 1994* (Prague: Academy of Sciences of the Czech Republic Main Library, 1996), 23–47.
3. John Martin Klassen, "Hus, the Hussites and Bohemia," in *The Cambridge History of Christianity: Christianity in Western Europe c. 1150–c. 1500*, eds. Miri Ruben and Walter Simons (Cambridge: Cambridge University Press, 2010), 372.
4. Vilém Herold, "The Spiritual Background of the Czech Reformation," in *A Companion to Jan Hus*, eds. Ota Pavlicek and František Šmahel (Madrid: Brill, 2015): 74. As of yet, there exists no publication of the Latin version nor an English translation of the work.
5. Vilém Herold, "The Spiritual Background," 73–74. Work has also been done to show the textual significance of this work on the thought of Hus as well; see n.18 in Herold for more information.
6. Herold, "Spiritual Background," 78.
7. Herold, "Spiritual Background," 81.
8. Herold, "Spiritual Background," 84.
9. This text is fascinating for the unusually wide range of authorities it borrows ideas and wholesale texts from, including the apocalyptic work of Guillaume de Sainte Amour; see Herold, "Spiritual Background," 87, for a wider list of the authorities he relied upon.
10. Thomas A. Fudge, *The Crusade against Heretics in Bohemia, 1418–1437* (Aldershot, UK: Ashgate, 2001), 1.
11. Herold, "Spiritual Background," 93–94.
12. Klassen, "Hus, the Hussites and Bohemia," 374.
13. Thomas A. Fudge, *Jan Hus between Time and Eternity: Reconsidering a Medieval Heretic* (Lanham: Lexington Books/Fortress Academic, 2015), 31.
14. Klassen, "Hus, the Hussites and Bohemia," 374.
15. Klassen, "Hus, the Hussites and Bohemia," 374.
16. Alfred Thomas and David Wallace, *Anne's Bohemia: Czech Literature and Society, 1310–1420* (Minneapolis: University of Minnesota Press, 1998), 141.
17. Klassen, "Hus, the Hussites and Bohemia," 375.

18. Klassen, "Hus, the Hussites and Bohemia," 376.
19. Vilém Herold, "How Wycliffite Was the Bohemian Reformation," in *The Bohemian Reformation and Religious Practice*, ed. David R. Holeton, vols. 1–2, *Papers from the XVIIIth World Congress of the Checoslovak Society of Arts and Sciences, Prague 1994* (Prague: Academy of Sciences of the Czech Republic Main Library, 1998), 27.
20. Peters, *Heresy and Authority*, 288.
21. Peters, *Heresy and Authority*, 289.
22. Herold, "Wyclif's Ecclesiology," 16.
23. Herold, "Wyclif's Ecclesiology," 17.
24. Peters, *Heresy and Authority*, 290.
25. Herold, "Wyclif's Ecclesiology," 27.
26. *Documenta* 234, reprinted in Herold, "Wyclif's Ecclesiology," 30.
27. Peters, *Heresy and Authority*, 296.
28. Peters, *Heresy and Authority*, 296–97.
29. Thomas A. Fudge, *The Memory and Motivation of Jan Hus, Medieval Priest and Martyr* (Tournhout: Brepols, 2013), xi.
30. Thomas A. Fudge, "Seduced by the Theologians: Aeneas Sylvius and the Hussite Heretics," in *Heresy in Transition: Transforming Ideas of Heresy in Medieval and Early Modern Europe*, eds. Ian Hunter, John Christian Laursen, and Cary J. Nederman (Aldershot, UK: Ashgate, 2005), 90.
31. Fudge, "Seduced by the Theologians," 100.
32. *Historia bohemica* 90, 92, as quoted by Fudge, "Seduced by the Theologians," 99. See also Dana Martínková, Alena Hadravová and Jirí Matl, eds., *Aeneae Silvii Historia Bohemica* (Prague: Academy of Sciences of the Czech Republic, 1998).
33. Thomson, "Orthodox Religion," 40.
34. For a more complete discussion of the history of the scholarship that required utter dependence to Wycliffe, see Herold, "How Wycliffite," 25–27. One limitation of this article is that it sees any attempts to find other sources of Hus, whether Czech or from elsewhere, to be furthering the idea that Czech work is derivative, rather than seeing it as integrative.
35. Vilém Herold, "The University of Paris and the Foundations of the Bohemian Reformation," in *The Bohemian Reformation and Religious Practice*, Eds. Zdeněk V. Davis and David R. Holeton, vol. 3 (Prague: Academy of Sciences of the Czech Republic Main Library, 2000), 15-16.

CHAPTER 9

1. Jonathan Durant and Michael D. Bailey, *Historical Dictionary of Witchcraft* (Lanham, MD: Scarecrow Press, Incorporated, 2012), 185. The authors point out that some of the fifteenth-century inquisitions into Waldensians became some of the earliest witch trials in Europe and that the word for the area where

Waldensians lived, *Vaudois*, was a word that could mean Waldensian but also came to mean witch by the late 1400s, despite there being no evidence the Waldensians ever engaged in anything similar to witchcraft.
2. Nancy Caciola, *Discerning Spirits: Divine and Demonic Possession in the Middle Ages* (Ithaca, NY: Cornell University Press, 2003), 16.
3. Christopher Mackay, *The Hammer of Witches* (Cambridge: Cambridge University Press, 2009), 21.
4. For the full range of vocabulary in Latin and Middle High German, used in identifying various types of witches, see J. B. Russell, *Dissent and Reform in the Early Middle Ages* (Berkeley, CA: University of California Press, 1965), 16.
5. Karen Louise Jolly, Catharina Raudvere, and Edward Peters, *Witchcraft and Magic in Europe: The Middle Ages* (London: Athlone, 2001), 15.
6. Isidore of Seville, *The Etymologies of Isidore of Seville*, trans. and eds. Stephen A. Barnaby, W. J. Lewis, J. A. Beach, and Oliver Berghof (New York: Cambridge University Press, 2006), VIII.ix.3 (181).
7. Isidore, *Etynologies*, VII.ix.9 (182).
8. Richard Kieckhefer, "Witch Trials in Medieval Europe," in *The Witchcraft Reader*, ed. Darren Oldridge (New York: Routledge, 2001), 25.
9. Kieckhefer, "Witch Trials in Medieval Europe," 15.
10. Michael Bailey, *Battling Demons: Witchcraft, Heresy and Reform in the Late Middle Ages* (University Park: Penn State University Press, 2003), 29.
11. Alan C. Kors and Edward Peters, *Witchcraft in Europe 400–1700: A Documentary History* (Philadelphia: University of Pennsylvania Press, 2001), 160.
12. Henry Charles Lea, *A History of the Inquisition of the Middle Ages*, 3 vols. (New York: Macmillan, 1887, 1922 reprint), 202.
13. Kors and Peters, *Witchcraft in Europe 400–1700*, 160.
14. Cohn, *Europe's Inner Demons*, 192.
15. Kors and Peters, *Witchcraft in Europe 400–1700*, 161.
16. See Wolfgang Behringer, "Detecting the Ultimate Conspiracy, or How Waldensians Became Witches," in *Conspiracies and Conspiracy Theory in Early Modern Europe. From the Waldensians to the French Revolution*, ed. Barry Coward and Julian Swann (Aldershot, UK: Ashgate, 2004), 18ff, for info on witches and walking with the dead, particularly in the light of the Waldensian trials.
17. Kors and Peters, *Witchcraft in Europe, 400–1700*, 162.
18. Peters, *Heresy and Authority*, 263–64.
19. H. C. Erik Midelfort, "Witchcraft," *Reformation and Early Modern Europe: A Guide to Research*, ed. David M. Whitford (Kirksville, MO: Truman State University Press, 2008), 21.
20. Bernardus Guidonis, *The Inquisitor's Guide*, 149.
21. Kieckhefer, "Witch Trials in Medieval Europe," 25–35.
22. Kieckhefer, "Witch Trials in Medieval Europe," 25.
23. Kieckhefer, "Witch Trials in Medieval Europe," 26.

24. Kieckhefer, "Witch Trials in Medieval Europe," 27.
25. Mackay, *Hammer of Witches*, 19–20.
26. Jolly, *Witchcraft and Magic*, 13.
27. Mackey, *Hammer of Witches*, 19.
28. Kieckhefer, "Witch Trials in Medieval Europe," 30.
29. Kors and Peters, *Witchcraft in Europe, 1100-1700*, 136.
30. Kieckhefer, "Witch Trials in Medieval Europe," 33.
31. Kors and Peters, *Witchcraft in Europe, 1100–1700*, 79.
32. Kors and Peters, *Witchcraft in Europe, 1100–1700*, 79.
33. Kors and Peters, *Witchcraft in Europe, 1100–1700*, 80–81.
34. H. C. Erik Midelfort, *Witch Hunting in Southwestern Germany 1562–1684: The Social and Intellectual Foundations* (Stanford: Stanford University Press, 1972), 20.
35. Kors and Peters, *Witchcraft in Europe, 400–1700*, 154.
36. Midelfort, *Witch Hunting in Southwestern Germany*, 12.
37. Lea, *History of the Inquisition*, 200.
38. Midelfort, *Witch Hunting in Southwestern Germany*, 15.
39. Midelfort, *Witch Hinting in Southwestern Germany*, 16. This explanation is in contrast to the previous misreading of the canon, which saw it as denying the existence of witchcraft.
40. Martin Le Franc's *Le Champion des Dames* (1450) was the first depiction of witches flying on broomsticks in art.
41. Kors and Peters, *Witchcraft in Europe, 1100–1700*, 85.
42. Kors and Peters, *Witchcraft in Europe, 1100–1700*, 85.
43. Kors and Peters, *Witchcraft in Europe, 1100–1700*, 87.
44. Kors and Peters, *Witchcraft in Europe, 1100–1700*, 88.
45. Kors and Peters, *Witchcraft in Europe, 400–1700*, 160.
46. Kors and Peters, *Witchcraft in Europe, 400–1700*, 161.
47. Bailey, *Battling Demons*, 18.
48. Bailey, *Battling Demons*, 3.
49. Mackay, *Hammer of Witches*, 8.
50. Behringer, "Detecting the Ultimate Conspiracy," 23.
51. See Ben Ray, *Satan and Salem: The Witch-Hunt Crisis of 1692* (Charlottesville: University of Virginia Press, 2017).

CHAPTER 10

1. Fudge, "Seduced by the Theologians, 89.
2. Lambert, *Medieval Heresy*, 65.
3. See Kienzle, "Religious Poverty," 47.

BIBLIOGRAPHY

PRIMARY TEXTS:

Actus Pontificum Cennomannis in Urbe Degentium, Publiés Par L'Abbé G. Busson et L'Abbé A. Ledru, Avec Une Table Alphabétique Des Noms Dressée Par Eugène Vallée. France: Au Siège de la Société, 1902.

Aeneas Sylvius. *Aeneae Silvii Historia Bohemica*. Edited by Dana Martínková, Alena Hadravová, and Jirí Matl. Prague: Academy of Sciences of the Czech Republic, 1998.

Amt, Emilie. *Women's Lives in Medieval Europe: A Sourcebook*. London: Routledge, 1993.

Barber, Malcom, and A. K. Bate. *The Templars: Selected Sources*. Manchester: Manchester University Press, 2002.

Bernard of Clairvaux. *In Praise of the New Knighthood*. Translated by Conrad Greenia. Kalamazoo: Cistercian Publications, 2000.

———. *Letters*. Translated by Bruno Scott James and introduced by Beverly Mayne Kienzle. Kalamazoo: Cistercian Publications, 1998.

———. *Sermons on the Song of Songs*. Vol. 3. Translated by Kilian Walsh, OCSO, and Irene M. Edmonds. Kalamazoo: Cistercian Publications, 1996.

Bernardus Guidonis. *The Inquisitor's Guide: A Medieval Manual on Heretics*. Edited and translated by Janet Shirley. Welwyn Garden City, UK: Ravenhall, 2006.

———. *Manuel de l'Inquisiteur*. Edited and translated by G. Mollat. Paris: Les Belles Lettres, 2006.

———. *Practica Inquisitionis Heretice Pravitatis, Auctore Bernardo Guidonis*. Edited by C. Douais. Paris: Alphonse Picard, 1886.

Besse, Guillaume. *Histoire des Ducs, Marquis et Comtes de Narbonne, autrement Appellez Princes des Goths, Ducs de Septimanie et Marquis de Gothie [Texte imprimé] [. . .] par le sieur Besse*. Paris: A. de Sommaville, 1660. http://catalogue.bnf.fr/ark:/12148/cb30099562b.

Biller, Peter, Caterina Bruschi, and Shelagh Sneddon. *Inquisitors and Heretics in Thirteenth-Century Languedoc: Edition and Translation of Toulouse Inquisition Depositions, 1273–1282*. Boston: Brill, 2010. ProQuest Ebook Central.

Desjardins, Robert Baron, François V. Pageau, and Andrew Colin Gow. *The Arras Witch Treatises: Johannes Tinctor's Invectives Contre la Secte de Vauderie and the*

Recollectio Casus, Status et Condicionis Valdensium Ydolatrarum by the Anonymous of Arras (1460). University Park: Pennsylvania State University Press, 2016. ProQuest Ebook Central.

Dondaine, Antoine. *Le Liber "De Duobus Principiis": Un Traité Néo-Manichéen Du Xiiie Siècle; Suivi D'un Fragment De Rituel Cathare*. Rome: Istituto Storico Domenicano S. Sabina, 1939.

Elliott, Alison Goddard. *The Vie de Saint Alexis in the Twelfth and Thirteenth Centuries: An Edition and Commentary*. Chapel Hill: UNC Dept. of Romance Languages, 1983.

Fredericq, Paul. *Corpus Documentorum Inquisitionis Haereticae Pravitatis Neerlandicae: Verzameling Van Stukken Pauselijke En Bisschoppelijke Inquisitie In De Nederlanden*. Gent: Vuylsteke, etc., 1889–1903. HathiTrust.

Garay, Kathleen E., and Madeleine Jeay. *The Life of Saint Douceline, a Beguine of Provence*. Woodbridge, UK: D. S. Brewer, 2001.

García y García, Antionio. *Constitutiones Concilii quarti Lateranensis una cum Commentariis glossatorum*. Vatican City: Biblioteca Apostolica Vaticano, 1981.

Halsall, Paul. "Internet Medieval Sourcebook." Last modified July 14, 2023. https://sourcebooks.fordham.edu/sbook.asp.

Hamilton, Janet, Bernard Hamilton, and Yuri Stoyanov. *Christian Dualist Heresies in the Byzantine World, c. 650–c. 1450: Selected Sources*. Manchester: Manchester University Press, 1998.

———, Sarah Hamilton, and Bernard Hamilton. *Hugh Ereriano: Contra Patarenos*. Leiden: Brill, 2004.

Hudson, Anne. *Selections from English Wycliffite Writings*. Cambridge: Cambridge University Press, 1978.

Isidore of Seville. *The Etymologies of Isidore of Seville*. Translated and edited by Stephen A. Barnaby, W. J. Lewis, J. A. Beach, and Oliver Berghof. New York: Cambridge University Press, 2006.

Kors, Alan C., and Edward Peters. *Witchcraft in Europe 400–1700: A Documentary History*. Philadelphia: University of Pennsylvania Press, 2001.

———. *Witchcraft in Europe 1100–1700: A Documentary History*. London: J. M. Dent & Sons, 1972.

Léglu, Catherine, Rebecca Rist, and Claire Taylor. *The Cathars and the Albigensian Crusade: A Sourcebook*. London: Routledge, 2014.

Mackay, Christopher. *The Hammer of Witches*. Cambridge: Cambridge University Press, 2009.

Maitland, S. R. *Facts and Documents Illustrative of the History, Doctrine, and Rites of the Ancient Albigenses and Waldensians*. Gloucester: Edward Power, 1832. HathiTrust.

Mansi, Giovan Domenico. *Sacrorum Conciliorum Nova et Amplissima Collectio: in qua Praeter ea quae Phil. Labbeus et Gabr. Cossartius [. . .] et Novissime Nicolaus*

Coleti in Lucem Edidere ea Omnia Insuper suis in Locis Optime Disposita Exhibentur, t.52. Paris: H. Welter, 1901–27.

Marguerite Porete. *The Mirror of Simple Souls*. Translated and introduced by Ellen L. Babinsky. New York: Paulist Press, 1993.

Meister Eckhart. *The Complete Mystical Works of Meister Eckhart*. Translated by Maurice O'C. Walsh. New York: Herder & Herder, 2009.

———. *The Essential Sermons, Commentaries, Treatises, and Defense*. Translated and introduced by Edmond College and Bernard McGinn. New York: Paulist Press, 1981.

———. *Teacher and Preacher*. Translated by Bernard McGinn, Frank Tobin, and Elvira Borgstädt. New York: Paulist Press, 1986.

Nelli, René. *Écritures Cathares: La Cène Secrète, Le Livre des Deux Principes, Le Rituel Latin, Le Ritual Occitan*. Paris: Éditions Denoël, 1959.

Peters, Edward. *Heresy and Authority in Medieval Europe: Documents in Translation*. Philadelphia: University of Pennsylvania Press, 1980.

Petri Venerabilis. *Contra Petrobrusianos Hereticos*. Corpus Christianorum Continuatio Medievalis X. Turnhout: Brepols, 1968.

Robinson, J. H. *Readings in European History*. Boston: Ginn, 1905. OpenLibrary.

Thomas de Cantimpré. *The Life of Christina the Astonishing*. Edited and translated by Margot H. King and David Wiljer. Toronto: Peregrina Publishing, 1999.

———. *Thomas of Cantimpré: The Collected Saints' Lives*. Edited by Barbara Newman. Translated by Margot H. King and Barbara Newman. Turnhout: Brepols, 2008.

Thompson, E. M. *Chronicon Angliae*. London: Longman and Company, 1874.

Thouzellier, Christine, ed. *Livre des Deux Principes*. Paris: Éditions du Cerf, 1973.

———. *Rituel Cathare: Introduction, Texte Critique, Traduction et Notes*. Paris: Éditions du Cerf, 1977.

Upton-Ward, J. M. *Rule of the Templars: The French Text of the Rule of the Order of the Knights Templar*. Woodbridge, UK: Boydell, 1992.

Wakefield, Walter Leggett, and Austin Patterson Evans, eds. *Heresies of the High Middle Ages*. New York: Columbia University Press, 1991.

William the Monk. *Guillaume Monachi: Contre Henri Schismatique et Hérétique suivi de Contre Les Hérétiques et Schismatiques*. Edited and translated by Monique Zerner. Paris: Les Éditions du Cerf, 2011.

SECONDARY TEXTS:

Abulafia, David, ed. *The New Cambridge Medieval History*. Vol. 5. New York: Cambridge University Press, 1999.

Angleton, Cicely d'Autremont. *Two Cistercian Preaching Missions to the Languedoc in the Twelfth Century, 1145 and 1178*. Washington, DC: Catholic University, 1984.

Arnold, John H. *Inquisition and Power: Catharism and the Confessing Subject in Medieval Languedoc*. Philadelphia: University of Pennsylvania Press, 2001. ProQuest Ebook Central.

Aston, Margaret. "Lollardy and Literacy." *History* 62, no. 206 (1977): 352–53. http://www.jstor.org/stable/24410786.

Audisio, Gabriel. *The Waldensian Dissent: Persecution and Survival, c. 1170–1570*. Translated by Claire Davison. Cambridge: Cambridge University Press, 1999.

Bailey, Michael. *Battling Demons: Witchcraft, Heresy and Reform in the Late Middle Ages*. University Park: Penn State University Press, 2003.

Barber, Malcolm. *The Cathars: Dualist Heretics in Languedoc in the High Middle Ages*. Harlow, UK: Longman, 2000.

———. "James of Molay, the Last Grand Master of the Order of the Temple." *Studia Monastica* 14 (1972): 91–124.

———. "Moving Cathars: The Italian Connection in the Thirteenth Century." *Journal of Mediterranean Studies* 10, no. 1 (2000): 5–19.

———. *The New Knighthood: A History of the Order of the Temple*. Cambridge: Cambridge University Press, 1994.

———. "Propaganda in the Middle Ages: The Charges against the Templars." *Nottingham Medieval Studies* 17 (1973): 42–57.

Bartlett, Robert. "Jacques de Vitry (d. 1240) and the Religious Life of His Time." *History (London)* 108, no. 379–380 (2023): 3–19. https://doi.org/10.1111/1468-229X.13345.

Benedetti, Marina, and Euan Cameron, eds. *A Companion to the Waldenses in the Middle Ages*. Leiden: Brill, 2022.

Berlioz, Jacques. *'Touz-les tous, Dieu reconnaîtra les siens': La croisade contre les Albigeois vue par Césaire de Heisterbach*. Portet-sur-Garonne: Loubatières, 1994.

Biller, Peter. "Goodbye to Waldensianism?" *Past and Present* 192 (August 2006): 3–33.

———. "The Waldenses 1300–1500." *Revue de L'Histoire Des Religions* 217, no. 1 (2000): 75–99. http://www.jstor.org/stable/43998779.

———, and Anne Hudson, eds. *Heresy and Literacy, 1000–1530*. Cambridge: Cambridge University Press, 1994.

———, and Barrie Dobson, eds. *The Medieval Church: Universities, Heresy and the Religious Life. Essays in Honour of Gordon Leff*. Woodbridge, UK: Boydell Press, 1999.

Bose, Mishtooni, and J. Patrick Hornbeck II, es. *Wycliffite Controversies*. Turnhout: Brepols, 2012.

Broedel, Hans Peter. *The Malleus Maleficarum and the Construction of Witchcraft: Theology and Popular Belief*. Manchester: Manchester University Press, 2003.

Brown, Elizabeth A. R., and Alan Forey. "*Vox in Excelso* and the Suppression of the Knights Templar: The Bull, Its History, and a New Edition." *Mediaeval Studies* 80 (2018): 1–58.

Bruschi, Caterina, and Peter Biller, es. *Texts and the Repression of Medieval Heresy*. Woodbridge, UK: York Medieval Press, 2003.

Burnham, Louisa. *So Great a Light, So Great a Smoke: The Beguin Heretics of Languedoc*. Ithaca, NY, and London: Cornell University Press, 2008.

Burr, David. "Early Olivi and the Parables." *Franciscan Studies* 78 (2020): 109–57. https://doi.org/10.1353/frc.2020.0005.

———. "Olivi, Christ's Three Advents, and the Double Antichrist." *Franciscan Studies* 74 (2016): 15–40. doi:10.1353/frc.2016.0017.

———. "Olivi, Maifreda, Na Prous, and the Shape of Joachism, ca. 1300." *Franciscan Studies* 73 (2015): 275–94. https://doi.org/10.1353/frc.2015.0010.

———. *The Spiritual Franciscans: From Protest to Persecution in the Century after Saint Francis*. University Park: Penn State University Press, 2001.

Caciola, Nancy. *Discerning Spirits: Divine and Demonic Possession in the Middle Ages*. Ithaca, NY: Cornell University Press, 2003.

Cameron, Euan. *The Reformation of the Heretics: The Waldenses of the Alps, 1480–1580*. Oxford: Clarendon Press, 1984.

———. *Waldenses: Rejections of Holy Church in Medieval Europe*. Oxford: Blackwell, 2000.

Carniello, Brian R. "Gerardo Segarelli as the Anti-Francis: Mendicant Rivalry and Heresy in Medieval Italy, 1260–1300." *Journal of Ecclesiastical History* 57, no. 2 (2006): 226–51.

Clark, J. M. *The Great German Mystics*. Oxford: Basil Blackwell, 1949.

Cohn, Norman. *Europe's Inner Demons: An Inquiry Inspired by the Great Witch Hunt*. New York: Pimlico, 1993.

Colish, Marcia L. "Peter of Bruys, Henry of Lausanne, and the Façade of St-Gilles." *Traditio* 28 (1972): 451–59.

Costagliola, Michel. "Fires in History: The Cathar Heresy, the Inquisition and Brulology." *Annals of Burns and Fire Disasters* 28, no. 3 (2015): 230–4.

Courtenay, William J. "Inquiry and Inquisition: Academic Freedom in Medieval Universities." *Church History* 58, no. 2 (June 1989): 168–81.

Coward, Barry, and Julian Swann, es. *Conspiracies and Conspiracy Theory in Early Modern Europe: From the Waldensians to the French Revolution*. Aldershot, UK: Ashgate, 2004.

Crowley, Sharon. *Toward a Civil Discourse: Rhetoric and Fundamentalism*. Namur: University of Pittsburgh Press, 2006. ProQuest Ebook Central.

David, Zdeněk V., and David R. Holeton, eds. *The Bohemian Reformation and Religious Practice: Papers from the IV. International Symposium on the Bohemian Reformation and Religious Practice under the Auspices of the Philosophical*

Institute of the Academy of Sciences of the Czech Republic Held at Vila Lanna, Prague 26–28 June 2000. 5 vols. Prague: Academy of Sciences of the Czech Republic Main Library, 2002.

Deane, Jennifer Kolpacoff. *A History of Medieval Heresy and Inquisition.* Lanham, MD: Rowman & Littlefield Publishers, 2011. ProQuest Ebook Central.

Dieudonné, A. *Hildebert de Lavardin, Évêque du Mans, Archevêque de Tours (1056–1133) Sa Vie.—Ses Lettres. Par A. Dieudonné.* Paris: A. Picard et fils, 1898.

Douie, Decima L. *The Nature of the Effect of the Heresy on the Fraticelli.* New York: AMS Press, 1978.

Durant, Jonathan, and Bailey, Michael D. *Historical Dictionary of Witchcraft.* Lanham, MD: Scarecrow Press, 2012. ProQuest Ebook Central.

Erbstosser, Martin. *Les Hérétiques au Moyen Age.* Montpellier: Presses du Languedoc, 1988.

Fearns, James. "Peter von Bruis une die Religiöse Bewegung des 12. Jahrhunderts." *Archiv für Kulturgeschichte* 48 (1966): 311–35.

Ferzoco, George, and Carolyn Muessig, eds. *Medieval Monastic Education.* London: Leicester University Press, 2000.

Fichtenau, H. *Heretics and Scholars in the High Middle Ages 1000–1200.* Translated by D. A. Kaiser. University Park: Penn State University Press, 1998.

Flood, David. "Peter Olivi and Franciscan Poverty." *Franciscan Studies* 74 (2016): 177–84.

Forey, A. J. "The Emergence of the Military Order in the Twelfth Century." *Journal of Ecclesiastic History* 36, no. 2 (1985): 175–85.

Forrest, Ian. *The Detection of Heresy in Late Medieval England.* Oxford: Clarendon Press, 2005.

Frale, Barbara. "The Chinon Chart: Papal Absolution to the Last Templar, Master Jacques de Molay." *Journal of Medieval History* 30, no. 2 (2004): 109–34. doi:10.1016/j.jmedhist.2004.03.004.

Frassetto, Michael. *Heresy and the Persecuting Society in the Middle Ages: Essays on the Work of R.I. Moore.* Leiden: Brill, 2006.

———. *Heretic Lives: Medieval Heresy from Bogomil and the Cathars to Wyclif and Hus.* London: Profile, 2007.

Fudge, Thomas A. *The Crusade against Heretics in Bohemia, 1418–1437.* Aldershot: Ashgate, 2001.

———. *Jan Hus between Time and Eternity: Reconsidering a Medieval Heretic.* Lanham, MD: Lexington Books, 2015. ProQuest Ebook Central.

———. *The Memory and Motivation of Jan Hus, Medieval Priest and Martyr.* Tournhout: Brepols, 2013.

Geybels, Hans. *Vulgariter Beghinae: Eight Centuries of Beguine History in the Low Countries.* Turnhout: Brepols, 2004.

Gilmont, Jean-François. "Les Vaudois: Sources et Méthodes." *Revue de L'Histoire Des Religions* 217, no. 1 (2000): 9–20. http://www.jstor.org/stable/43998775.

Giraudo, Andrea. "The Critical Edition of the Medieval Waldensian Sermons." *Medieval Sermon Studies* 59, no. 1 (2005): 74–77. doi:10.1179/1366069 115Z.00000000024.

Given, James. *Inquisition and Medieval Society: Power, Discipline and Resistance in Languedoc.* Ithaca, NY, and London: Cornell University Press, 1997.

———. "The Inquisitors of Languedoc and the Medieval Technology of Power." *The American Historical Review* 94, no. 2 (1989): 336–59.

Gonnet, Giovanni. "The Influence of the Sermon on the Mount upon the Ethics of the Waldensians of the Middle Ages." *Brethren Life and Thought* 35, no. 1 (Winter 1990): 34–40.

Goodich, Michael, ed. *Other Middle Ages: Witnesses at the Margins of Medieval Society.* Philadelphia: University of Pennsylvania Press, 1998. ProQuest Ebook Central.

Grundmann, Herbert. *Religious Movements in the Middle Ages: The Historical Links between Heresy, the Mendicant Orders, and the Women's Religious Movement in the Twelfth Century, with the Historical Foundations of German Mysticism.* Translated by Steve Rowan. Notre Dame and London: University of Notre Dame Press, 1995.

Hamilton, Bernard. *Crusaders, Cathars and the Holy Places.* Aldershot, UK: Ashgate, 2002.

———. "The Albigensian Crusade and Heresy." In *The New Cambridge Medieval History*, edited by David Abulafia, 164–81. Cambridge: Cambridge University Press, 1999.

Holeton, David. R., ed. *The Bohemian Reformation and Religious Practice: Papers from the XVIIIth World Congress of the Checoslovak Society of Arts and Sciences, Prague 1994.* Vols. 1–2. Prague: Academy of Sciences of the Czech Republic Main Library, 1996–8.

Hoose, Adam L. "Durán of Huesca (c. 1160–1230): A Waldensian Seeking a Remedy to Heresy." *Journal of Religious History* 38, no. 2 (2014): 173–89.

Housley, Norman, ed. *Knighthoods of Christ: Essays on the History of the Crusades and the Knights Templar Presented to Malcolm Barber.* Aldershot, UK: Ashgate, 2007.

Hudson, Anne. "From Oxford to Prague: The Writings of John Wyclif and His English Followers in Bohemia." *The Slavonic and East European Review* 75, no. 4 (1997): 642–57. http://www.jstor.org/stable/4212488.

———. *Lollards and Their Books.* London: Hambledon Press, 1985.

———. *The Premature Reformation: Wycliffite Texts and Lollard History.* Oxford: Oxford University Press, 1988.

———. *Studies in the Transmission of Wyclif's Writings.* Burlington, VT: Ashgate, 2008.

Hunter, Ian, John Christian Laursen, and Cary J. Nederman, eds. *Heresy in Transition: Transforming Ideas of Heresy in Medieval and Early Modern Europe.* Aldershot, UK: Ashgate, 2005.

Iogna-Prat, Dominique. *Order and Exclusion: Cluny and Christendom Face Heresy, Judaism, and Islam, 1000–1150*. Translated by Graham Edwards. Ithaca, NY, and London: Cornell University Press, 2002.

Jolly, Karen Louise, Catharina Raudvere, and Edward Peters. *Witchcraft and Magic in Europe: The Middle Ages*. London: Athlone, 2001.

Jurkowski, Maureen. "Lollardy and Social Status in East Anglia." *Speculum* 82 (2007): 120–52.

Kaelber, Lutz. "Other- and Inner-Worldly Asceticism in Medieval Waldensianism: A Weberian Analysis." *Sociology of Religion* 56, no. 2 (Summer 1995): 91–119. https://doi:10.2307/3711758.

———. "Weavers into Heretics? The Social Organization of Early-Thirteenth-Century Catharism in Comparative Perspective." *Social Science History* 21, no. 1 (Spring 1997): 111–57.

Kaminsky, Howard. "Wyclifism as Ideology of Revolution." *Church History* 32, no. 1 (1963): 57–74.

Kelly, Henry Ansgar. "Trial Proceedings against Wyclif and Wycliffites in England and at the Council of Constance." *Huntington Library Quarterly* 61, no. 1 (1998): 1–28.

Kieckhefer, Richard. *Magic in the Middle Ages*. Cambridge: Cambridge University Press, 2000.

Kienzle, Beverly Mayne. "Cathars." In *Encyclopedia of Genocide and Crimes against Humanity*, edited by Dinah L. Shelton, 151–55. Vol. 1. Detroit: Macmillan Reference USA, 2005. Gale eBooks.

———. *Cistercians, Heresy and Crusade in Occitania, 1145–1229: Preaching in the Lord's Vineyard*. Woodbridge, UK: York Medieval Press/Boydell Press, 2001.

Klassen, John Martin. *The Nobility and the Making of the Hussite Revolution*. New York: Columbia University Press, 1978.

Lambert, Malcolm D. *Medieval Heresy: Popular Movements from Bogomil to Hus*. Oxford: Blackwell, 2002.

Laursen, John Christian, Cary J. Nederman, and Ian Hunter, eds. *Heresy in Transition: Transforming Ideas of Heresy in Medieval and Early Modern Europe*. Aldershot, UK: Ashgate, 2005.

Lea, Henry Charles. *A History of the Inquisition of the Middle Ages*. 3 vols. New York: Macmillian, 1887, 1922 reprint.

Leclercq, Jean. "Un document sur les Débuts des Templiers." *Revue d'Histoire Ecclésiastique* 52 (1957): 81–91.

Leff, Gordon. *Heresy in the Later Middle Ages: The Relation of Heterodoxy to Dissent, c. 1250–1450*. Manchester, UK: Sandpiper Books, 1999.

———. "The Making of the Myth of a True Church in the Later Middle Ages." *Journal of Medieval and Renaissance Studies* 1, no. 1 (1971): 1–15.

———. "Wyclif and Hus: A Doctrinal Comparison." *Bulletin of the John Rylands Library, Manchester* 50 (1967–68): 387–410.

LeGoff, Jacques. *The Birth of Purgatory*. Chicago: University of Chicago Press, 1984.
Lerner, Robert E. "A Case of Religious Counter-Culture: The German Waldensians." *American Scholar* 55 (Spring 1986): 234–47. http://www.jstor.org/stable/41211314.
———. *The Heresy of the Free Spirit in the Later Middle Ages*. Notre Dame and London: University of Notre Dame Press, 1972.
Lewis, Warren. "Peter John Olivi, Prophet of the Year 2000: Ecclesiology and Eschatology in the Lectura Super Apocalypsim; Introduction to a Critical Edition of the Text." PhD diss., Universität Tübingen, 1976. CRL Digital Delivery System.
Little, Lester K. *Religious Poverty and the Profit Economy in Medieval Europe*. London: Paul Elek, 1978.
Lord, Evelyn. *The Knights Templar in Britain*. London: Longman, 2002.
Macek, Josef. *The Hussite Movement in Bohemia*. Prague: Orbis, 1958.
Manselli, Raoul. "Il monaco Enrico e la sua eresia." *Bolletino dell'Istituto Storico Italiano per il Medioevo e Archivo Muratoriano* 65 (1953) 1–63.
Marshall, Peter. "Identifying Heresy in Sixteenth-Century England." *Saint Anselm Journal* 14, no. 2 (Spring 2019): 59–81.
Marthaler, B. "Forerunners of the Franciscans: The Waldenses." *Franciscan Studies* n.s. xviii, no. 2 (June 1958): 133–42.
Matenaer, James M. "Franciscan Poverty as Virtual Perfection: The Description of the Apostolic Life in Peter of John Olivi's Matthew Commentary." *Cithara* 62, no. 1 (November 2022): 18–32.
McDonnell, Ernest W. *The Beguines and Beghards in Medieval Culture*. New Brunswick, NJ: Rutgers University Press, 1954.
Menache, Sophia. "Contemporary Attitudes Concerning the Templars' Affair: Propaganda's Fiasco?" *Journal of Medieval History* 8 (1982): 135–47.
Merlo, Grado Giovanni. "Frammenti Di Storiografia e Storia Delle Origini Valdesi." *Revue de L'Histoire Des Religions* 217, no. 1 (2000): 21–37. http://www.jstor.org/stable/43998776.
Mews, Constant. "Accusations of Heresy and Error in the Twelfth-Century Schools: The Witness of Gerhoh of Reichersberg and Otto of Friesing." In *Heresy in Transition: Transforming Ideas of Heresy in Medieval and Early Modern Europe*, edited by Ian Hunter, John Christian Laursen, and Cary J. Nederman, 43–57 Aldershot, UK: Ashgate, 2005.Midelfort, H. C. Erik. *Witch Hunting in Southwestern Germany 1562–1684: The Social and Intellectual Foundations*. Stanford: Stanford University Press, 1972.
Monfasani, John. *Renaissance Society and Culture: Essays in Honor of Eugene F. Rice, Jr.* New York: Ithaca Press, 1991.
Moore, Robert Ian. *The Formation of a Persecuting Society. Authority and Deviance in Western Europe, 950–1250*. Oxford: Blackwell, 2007.
———. *The War on Heresy: Faith and Power in Medieval Europe*. London: Profile, 2012.

Morgan, Nigel J., and Rodney M. Thomson, eds. *The Cambridge History of the Book in Britain*. Vol. 2, *1100–1400*. Cambridge: Cambridge University Press, 2008.

Mundy, John H., Richard W. Emery, and Benjamin N. Nelson, eds. *Essays in Medieval Thought: Presented in Honor of Austin Patterson Evans*. New York: Columbia University Press, 1955.

Nicholson, Helen, Paul F. Crawford, and Jochen Burgtorf. *The Debate on the Trial of the Templars (1307–1314)*. Farnham: Taylor & Francis Group, 2010. ProQuest Ebook Central.

Nicholson, Helen J. *Knights Templar, 1120–1312*. Oxford: Osprey, 2004.

——. *The Proceedings against the Templars in the British Isles*. Farnham: Ashgate, 2011.

Nieto-Isabel, Delfi I. "Beliefs in Progress: The Beguins of Languedoc and the Construction of a New Heretical Identity." *Summa* 15 (Spring 2020): 95–117.

Noutsou, Stamatia. "'We are not to believe that he hesitated to give correction, for his ministry is applauded': Politicizing the Fight against Heresy in the Writings of Geoffrey of Auxerre." *Cistercian Studies Quarterly* 57, no. 1 (2022): 57–93.

Oldridge, Darren, ed. *The Witchcraft Reader*. New York: Routledge, 2001.

Pavlicek, Ota, and František Šmahel, eds. *A Companion to Jan Hus*. Madrid: Brill, 2015. ProQuest Ebook Central.

Pegg, Mark Gregory. *A Most Holy War: The Albigensian Crusade and the Battle for Christendom*. Oxford: Oxford University Press, 2008.

——. "On Cathars, Albigenses and the Good Men of Languedoc." *Journal of Medieval History* 27, no. 2 (2001): 181–95.

Phillipen, L. J. M. *De begijnhoven: oorsprong, geschiedenis, inrichting*. Antwerp: Veritas, 1918.

Poole, Reginald L. "The Thirty-Seven Conclusions of the Lollards." *The English Historical Review* XXVI (1911): 738–49.

Prudlo, Donald, ed. *Origin, Development and Refinement of Medieval Religious Mendicancies*. Leiden: Brill, 2011.

Ratzinger, Joseph. *The Theology of History in St. Bonaventure*. Translated by Zachary Hayes. Chicago: Franciscan Herald Press, 1971.

Ray, Ben. *Satan and Salem: The Witch-Hunt Crisis of 1692*. Charlottesville: University of Virginia Press, 2017.

Rex, Richard. *The Lollards*. Basingstoke: Palgrave, 2002.

Roach, Andrew P. "Penance and the Making of the Inquisition in Languedoc." *Journal of Ecclesiastic History* 52, no. 3 (July 2001): 409–33.

——, and James R. Simpson, eds. *Heresy and the Making of European Culture: Medieval and Modern Perspectives*. London: Taylor & Francis Group, 2013. ProQuest Ebook Central.

Ruben, Miri, and Walter Simons, eds. *The Cambridge History of Christianity: Christianity in Western Europe c. 1150–c. 1500*. Cambridge: Cambridge University Press, 2010.

Russell, J. B. *Dissent and Reform in the Early Middle Ages*. Berkeley: University of California Press, 1965.

Satto, Gloria. "The Last Beguine." *L'Osservatore Romano*, September 26, 2020. https://www.osservatoreromano.va/en/news/2020-09/the-last-beguine.html.

Schulevitz, Deborah. "Following the Money: Cathars, Apostolic Poverty, and the Economy in Medieval Languedoc, 1237–1259." *Journal of Medieval Religious Cultures* 44, no. 1 (2018): 24–59.

Sennis, Antonio, ed. *Cathars in Question: Heresy and Inquisition in the Middle Ages*. Woodbridge, UK: York Medieval Press, 2016.

Simons, Walter. *Cities of Ladies: Beguine Communities in the Medieval Low Countries, 1200–1565*. Philadelphia: University of Pennsylvania Press, 2001.

Smelyansky, Eugene. "Heretical Refugees and Persecution of German Waldensians, 1393–1400." *Journal of Medieval History* 48, no. 3 (2022): 396–416. https://doi.org/10.1080/03044181.2022.2073463.

Somerset, Fiona, Jill C. Havens, and Derrick G. Pitard, eds. *Lollards and Their Influence in Late Medieval England*. Woodbridge, UK: Boydell, 2003.

Sumption, Johnathan. *The Albigensian Crusade*. London, Faber & Faber, 1978.

Tarrant, Jacqueline. "The Clementine Decrees on the Beguines: Conciliar and Papal Versions." *Archivum Historiae Pontificiae* 12 (1974): 300–308. http://www.jstor.org/stable/23563645.

Thomas, Alfred, and David Wallace. *Anne's Bohemia: Czech Literature and Society, 1310–1420*. Minneapolis: University of Minnesota Press, 1998.

Thomson, J. A. F. "Orthodox Religion and the Origins of Lollardy." *History* 74, no. 240 (1989): 39–55.

Tsougarakis, Nickiphoros I. "Heretical Networks between East and West: The Case of the Fraticelli." *Journal of Medieval History* 44, no. 5 (2018): 529–42. doi: 10.1080/03044181.2018.1509802.

Uitti, Karl D. "The Old French 'Vie de Saint Alexis': Paradigm, Legend, Meaning." *Romance Philology* 20, no. 3 (1967): 263–95. http://www.jstor.org/stable/44940258.

Van Engen, John. "The Christian Middle Ages as a Historiographical Problem." *American Historical Review* 19, no. 3 (1986): 519–52.

Vedder, Henry C. "Origin and Early Teachings of the Waldenses, According to Roman Catholic Writers of the Thirteenth Century." *The American Journal of Theology* 4, no. 3 (1900): 465–89. http://www.jstor.org/stable/3152828.

Wakefield, Walter Leggett. *Heresy, Crusade, and Inquisition in Southern France 1100–1250*. London: George Allen and Unwin, 1974.

Wakefield, Walter L. "Notes on Some Antiheretical Writings of the Thirteenth Century." *Franciscan Studies* 27 (1967): 285–321. http://www.jstor.org/stable/41974781.

Wallace, David, ed. *Cambridge History of Medieval English Literature*. Cambridge: Cambridge University Press, 1999.

Whalen, Brett. "Joachim of Fiore, Apocalyptic Conversion, and the 'Persecuting Society.'" *History Compass* 8/7 (2010): 682–91.
Whitford, David M., ed. *Reformation and Early Modern Europe: A Guide to Research*. Kirksville: Truman State University Press, 2008.
Zerner, Monique, ed. *Inventer l'hérésie? Discours polémique et pouvoir avant l'inquisition*. Nice: Centre d'Études Médiévales de Nice, 1998.

INDEX

Abbey of Fontevrault 9, 13, 56
Ad Abolendam (*Toward Abolishing*) 45–46, 68–69
Ad Nostrum (*In Our Time*) 78, 88, 90, 93
Ad providam (*To Provide*) 118
Aeneas Sylvius 183
affective theology 86, 106, 165
Albertus Magnus 76, 205
Albigensian Crusade 28, 31, 35, 47–49, 51, 71, 139
Alexander III (Pope) 44, 67, 70, 72
Alexander IV (Pope) 201
Alexander V (Pope) 178, 207
Angelo of Clareno 130–31
annihilation of soul 88, 95, 182
antimaterialism 19, 20, 23, 34, 40–42, 64, 76, 88
antisacerdotalism 19, 20, 23, 34, 40–42, 64, 76, 88, 202, 222 n 17
apocalypticism 25, 121–23, 125–34, 139–40
Archbishop Zbyněk 178
Arians 1, 3, 11, 26
Arnoldists 68, 130
auto–da–fé xi, 1, 75, 89, 112, 139, 225 n 2

Baldwin II, King of Jerusalem 100–101
Baphomet 117, 195, 198
Béguins of Languedoc 123, 127, 133–34, 136–41, 196, 206, 215
beguinages 75, 79, 81–3, 97, 218, development 81–83
beguines 6, 75–98, 99, 123, 134, 141, 171, 176, 189, 209, 212, 214, 218, 219
Benedict of Nursia 26
Benedict XI (Pope) 116
Benedictine order 27, 37, 51, 80, 144, 147, 155, 201, 209
Berengar of Narbonne 50
Bernard of Caux 49
Bernard of Clairvaux 18, 21–22, 24–29, 35, 45, 51, 57, 83, 86, 88, 101–103, 105–109, 189
Bernardo Gui 40–41, 50, 54–55, 62, 66, 137–39, 141, 196, 207, 215
bizzoche 80, 121, 136
black death 159, 189
Blackfriars Council 149, 157, 159
Bogomil 8, 34–35, 38
Boniface VIII (Pope) 112, 116, 131
The Book of Two Principles 36, 40
Brautmystik 86

Burchard of Ursperg 62
Bury St. Edmunds 144, 159

Caesarius of Heisterbach 76
Callixtus II (Pope) 21
Canons of Toulouse (1229) 49
Carthusian Order 13
Cathars 2–3, 6–7, 28, 30, 31–52,
    53–54, 57–58, 59, 61, 65, 67, 69,
    80, 102, 119, 133, 137, 139, 184,
    187, 193, 194, 195, 196, 198–99,
    207, 211, 214–17
Catholic Poor 70, 73, 231 n 63
Celestine II (Pope) 103
Celestine V (Pope) 131–32
Charlemagne 11
King Charles IV of Bohemia 169–71,
    173–75
Charles University 168, 169, 173, 174,
    177–78, 187
Chinon parchment 116–17
Christina Mirabilis 81–82, 84–85
Chronicon Urspergense (*Ursperger Chronicle*) 62
Cistercian Order 13, 17, 21–22, 24–26,
    28, 29, 45, 47, 55, 57, 69, 80, 83,
    88, 98, 101, 108, 126, 216
Cîteaux 17, 22, 31, 69
Clement V (Pope) 49, 91, 113, 116–18,
    134, 136
Cluniac reform 13
Cluny 14, 19, 101
Compactata (*Compacts*) *of Basel* 184
Compilatio de novo spiritu (*Compilation of the New Spirit*) 76

Conrad Waldhauser 169–70, 179, 185
Considerantes dudum (*Considering Time*) 118
consolamentum 33, 38–39, 41–43,
    227 n 32
Constitutions against Gospellers 146
Contra Henricum schismaticum et hereticum (*Against the Henrician Schismatics and Heretics*) 22
Contra Petrobrusianos (*Against the Petrobrusians*) 19, 23
Convensa 40
Conventuals 124–28, 132
Cosmas 8, 34
Council of Basel 209, 211
Council of Constance 150, 164, 176,
    179–80, 182, 209
Council of Lyon (1180–81) 57
Council of Nablus 101
Council of Pisa (1135) 17, 22
Council of Pisa (1409) 177–78
Council of Rheims (1148) 18, 45, 55
Council of Toulouse (1056) 43
Council of Toulouse (1119) 21, 29, 45
Council of Verona (1184) 45
crusades 3, 14, 21, 22, 24, 28, 31, 33, 35,
    46, 47, 100, 102, 105, 106, 107,
    111, 113–14, 116, 218
Cum de quibusdam mulieribus (*Concerning Certain Women*) 89, 91

De civili dominio (*Of the Civil Dominion*) 147, 151, 154
De heretico comburendo (*Regarding The Burning of the Heretic*) 145

De laude novae militie (*In Praise of the New Knighthood*) 101, 107
Denis, King of Portugal 113
diabolism 1, 195, 196, 198–99, 204, 205, 209, 212, 213
Dominicans xi, 8, 9, 30, 46, 49, 54, 55, 70, 76, 77, 80, 82, 83, 92–95, 121–22, 132, 135, 144, 199, 203, 205, 207–10, 212, 215
Donatists 64, 67, 70, 153, 170
Douceline 85
Durand of Huesca 58, 64, 69–70, 73

Eckbert of Schönau 35, 51
Edward I, King of England 113
Edward II, King of England 117
Edward III, King of England 148
Elizabeth of Schönau 51
Emperor Alexius I 34
Errores Gazariorum (*The Errors of the Cathars*) 193, 195, 207–208
Eudes de l'Étoile 55
Eugene III (Pope) 18, 24, 104
Eugene IV (Pope) 204, 211
eucharist 12, 19, 21, 29, 41, 64, 71, 147, 149, 151–52, 156, 158–61, 173, 177, 184, 202–203, 223 n 19
Euthymius Zigabenus 34
Everwin of Steinfeld 28, 35
Excommunicamus et anathematisamus (*We Excommunicate and Anathematize*) 48
Exiit qui seminat (*A Sower Went Forth*) 128, 134
Exivi de paradiso (*When I Went Forth from Paradise*) 134

Faciens misericordiam (*Granting Forgiveness*) 116
Flagellum haereticorum fascinariorum (*The Scourge of Heretical Witches*) 207
Formicarius (*The Anthill*) 204, 209, 210
Four Articles of Prague 171, 184
Fourth Lateran Council (1215) 46, 48, 54, 64, 70, 71, 77, 79, 91, 98, 163, 213, 216
Francis of Assisi 72, 86, 122–123, 126, 128, 129, 131, 135, 136, 138, 139
Franciscan *Rule* 123, 125, 127–28, 131, 134, 136, 138
Franciscans 30, 77, 85, 92, 121–41, 176, 200, 215
Fulk of Toulouse (Bishop) 70

Gelasius II (Pope) 13
Gerardo Segarelli 131–32
Gilbert of Tournai 77, 92
Gilles de Rais 200
Gregorian reform 4, 7, 13–14, 17, 29, 50, 216–17, 222 n 17
Gregory VII (Pope) 13; see also Gregorian Reform
Gregory IX (Pope) 46, 47, 49, 51, 127–28, 193
Gregory X (Pope) 132
Gregory XI (Pope) 148, 177
Guglielma 132–33

Henry of Agro 91
Henry of Lausanne 11–12, 14–29, 32, 55, 57, 66
Henry II, King of England 45, 112

Henry IV, King of England 145
Henry V, King of England 161, 162
heresy, definition 2–3
Heresy of the Free Spirit 75–76, 78, 89–90, 92, 97–98, 123, 134, 187, 190, 197, 213, 232 n 2
Heresy Act of 1382, 145
Hermits of Saint Augustine 70
Hildebert of Lavardin 16–17, 29, 223 n 26
Honorius III (Pope) (1150–1227) 97, 105
Honorius IV (Pope) 132
Hospitallers 100, 101, 104, 111–13, 115, 118–19
Hugh of Champagne 101
Hugh of Payens 100–101, 109, 114–15
Humbert of Romans 77
Humiliati 68, 70, 81, 130, 231 n 63
Hussites 167–87, 209, 213

infant baptism 19, 20, 21, 23, 28, 29, 223 n 19, 223 n 26
infanticide 199–200
Innocent II (Pope) 29, 103
Innocent III (Pope) 46–47, 69–73, 122
Innocent VIII (Pope) 203, 210
Interrogatio Iohannis (*The Questions of John*) 40
Isidore of Seville 191

Jacques de Molay 113–19
Jacques de Vitry (ca. 1160–1240) 81, 82, 97
James II, King of Aragon 114, 117
Jan Hus 143, 167–187; death of Hus 180–82; Hus and Bible translations 176, 185; Jan Hus at Charles University 176–79; Hus at Bethlehem Chapel 172–73, 174, 178, 180
Jan von Ruusbroec 93
Jan Žižka 183
Jean des Bellesmains, Archbishop of Lyon 68
Jerusalem 47, 81, 100–104, 106–107, 110, 111, 126, 164, 171
Joachim of Fiore 125–28, 237 n 28
John XXII (Pope) 91, 135, 136, 202, 203
John of Gaunt 146, 148
John Milíč of Kroměříž 170
John Nider 199, 208–10
John of Winterthür 193
John Wycliffe 143–66, 168, 173–78, 180–81, 184, 186, 187; Wycliffe on church authority 158–60; Wycliffe on sacraments 155–57; Wycliffe's anticlericalism 152–53; Wycliffe on universals 151–52; Wycliffe on disendowment 153–54; Wycliffe on church practices 154–55
Julian of Norwich 83, 163

Languedoc 7, 11, 15, 18, 28, 32–37, 45–46, 48, 50, 52, 53, 68–69, 73, 122–23, 133–36, 139–41, 167, 187, 196, 215–16, 219
Legenda Major (*Life of Saint Francis*) 126
Liber antihaeresis (*Book Against Heresy*) (1210) 58, 64, 69
Liber sententiarum (*Book of Sentences*) 137

Index

Lollard *Twelve Conclusions* 160–61
Lollards 143, 146, 151, 157–66
Lollard literature 162–64
Lombard Reconciled Poor 71, 73
Louis VII, King of France 44–45
Louis VIII, King of France 48
Louis IX, King of France 49
Lucius III (Pope) 45, 68, 126, 231 n 63
Lutgard of Aywières (1182–1246) 82

maleficium 191, 193, 195, 196, 197, 203–204, 208, 210
Malleus Maleficarum (*Hammer of Witches*) 199, 203, 204, 207–10
Manicheans 2, 3, 8, 11, 33, 35, 215, 217
Margerite d'Ypres (1216–37) 82
Marguerite Porete 1, 75, 76, 87–89, 92, 96, 213, 215
Marie d'Oignies (1177–1213) 81, 84, 97, 233 n 2
Matěj of Janov 171–72, 179, 185, 187
Matthew Paris 18
Meister Eckhart 78, 84, 93–96, 98, 165
Milites Templi (*Soldiers of the Temple*) 103
Militia Dei (*Soldiers of God*), 104
mulieres religiosae 80
Multorum querela (*The Complaint of Many*) 49

Na Prous Boneta 134, 140
Nicetas 35, 38, 225 n 10
Nicholas Eymeric 196, 205–207, 210
Norbert of Xanten 13
Nuremburg Handbook 190

Olim felicis recordationis (*Once Upon A Happy Memory*) 132
Omne Datum Optimum (*Every Perfect Gift*) 103
Order of Saint James 100

papal bulls condemning Wycliffe 148, 149, 153, 155
Paris and Oxford condemnations 94
Passau Anonymous 60, 66
Pastoralis praeeminentiae (*Pastoral Preeminence*) 117
Patarines 48, 68
Peasants' Revolt 1, 159–60, 167
Pelagians 1, 3
periods in the development of witchcraft accusations 197–201
Peter of Bruys 11, 14, 16–17, 19, 21–24, 27, 32, 55, 57
Peter Damian 55
Peter of Mladoňovice 180–82
Peter of John Olivi 121, 124, 127–30, 133–36, 139, 140, 206
Peter Valdesius 53–58, 66–68, 70–72
Peter the Venerable 15, 19, 22–24, 26, 28, 29, 51, 101
Peter Zwicker 55, 229 n 13
Philip II, King of France 112, 113
Philip IV, King of 115–17
pilgrimage 44, 100, 101, 104, 126, 130, 147, 160–61, 164
prayers for the dead 19, 23, 58, 66–67, 73, 84, 147, 156, 161
predestination 153, 156–57, 161, 174, 179
proto–Protestants 72, 185–86
purgatory 28, 66, 71, 73, 84, 155

Quorundam exigit 136

Ratio recta (*Correct Reasoning*) 91
Raymond VI, Count of Toulouse 46–48
Regnans in coelis (*Reigning in Heaven*) 116
Religionum diversitatem nimiam (*The Diversity of Religions is Too Great*) 132
Rituel de Florence 36–37
Rituel de Lyon 36–37
Robert of Arbrissel 9, 13, 55–56
Robert of Sorbon 76, 97
Rule of Saint Augustine 13, 109
Rule of Saint Benedict 109
Rule of the Templars 101, 103, 107–10

Sancta Romana (*Holy Roman*) 134, 136
Second Lateran Council (1139) 29, 45
Second Council of Lyon (1274) 77, 89, 132
sexual misdoings, accusations of 1, 3, 62, 76, 94, 100, 112, 114, 115, 120, 141, 175, 193, 199–200, 208
Simon of Montfort 47–48
Sister Catherine Treatise 93, 96
sodomy 113, 117, 161, 197, 200
Spiritual Franciscans 61, 122–41
spitting on the cross 114, 116, 117
Summis desiderantes affectibus (*Desiring with Supreme Ardor*) 203
Super illius specula (*Upon His Watchtower*) 203

Synod of St Félix-de-Caraman 38, 227 n 33

Tanchelm of Antwerp 12
Templars 1, 3, 6, 99–120, 143, 184, 195, 197, 198, 205, 211, 212, 213, 215, 219
Templar trials 112–19
Third Lateran Council (1179) 67
Thomas Arundel, Archbishop of Canterbury 145–46
Thomas de Cantimpré 81, 84
transubstantiation 147, 149, 151, 155, 156, 158, 160, 177, 223 n 19
transvection 193, 199, 205, 207–208, 244 n 40
Treaty of Paris (1229) 48

universities xi, 4, 26, 34, 46, 76, 93–95, 97, 113, 123–124, 127–28, 131, 143–44, 146–49, 152, 157–8, 164–5, 168–178, 182–83, 185, 187, 188, 191, 204, 207
Urban II (Pope) 13
Urban III (Pope) 126
Urban V (Pope) 147
Urban VI (Pope) 150
usus pauper 123–24, 127–29, 134, 136
utraquism 171, 179, 184

veneration of the cross 19, 34
Vergentis in senium (*Inclining toward Decay*) 46–47

Index

vernacular writings 4, 56, 57, 63, 67, 69, 77, 84, 86–88, 92–95, 130, 134, 143, 144, 146, 150, 154, 159, 160, 162–63, 165, 177, 186
Vox in excelso (*A Voice from on High*) 118
Vox in Rama (*A Voice in Ramah*) 193

Waldensians 6, 49, 53–74, 81, 92, 99, 119, 122, 167, 184, 186, 193–99, 207, 211, 214–15

wandering preachers 1, 4, 11–17, 20, 24, 28, 52, 53, 55, 57, 59, 62–63, 65, 70, 126, 212, 213, 214
Wenceslas IV, King of Bohemia 169, 177, 184
Archbishop William Courtenay 148, 149, 160
William of Tyre 101, 103, 108
William the Monk 20–22